BIOGRAPHY

JAN   1989

SHELLEY'S MAJOR VERSE

Henry Fuseli, *Prometheus Rescued by Hercules*. Courtesy of the Trustees of the British Museum.

SHELLEY'S MAJOR VERSE

The Narrative and Dramatic Poetry

Stuart M. Sperry

HARVARD UNIVERSITY PRESS

Cambridge, Massachusetts, and London, England   1988

Publication of this book has been aided by a grant from
the Andrew W. Mellon Foundation.

This book is printed on acid-free paper, and its binding
materials have been chosen for strength and durability.

Library of Congress Cataloging-in-Publication Data

Sperry, Stuart M.
    Shelley's major verse : the narrative and dramatic
poetry / Stuart M. Sperry.
        p.   cm.
    Includes index.
    ISBN 0-674-80625-5 (alk. paper)
    1. Shelley, Percy Bysshe, 1792–1822—Criticism and
interpretation. I. Title.
PR5438.S65 1988   87-35923
821'.7—dc19   CIP

For Sophie again

CONTENTS

PREFACE

Shelley has been increasingly viewed as a thinker who evolved an intellectual philosophy in isolation from life. There is no doubt that throughout his career Shelley was intensely preoccupied by the great philosophical questions—epistemological, social, and historical. From an early age he was a keen student of ideas who read widely and was strongly influenced by the thought of others. In his prose he sought to write clearly and rigorously about fundamental issues; and there is no question that his writings possess a high degree of intellectual coherence. Nevertheless, the attempt to reduce his work to a philosophical system has been in many ways unfortunate. For one thing, it has ignored that Shelley was above all a poet and, like all great poets, composed verse of emotional power and feeling that cannot be explained in terms of ideas alone. For another thing, it has steadily divorced the writer from his life, as if the poet who was inspired to write his great narrative, dramatic, and visionary poems were a being totally distinct from the child who was deeply loved, the youth who suffered the myriad trials of adolesence, or the grown man who sought to recreate a lost harmony through a network of extraordinarily idealized personal relationships.

This book attempts to rectify the imbalance by beginning to reintegrate the poetry with the life. We know relatively little about Shelley's earliest days. There can be little doubt, however, that as an infant and a child he knew the force of love, inevitably in the first instance from his mother. It is my argument that this love provides the life force of Shelley's verse and that it accounts for the enduring quality and power of his voice. The recent emphasis on Shelley as not only a philosopher but a philosopher of a specifically skeptical cast has obscured the fact that he is one of the great visionary idealists of world literature, a truth perceived from the outset of his critical reception and for which he has been alternately admired and derided. No doubt the pronounced hostility of some Victorian and modern critics has impelled Shelley's recent defenders, struggling to overcome the stigma of the "ineffectual angel," to stress his intellectual vigor and tough-mindedness. However understandable and even salutary, the effort to present Shelley as an intellectual and rationalist has cut him off from the true sources of his poetry, from the emotions that lie hidden in the earliest of his childhood experiences. Nor has recent criticism always appreciated the fact that, as Plato demonstrates, the most extreme forms of skepticism and idealism are frequently compatible.

This study is not a "thesis" book. As I have said, I have sought to present Shelley above all as an idealist and to study the life forces that nourished and directed the power of his visionary impulse. However, it has not seemed practicable to come at each of the major works I consider in precisely the same way, and the reader who expects to find one kind of approach pressed throughout will be disappointed. Whatever underlying unity we may discern, there exist among the central works of any artist of significance important qualitative differences. Such differences involve much more than questions of comparative excellence. They have to do, in a more profound way, with matters of occasion, forethought, and conceptualization. Every poet or artist composes in response to different needs, in various states of haste or deliberation, and with varying degrees of intellectual or emotional realization. Different works both spring from and reflect different levels of conscious or unconscious awareness. Such distinctions loom especially large in the case of Shelley, who wrote in such an extraordinary range of genres, in reaction to such varied social or personal compulsions, and at such different rates of speed and concentration.

In the chapters that follow, therefore, I have not hesitated to alter my approach in ways that seemed genial to the distinctive nature of each work, even at the cost of what may seem to some readers disconcerting shifts of critical focus. The chief perspective of a number of the chapters is psychological, employing concepts and even language that is psychoanalytic in origin. *Alastor,* as I read it, is a deeply introverted work which grows directly out of the psychological tensions generated by the turbulence and distress of Shelley's involvement with Harriet Westbrook and Mary Wollstonecraft Godwin. *Epipsychidion,* in the personal allegory of its central section and in its thinly disguised allusions to Mary, Claire Clairmont, Harriet, and some of the most traumatic events of the poet's life, dramatizes a symptomatic and recurring crisis of identity. Even Shelley's longest poem, *The Revolt of Islam,* a fable intended to rekindle man's faith in historical progress and the ultimate triumph of justice and enlightenment, draws on the events of Shelley's childhood and upbringing and his relationship with Mary. In the case of *Queen Mab,* I have deliberately eschewed the poem's lode of ideas, so thoroughly mined in the past, to concentrate on neglected but revealing aspects of the poem's framework that introduce and illuminate recurring patterns of the life.

With *Prometheus Unbound* and, to some extent, *The Triumph of Life,* we encounter works that mark major watersheds in Shelley's career, poems that reflect a superior degree of self-consciousness and intellectualization. Shelley undertook the writing of *Prometheus* as his avowed masterpiece. He composed, added to, and revised the drama with exceptional care over an extended period of time; and the work springs far less from any immediate or personal preoccupations than from his desire to project a vision embodying long-studied conclusions as to the nature of man, life, and destiny. Certainly the actors and agents within the highly idealized drama he created possess a strongly psychological character. In his "Preface" to the drama Shelley himself declared that he had deliberately sought through his use of imagery to represent "the operations of the human mind." Nevertheless, those agents and reactions are universalized at a high level of intellectual abstraction in the effort to represent the permanent and inalienable powers of the human psyche. Consequently, in dealing with *Prometheus* and to a lesser extent with *The Triumph of Life* I have sought to step back from the history of Shelley's personal involvements in order to concentrate on his conscious intention and design. This is not to say that during the time he was at work on *Prometheus* Shelley was unmoved by domestic tragedy or the growing strains of his relationship with Mary or doubts occasioned by the slowness and uncertain course of earthly revolution. Such fears and reservations were, however, in great part subsumed within the darker forces of his allegory, the Furies and to some degree Demogorgon—abstractions whose power and comprehensiveness resist easy psychological reduction. No doubt distinctions between the conscious and unconscious significance any work possesses are matters of individual judgment, and in any case involve differences of degree rather than of kind; but they are no less important to the task of criticism. While I have attempted throughout my study to pursue the life forces that animate the poetry, I have sought at the same time to recognize that those energies are reflected from poem to poem at different levels of the poetic psyche and that not every work of art is best illuminated by the same method of critical analysis.

It may be asked why I have chosen to restrict myself to the narrative and dramatic poetry or why, for that matter, I have limited my examination to the particular poems I have singled out. Even though he died while still in his twenties, Shelley wrote prolifically, and his work, in both prose and verse, bulks large. Some manageable limit had to be set for the present study. Furthermore, as I have partly indicated, my intention is not to provide a general commentary on the whole of Shelley's work or even to give a complete account of his narrative and dramatic artistry. My purpose is, rather, to trace the life force of his poetry and its transformation and efflorescence in the course of his development. The great narrative and dramatic compositions that run chronologically from the start to the end of his poetic career provide a kind of backbone or central nervous column to which all the shorter pieces are attached. When it seemed useful, I have alluded to these connections, seeking at the same time to keep my eye upon the principal divisions into which the career falls. To sense the difference between the playfulness and comic irony of *The Witch of Atlas* and the fatalism and darkness of *The Triumph of Life* is to appreciate the extraordinary range of Shelley's responsiveness, the extremes of his mature reaction to essentially the same set of human circumstances. It is also to fathom certain deeper shifts of mood and perception within a transition cut short by death. In my discussions of the poems that I have chosen, I hope to convey my sense of Shelley's essential evolution as a poet, to make the vital balance between continuity and development clear. Some may ask why there are no chapters on the narratives of *Rosalind and Helen, The Sensitive Plant,* and *Julian and Maddalo* and none on the important late drama, *Hellas*. To have considered all of these works would have added greatly to the length of my volume and imposed on the patience of the reader more than I already have.

Anyone writing seriously on Shelley today is of necessity indebted to a host of scholars and critics who have preceded him. In the documentation I hope to have given some indication of how great my indebtedness is. At the same time one is always apprehensive, when recognizing particular obligations, of ignoring or overlooking those of a deeper or a subtler kind. The silent assimilation of a major line of critical argument is often more important and difficult to acknowledge than is the acceptance of particular facts or details. I can only say that I am immensely obligated to the wealth of Shelley scholarship and criticism and apologize in those cases where I may have failed to make my indebtedness sufficiently clear or precise.

Several general obligations require particular mention. Carlos Baker gave me my first introduction to Shelley as an undergraduate, and I have sought to emulate, if I have been unable to achieve, the balance, sanity, and acumen of his pioneering study, *Shelley's Major Poetry: The Fabric of a Vision* (Princeton: Princeton University Press, 1948). As some readers will have already inferred, my own approach to Shelley is partly a deliberate reaction against the unremitting analysis and philosophical reductiveness of Earl R. Wasserman. It remains to say, however, that he is one of the poet's most penetrating critics and that I have learned much from his work, particularly his *Shelley: A Critical Reading* (Baltimore and London: Johns Hopkins University Press, 1971). I have also benefited greatly from the knowledge and good sense of Kenneth Neill Cameron, and his work, especially his important biographical and critical compendium, *Shelley: The Golden Years* (Cambridge, Mass.: Harvard University Press, 1974), has never been far from my hand. Donald H. Reiman gave the typescript a careful and generously sympathetic reading and provided a sheaf of notes and comments that recommended improvements and saved me from a number of errors. Long before this, however, he was a friend who encouraged me in our conversations and inspired me by his example. I am greatly indebted to his work, both scholarly and critical, from my reliance on his text to the critical perceptiveness concentrated in his excellent introductory *Percy Bysshe Shelley* (New York: Twayne, 1969). My indebtedness to Shelley's many American critics does not mean that I have neglected the contribution of their distinguished British counterparts. I have benefited greatly from the work of Richard Holmes and Timothy Webb, to cite only two. Ronald Tetreault's *The Poetry of Life: Shelley and Literary Form* (Toronto: University of Toronto Press, 1987), appeared too late for me to take into account.

Leon Waldoff's essay, "The Father-Son Conflict in *Prometheus Unbound:* The Psychology of a Vision," *The Psychoanalytic Review,* 62 (1975), gave me important help in formulating a psychological context for Shelley. In addition, his friendship, generous counsel, understanding, and enthusiasm have been invaluable. Stuart Curran, with whom I have collaborated over many years in work involving both Keats and Shelley, was good enough to send me a copy of his important revision of the Shelley bibliography prior to its publication in *The English Romantic Poets: A Review of Research and Criticism,* ed. Frank Jordan (New York: Modern Language Association, 1985). Over and beyond that particular kindness, I have long been the beneficiary of his intelligence and quiet encouragement. Robert and Jo Gittings, Betty Bostetter, and Christina Gee all helped in various ways to raise my spirits when I needed it. Closer to home, my colleagues at Indiana University, Charles Forker, Alfred and Linda David, Bill and Hana Wilson, Mary Gaither, James Justus, Wallace Williams, Judith Anderson and the late E. Talbot Donaldson, all friends of many years' standing, cheered me on vital occasions. My former student, Michael Shelden, has long encouraged me to think I had something worthwhile to say about Shelley and has been a valued and sustaining friend. Undoubtedly my greatest debt is to my wife, who typed several preliminary drafts and helped in any number of ways to get me through.

I am grateful to former and present department heads Donald J. Gray, Paul Strohm, and Mary Burgan for their help and cooperation and to Indiana University for a sabbatical leave. It is a pleasure to acknowledge the skill and kindness of the staff at London Library, in whose reading room this book was principally written. Brad Stiles and Fiona Crosskill typed the final draft swiftly and efficiently under difficult circumstances on different sides of the Atlantic.

Chapter 3 appeared in an earlier form as "The Sexual Theme in Shelley's *The Revolt of Islam,*" *Journal of English and Germanic Philology,* 82 (1983), 32–49. Chapter 4 adapts several paragraphs from my "Necessity and the Role of the Hero in Shelley's *Prometheus Unbound,*" *PMLA,* 96 (1981), 242–54. Chapter 7 appeared in a slightly different form as "The Ethical Politics of Shelley's *The Cenci*" in *Studies in Romanticism,* 25 (1986), 411–27, published in honor of Carl Woodring. I am grateful to these journals and their editors for permission to republish. I am also grateful to W. W. Norton & Company, Inc., for permission to reprint material from *Shelley's Poetry and Prose,* copyright © 1977 by Donald H. Reiman and Sharon B. Powers, and to Oxford University Press for permission to reprint material from *The Letters of Percy Bysshe Shelley,* edited by Frederick L. Jones, and *Shelley: Poetical Works,* edited by Thomas Hutchinson and revised by G. M. Matthews.

SHELLEY'S MAJOR VERSE

one

OUR PROPER DESTINY

Queen Mab

Shelley was only nineteen when he began the composition of *Queen Mab*. The poem has many weaknesses, from its mediocre verse to its derivative ideas. Shelley's first major work, however, is remarkably ambitious in design and scope—the vision of an attainable, indeed a preordained perfection that was alternately to inspire and to haunt the poet to the end of his career.

Queen Mab is above all a poem of ideas, "an unsuccessful emulsion," as Carlos Baker has written, "of anti-Christian, pantheistic, deistic, materialistic, and necessitarian principles."[1] None of the ideas was original, and all have been traced back to sources in Shelley's reading such as Baron Holbach, Erasmus Darwin, and William Godwin.[2] Nevertheless the poem breathes the spirit of a reforming ardor, and the ideals and programs it endorses are the result of strenuous and sustained intellectual assimilation. A revolutionary work that rails against tyrants and monarchs, it depicts the myriad evils of society while at the same time advocating trust in the ultimate disappearance of vice and even physical disease through the operation of the laws of a benign necessity. The machinery Shelley devised for projecting this millennial vision was as derivative as the perfectionist ideals to which the poem is committed and draws heavily on the conventions of the moral allegory and dream vision.[3] Descending in her chariot, Shelley's omniscient preceptress, the Fairy Mab, conducts the soul of his heroine, the sleeping Ianthe, on a visionary tour of the carnage and misrule of the centuries, a desolation redeemed in the end by the force of an irresistible necessity. The purpose of this guided survey of past, present, and future is to educate Ianthe to take her place by the side of her lover; and the poem begins and ends as Mab first elevates and then returns Ianthe's soul beneath the gaze of the watchful and adoring Henry. The vision represents a fusion of melioristic, necessitarian, and radically reformist ideas Shelley was to revise in various ways but never entirely to abandon.

The intellectual character of the work has been emphasized ever since it was issued in a limited number of copies in the spring of 1813, accompanied by lengthy explanatory prose notes that are as long as the poem itself and have drawn a greater share of attention. In 1821, the year before the poet drowned, the book was pirated by a London bookseller. By 1840 more than fourteen editions had appeared, an unanticipated popularity Shelley partly foresaw, with keen irony in view of the neglect of virtually all his major writing. He considered attempting to have the pirated edition suppressed by legal injunction and composed a letter printed in Leigh Hunt's *Examiner* in July 1821 characterizing the work as "crude and immature" and "perfectly worthless in point of literary composition."[4] Behind such disclaimers one can sense a certain wry amusement and even an element of personal gratification. Throughout the nineteenth century several generations of leaders in the British labor movement found the volume, especially the prose notes, an inspiring and important source of radical ideology. Modern scholarship, although providing a more balanced assessment of the work in the context of Shelley's career, has continued to analyze its ideas and their sources as the principal evidence of the poet's intellectual background and early development.

Even in the case of a writer as devotedly intellectual as Shelley, however, ideas do not find their way into verse except through the pressure of emotion. Nor do they generate their own human interest and appeal. They require the emotional tensions and oppositions that a longer poem, even an overtly didactic one, creates by dramatizing its argument through story, myth, and symbol. Admittedly, Shelley's adaptation of long-standing narrative conventions provided a ready platform for propounding his reformist principles. Once the soul of Ianthe has been disencumbered of her body in charmed sleep, the tutelary Mab and her magic car provide an ideal vehicle for surveying the inevitable progress of the world from superstitious darkness to rational enlightenment and for demonstrating how individual fulfillment lies in cooperating with rather than impeding the forward march of civilization. Yet for all the attention scholars have devoted to these ideas and their origin in Shelley's reading, little has been said of the poem's connection with the deeper springs and sources of his emotional life. *Queen Mab* may project the vision of a grand and irresistible destiny, but it does so with a play of light and shade and a host of hesitations that suggest that the task was for Shelley neither so clear-cut nor logical an undertaking as many have assumed.

For all its apparent simplicity, the framework of *Queen Mab* is particularly revealing in the way it serves to focus and set off its visionary argument. The three brief epigraphs from Voltaire, Lucretius, and Archimedes relate directly to the poem's burden of ideas and testify to different kinds of intellectual indebtedness. The dedicatory verses to Harriet, Shelley's first wife, confess to a reliance of an emotional and deeper kind:

> Whose is the love that, gleaming through the world,
> Wards off the poisonous arrow of its scorn?
>> Whose is the warm and partial praise,
>> Virtue's most sweet reward?
>
> Beneath whose looks did my reviving soul
> Riper in truth and virtuous daring grow?
>> Whose eyes have I gazed fondly on,
>> And loved mankind the more?
>
> Harriet! on thine:—thou wert my purer mind;
> Thou wert the inspiration of my song . . .[5]

Carried forward by the surge of insistent questions, the verses, with their conventional figures and poetic diction, hardly compose the most subtle or affecting of tributes. Nevertheless there is an undeniable power in the way the flow of rhetorical interrogation culminates in the answer of Harriet's name. Nor is there any point, for all the signs of poetic immaturity, in doubting the sincerity of Shelley's gratitude. *Queen Mab* is a work of concentrated intellectual effort; but the emotional power that informs it springs from the poet's relationship with his first wife. Behind the connection with Harriet stands his relationship with his family, especially his father, the disastrous development of which largely accounts for his first and ultimately tragic marriage.

For a work of such strong didactic intention, *Queen Mab* opens on a curiously tentative note:

> How wonderful is Death,
> Death and his brother Sleep!
> One, pale as yonder waning moon
> With lips of lurid blue;
> The other, rosy as the morn
> When throned on ocean's wave
> It blushes o'er the world.   (I.1–7)

The odd juxtaposition of the two states, the one healthful and life-restoring, the other life-denying, yet superficially so like each other, establishes an aura of wonder and trepidation around our first view of the poem's sleeping heroine:

> Will Ianthe wake again,
> And give that faithful bosom joy
> Whose sleepless spirit waits to catch
> Light, life and rapture from her smile?   (I.27–30)

Even before we are aware of the identity of the attendant Henry or of Mab's fated mission, the scene seizes us with something of the wonder of a fairy tale. Henry gazes on Ianthe rather as the Prince kneels above the Sleeping Beauty just before the moment when he awakens her with his kiss and is rewarded with her answering smile of love. The moment, together with the peculiar uncertainty that surrounds it, is the more memorable for the reason that the poem returns to it, including the repetition of some of the very verses that describe it, at its close. When at the end the poem has come full circle and Mab's chariot reappears, the celestial mentor takes leave of her newly enlightened pupil with the charge:

> "Go, happy one, and give that bosom joy
> Whose sleepless spirit waits to catch
> Light, life and rapture from thy smile."   (IX.209–11)

As the chariot withdraws, our last view in the poem is of Henry, waiting as Ianthe's dark blue eyes begin to open while he "kneel[s] in silence by her couch, / Watching her sleep with looks of speechless love" (IX.237–38). Indeed the whole framework Shelley constructs for his central vision of the dawning of a brighter future seems calculated to produce the magic moment on which the poem hovers as it closes without ever quite achieving: the moment when Ianthe reawakens and smiles.[6]

The interrelationship between the poem's framework and its visionary argument may begin to suggest how, even in a work so seemingly cerebral as *Queen Mab*, reason and emotion, the dialectics of necessity and the human craving for approval and affection, were from the first in Shelley dependent on each other. In order to appreciate the significance of the moment the ending of the poem so strongly anticipates yet curiously withholds, it is necessary to remember, or rather to anticipate, the recurrence of the smile and its power throughout Shelley's poetry. One recollects, first of all, the sudden unexpected moments of rapture his lovers, such as Laon and Cythna, exchange: "She turned to me and smiled—that smile was Paradise!"[7] Later the Guido Reni portrait of Beatrice Cenci, with features so like his own, and particularly her haunting smile, drew him on to the portrayal of his most moving heroine. Again, it was the smile of his second wife, Mary, as "serene" as the "eternal smile" (15–16) of day itself, that he portrayed, in dedicating to her his *Witch of Atlas*, as the necessary atmosphere of his poetic creativity. Other examples could be cited. It is enough, however, to declare that for Shelley all poetry aspired to the condition of the human smile. Like Byron, he was extraordinarily susceptible to the power of eyes, the speaking glance across the ballroom that in an instant revealed, for the older poet, the magnetic current of an unsuspected attraction; the longer, deeper glance behind which, for the younger, the whole soul lay exposed. As Shelley knew, the smile best disarms suspicion and fear, relaxes doubt and prejudice, drawing one into the charmed circle of community and fellow feeling. It is the natural hypnotism of the soul, and he was continually impelled to see the smile reflected in the disposition of the stars and planets and in the changing features of the heavens, especially at dawn and sunset. Similarly for Shelley the essence of evil is the assumed smile of cunning calculation and deliberate malice, precisely because it subverts the most benign, unthinking, and instinctive of all human responses.

Beyond his continuous fascination with the smile, however, one senses his infatuation above all with its archetypal instance: the dawning smile of love and reassurance, virtually the kiss of life, with which a mother welcomes her newborn infant into the world. One can only imagine that Shelley must himself have experienced the power of that original smile in the deepest possible way, for he forever after attempted to recapture and reduplicate its effect within his poetry. As he wrote in the best-known of his essays, "On Love": "We are born into the world and there is something within us which from the instant that we live and move thirsts after its likeness. It is probably in correspondence with this law that the infant drains milk from the bosom of its mother; this propensity developes itself with the developement of our nature."[8] The smile was all the more fascinating to him because it involved that mirroring effect that was for him so close to the essence of love: the way a mother, in smiling at her infant, intuitively teaches it to smile, unconsciously shaping its features, its powers of responsiveness, by the force of her own charm and protectiveness, even as a greater planet attracts and guides a lesser that comes within its orbit. At the crucial point at which *Queen Mab* both opens and closes, the rapturous and expectant Henry kneels by the side of Ianthe's couch, waiting for her to awaken and to smile. In a sense the scene depicts Shelley in the person of Henry assisting, with the help of his celestial midwife Mab, at the birth of his own intellectual offspring, the child bride he had recently married.

Queen Mab is intimately related to Shelley's first marriage, and it is possible to see them as parts of a single reaction—an act of necessary defiance and the reflection of a special need for reassurance. The poem is, in fact, Shelley's youthful *Paradise Regained*, a poem written to recompense him for the world of prerogative and self-assurance he himself had largely destroyed. The unwritten *Paradise Lost* preceding it was the story of the collapse of his relationship with his family and more especially with his father. Despite the reign of injustice and misery the poem surveys, it enunciates an optimistic view of man's earthly situation, an optimism founded on the belief in an ultimate perfectibility already in progress through the iron laws of necessity. The security Shelley demanded could not, however, be restored by purely intellectual means, not even by a pronunciamento as forceful and sweeping as *Queen Mab*. The interrelationship of the poem and its framework reveal how essential to Shelley from the start was some acknowledgment or response from an audience, even one so limited as the sleeping Ianthe. Beginning with his elopement with Harriet Westbrook, Shelley's struggle to fulfill that need can be seen in the relationship he attempted to create with her and in the circle of friends he sought to assemble about her and their children, the firstborn of whom the couple named Ianthe. At various times the little community included, among others, his sister-in-law, Eliza Westbrook; Elizabeth Hitchener, the Sussex schoolteacher and newfound "sister of his soul"; Thomas Jefferson Hogg, the closest of his early friends; Thomas Love Peacock, the best of those he made later; and even his spiritual father, William Godwin. *Queen Mab* grew out of an ethos that was as emotional as intellectual, out of Shelley's need for the security of a new orientation.

The need for that reorientation was in great part the result of Shelley's break with his father. For all the comment that the obvious Oedipal strains within the poet's development have drawn, the true complexity of his relationship with Timothy Shelley has been rarely understood. That important relationship emerges from a background of family connections that are varied and partly obscure. The facts about the poet's childhood are hardly as full as one might like. Among other accounts, however, there stands out the picture of the older brother happily leading his four admiring little sisters in adventures around their Sussex home, Field Place, alternately beguiling and terrifying them with stories of the great tortoise that lived in Warnham Pond or of the ancient alchemist with beard and books and lamp who occupied a garret beneath the roof of the family dwelling, entered by a trapdoor. The family circle provided security and encouragement for the cultivation of those early imaginative abilities, and it is significant that his first volume of verse, the *Original Poetry by Victor and Cazire*, was written in collaboration with his oldest sister, Elizabeth. There is no evidence that Sir Timothy and his wife, however conservative in thought and manner, treated Bysshe any less lovingly than their other offspring, by whom they were affectionately remembered. In the autumn of 1810 Timothy accompanied Bysshe to Oxford and helped him settle in at his old college, University, requesting the local bookseller and printer, Henry Slatter, to humor his son's "literary turn" and "indulge him in his printing freaks," an instruction that suggests a parental pride in Bysshe's authorial talents.[9] The days of Bysshe's early schooling, when he was forced to leave the happy family circle for Syon House Academy at Brentford and thereafter Eton, were turbulent and often unhappy, but they set him on the path he seemed destined to follow: a successful university career; the inheritance, as elder son, of a substantial fortune and the family estate in Sussex; succession in time to his father's seat in Parliament as Whig member for New Shoreham; and the patronage and support of family, county, and important political figures, beginning with the Duke of Norfolk. These prospects were put in most serious jeopardy by the expulsion from Oxford that followed on Shelley and Hogg's publication in February 1811 of *The Necessity of Atheism*.

Hogg's biography of Shelley is notoriously untrustworthy in detail even while it provides the fullest sense we have of the earlier part of the poet's life. The description of Shelley's shock immediately after being expelled has the ring of verisimilitude:

> He was terribly agitated. I anxiously inquired what had happened.
>
> "I am expelled," he said, as soon as he had recovered himself a little, "I am expelled!" . . .
>
> He sat on the sofa, repeating, with convulsive vehemence, the words, "Expelled, expelled!" his head shaking with emotion, and his whole frame quivering.[10]

It was a clever joke that had gone badly wrong. Indeed *The Necessity of Atheism* shares the same impulse as those baiting letters Shelley had written with Hogg's connivance, under a pseudonym such as Jeremiah Stukely, addressing selected clergymen with some horrendous contradiction between Christian doctrine and moral or scientific reasoning and requesting, in apparent guilelessness, some resolution to a soul's distress.

The practice led to exchanges that exercised Shelley's wit and skill at argument, and the replies it elicited proved a source of endless amusement.[11] At the time the little pamphlet was published anonymously, Shelley and Hogg contrived to help its notoriety if not its sales by sending copies to various bishops, heads of colleges, and faculty. The combination of the covert and the disingenuous, the mischievous and the serious, the naive and the calculating is striking. They were like gamblers pressing their luck. When the offending treatise was apprehended in the window of the booksellers Munday and Slatter and the authorities cracked down, there came from the culprits the predictable outcry of righteous protest. How was it possible in post-Enlightenment Europe to impugn the propriety of a reasoned argument drawing its conclusion from the logic and methods of thinkers long acknowledged for their intellectual mastery? Do great universities exist for the discussion and testing of ideas or for their suppression? Even if one is convinced of another's error, is it proper to deny him the right to express his belief, or his doubt? Should one not rather encourage him to articulate his views with the hope of correcting his erroneous notions with superior arguments? The logic was impeccable, but within the context of events its effect was like that of the final line of *Hedda Gabler*—"Good God!—people don't do such things"—after the pistol has gone off. It was not so much the content as the circumstances under which *The Necessity of Atheism* was published that made it seem contrived to elicit the reaction it implicitly condemns.

The dismissal from Oxford need not have led to the more important alienation of Shelley from his father. Quite possibly even his former standing with the university was not irretrievable. "He wants me," he wrote of his father to Hogg in April, "to go to Oxford to apologise to Griffiths" (I,74). The latter was Dr. James Griffith, Master of University College, and behind Sir Timothy's demand one senses the tacit hope, assuming a suitable apology on Bysshe's part, of a reconciliation with the college authorities and readmission. The correspondence between father and son immediately following the expulsion conveys Sir Timothy's conviction that a period of rustication with his family might provide the necessary interval for his son to absorb the repercussions of his action and come to his senses, an undertaking for which he had perhaps already canvassed official support. Timothy's own religious views, as known to his friends, were broad-minded, and it was clear to Shelley that his father had no real concern for his religious opinions. All his father demanded was the modicum of outward deference to conventional belief necessary for his son to pursue his academic career and to occupy a place appropriate to him in society. It was one thing to doubt in the quietness of one's conscience and another thing to flaunt a set of gratuitous questions before the eyes of the world. Timothy, however, had seen the storm building from afar and knew that if the crisis in his son's affairs were to have a salutary result, it must be treated with the utmost seriousness as the occasion for compelling him to accept the need for a genuine change in his style and habits.

Having received Bysshe's letter informing him of the expulsion, Timothy wrote to his son with a list of conditions for his continued financial support: to return to Field Place, to break off his correspondence with Hogg, to receive instruction from mentors his father would appoint.[12] Shelley and Hogg replied with counterproposals, which Timothy rejected. Old Sir Bysshe, the poet's grandfather, wrote urging Timothy to accept nothing less than "unconditional Submission."[13] In the meantime Timothy, in exasperation, had given the task of negotiating with his son to his solicitor, William Whitton, whose design seems to have been to starve Bysshe into surrender. Inexorably, father and son were compelled to reenact the drama of the Promethean situation that was to exercise an increasing fascination over the poet's imagination: the contest of wills between an unappeasable father using his full power to force compliance with his authority and an isolated, suffering, but defiant offspring clinging to his integrity and the conviction of his eventual triumph.

Paradoxically Bysshe was always in the stronger position, not simply because he was the more intelligent of the two, but because he had more to lose and was willing, if necessary, to lose it. Although he tried from the first to reason with his father, his contempt for Timothy's conventional beliefs and abilities emerges in the first of his surviving letters to his parent—"Supposing twelve men were to make an affidavit before you that they had seen in Africa, a vast snake three miles long, suppose they swore that this snake eat nothing but Elephants" (I,50)—and rises into open insult later when, cut off, his need for his father's financial support deepened—"The institutions of society have made you, tho' liable to be misled by passion and prejudice like others, the *Head of the family;* and I confess it is almost natural for minds not of the highest order to value even the errors whence they derive their importance" (I,146–47). Such expressions were the result of anger and frustration in the face of Timothy's intransigence. It would be a mistake to imagine, however, that such contempt came easily to Shelley or that he paid no price for exercising it. It was easy for him to see his father as the hypocritical conservative, shielding the none too respectable background of the family and its fortune behind the cloak of social and religious respectability. Timothy, in turn, could berate the Eton boy, so privileged and so thankless, full of crackpot radical ideas gathered at secondhand and without any practical knowledge of life.

Beyond their manifest differences and obvious misjudgments, they were, like most fathers and sons, united at a deeper level of understanding. In introducing himself to both Leigh Hunt and William Godwin, Bysshe was quick to associate himself with his father's position, wealth, and influence, whereas Timothy was able to anticipate a number of his son's actions—for example, that Bysshe later left Harriet in the hands of the untrustworthy Hogg at York.[14] In their very opposition to each other they were alike in their unyielding dedication to principle as they saw it, and the determination of one only hardened the resistance of the other.

Bysshe knew his father well enough to wound him at his most sensitive points. His offer to renounce the family entail in return for a division of property between his mother and sisters and an annuity for himself of two hundred pounds deeply shocked and hurt his father. As Newman I. White has written, the offer "completely reversed the situation" as regards Timothy's threats to cut him off. "*He* [Bysshe] was proposing to throw the family overboard, to accept a severing of all formal connections."[15] Beyond this Bysshe knew that the way to hurt his father most, in view of all the hope and pride Timothy had invested in his son, was to marry beneath him. It was the one act for which he would never be forgiven. It was also the way of declaring his absolute independence of his family. Not yet sixteen, Harriet Westbrook was lovely, charming, and intelligent, and immediately took to Bysshe's tutelage when he was introduced to her by his sisters. Though wealthy and successful, her father, John Westbrook, owed his modest fortune to the coffeehouse and tavern trade and therefore was unacceptable to Timothy. Harriet warmed to Shelley's atheistic teachings, for which she was promptly persecuted at school in a way that reminded Shelley of his own unhappy schooldays. In a sense she was a second Harriet to replace his first love, his cousin Harriet Grove, who had given him up some months earlier, partly under family pressure because of his antireligious opinions. "*She* has thrown herself upon *my* protection!" (I,131) he wrote excitedly to Hogg when Harriet's father threatened to compel the unhappy girl to return to school. At various later times Shelley found it convenient to imply that he had been deliberately led on by the Westbrooks (who never demonstrated opposition to the match), especially by Harriet's close friend and older sister, Eliza, whom Shelley also befriended but came in time to look on as an evil genius. Whatever truth may lie in such suspicions, it is nevertheless clear that the impetus for the famous elopement of August 1811 came from Shelley himself. It was the logical result of the position in which he had placed himself. It was his climactic act of self-assertion and retaliation against his father, a declaration of independence from the world of privilege and security he thus deliberately disowned.

During the months following his marriage the impulsiveness and unpredictability of Shelley's conduct reveals a complication of feeling whose intensity frightened his family and which they never understood. On September 27, after long delay, Bysshe at last openly acknowledged to his father the marriage which Timothy had for some time suspected.

> Let us admit even that it is an injury that I have done, let us admit that I have wilfully inflicted pain on you, & no moral considerations can palliate the heinousness of my offence— Father, are you a Christian? it is perhaps too late to appeal to your love for me. I appeal to your duty to the God whose worship you profess, I appeal to the terrors of that day which you believe to seal the doom of mortals, then clothed with immortality.—Father are you a Christian? judge not then lest you be judged.—Remember the forgiveness of injuries which Christians profess and if my crime were even deadlier than parricide, forgiveness is your duty.—What! will you not forgive? How then can your boasted professions of Christianity appear to the world, since if you forgive not you can be no Christian.   (I,142)

There is a fierce, compulsive pleasure in the way Shelley turns the moral logic of his father's position against him. The driving intensity of the legal argument is the more striking in the way it gainsays the normal ties of understanding and affection between father and son, the existence of a "love for me" to which "it is perhaps too late to appeal." It is remarkable that Harriet is never named in Shelley's letter. Her recommendations as a woman or her qualifications as a spouse are never cited. The entire force of Shelley's argument is centered in the attack on his father, not with the aim of converting him or winning his forgiveness but rather with the purpose of exposing the hypocrisy and shallowness of his position, of making him feel something of the guilt and pain the letter so obviously reflects.

The depth of Shelley's fixation with his family during the first months of his marriage is revealed by a strange episode. The affair is particularly interesting because it throws a suggestive light on Bysshe's relationship with his mother, about which we know so little other than that she was from the time of his early childhood much attached to her son. The story concerns the extraordinary accusations Shelley made against his mother and Edward Graham. A young man of musical abilities, Graham was befriended by Timothy, who took him into his house where he served as music master and where "he was treated as a member of the family," according to one account virtually as a brother to Bysshe.[16]

Graham became a close friend to Bysshe and acted for him on several occasions as agent. In May 1811 Shelley reported to Graham, then in London, that the family had received an odd letter accusing Shelley's mother Elizabeth "of being more intimate with *you* [Graham] than with my father himself" (I,85). Elizabeth was then forty-eight and Graham only five years older than Bysshe, and the Shelley family seems to have taken the accusation as a tremendous joke. Bysshe even wrote a playful little poem to Graham acquitting him "Of having let one wild wish glow / Of cornuting old Killjoys brow" (I,87).[17]

Four months later, however, the joke turned around savagely in Shelley's imagination. Bysshe heard a report, perhaps from his uncle, Captain Pilfold, that his mother was encouraging a match between Graham and his favorite sister, Elizabeth, whom he had earlier sought to interest in Hogg. Immediately he sent a furious letter to his mother, enclosed in a note to Timothy, accusing her of promoting the liaison as a way of concealing her own adultery (I,155). The charge would seem almost comical if Bysshe hadn't taken it so seriously, describing to Elizabeth Hitchener his mother's "depravity" (I,163) and writing to his sister to implore her to "speak truth" (I,156). Not content with writing, Bysshe left Harriet with Hogg at York and descended on Field Place, perhaps during his father's absence, to confront his mother and sister in a terrifying scene that left even Timothy shaken. "He frightened his mother and sister exceedingly," Timothy wrote to Whitton on October 25, describing "the present perturbed state of P. B.'s mind, which will not suffer it to rest until it has completely and entirely disordered his whole spiritual past."[18] The little drama reads like a reenactment of scenes from *Hamlet*. Barely returned from Scotland and his honeymoon with Harriet, Shelley was drawn back yet again, through his obvious identification with Graham, into the web of compulsive desires, guilts, and insecurities of his earliest romance with his family.

The history of Shelley's tortured relationship with his family, culminating in the decisive elopement with Harriet, provides the vital context for a reading of *Queen Mab*. As dispassionate and inflexible as it seems, the poem's philosophical machinery is driven by guilts, hopes, and fears not far beneath the surface. In republishing the poem in her first collected edition of 1839, Mary Shelley suppressed the dedicatory stanzas to Harriet. She also added a note to the poem portraying the spirit of humanitarian disinterestedness in which Shelley had composed it:

He was animated to greater zeal by compassion for his fellow-creatures. His sympathy was excited by the misery with which the world is burning. He witnessed the sufferings of the poor, and was aware of the evils of ignorance . . . He saw, in a fervent call on his fellow-creatures to share alike the blessings of the creation, to love and serve each other, the noblest work that life and time permitted him. In this spirit he composed *Queen Mab*.[19]

Such is, however, a very one-sided account of the poem's genesis. As Richard Holmes has written of the work, "the overwhelming impression is one of anger and accusation."[20] Nor are the anger and accusation directed solely at society. When Mab addresses the evils of kingship and the question of why the common man delights in his servitude when he might, rather, hurl the tyrant from his throne, she declares:

> No—'tis not strange.
> He, like the vulgar, thinks, feels, acts and lives
> Just as his father did; the unconquered powers
> Of precedent and custom interpose
> Between a king and virtue.   (III.95–99)

Shelley's attack is directed against the institution of monarchy; but the analogy between king and father, so frequent throughout the poem, suggests how much his resentment against the tyranny of tradition draws its animus from the pressures to conform as they operated in his own case. The poem is often balanced awkwardly between two opposite impulses. One is a long-range Godwinian trust in evolutionary progress, by which, as Mab explains it, kingship will quietly disappear through the growth of reason:

> When man's maturer nature shall disdain
> The playthings of its childhood;—kingly glare
> Will lose its power to dazzle; its authority
> Will silently pass by.   (III.131–34)

At the same time the poem manifests a burning impatience as to why

> not one slave, who suffers from the crimes
> Of this unnatural being; not one wretch,
> Whose children famish, and whose nuptial bed
> Is earth's unpitying bosom, rears an arm
> To dash him from his throne!   (III.102–6)

The spirit of a lofty philosophical quietism alternates uneasily with the imperative of the poem's epigraph from Voltaire, "Ecrasez l'infame!"

It is remarkable how much *Queen Mab* is dominated by the imagery of mother, father, and child, and how many of the hopeful progressions it anticipates take as their model the metaphor of the child's development from infancy to maturity. Canto VI presents a long anthropological analysis of the evolution of religion, an argument that in many respects looks forward to the brilliant dialectics of Browning's "Caliban upon Setebos." The infant's natural reverence for the stars, trees, and clouds that surround it gradually develops into superstitious belief in ghosts and spirits, in the kind of necromancy and alchemy that fascinated Shelley in his own boyhood. Faced with the inexplicable wonders of the universe, the human soul, "Baffled and gloomy" (VI.94) in its ignorance, at last escapes from the pain of its uncertainty by personifying the power it intuits in the figure of a God, a figure that becomes the reflection of corrupt desire and misrule. Religion, however, is already past its prime and descending through old age and senility toward "the darksome grave" (VI.140) of superannuated beliefs. This type of hopeful paradigm is one Shelley uses throughout his study of the various aspects of human evolution. Although the human soul seems born into the world to suffer, Shelley makes it clear that the influences so blighting to human development can at any moment be eliminated, as in time they inevitably must. Indeed the instruction Ianthe receives as Mab's pupil, between the time she leaves until she returns to the adoring gaze of Henry, dramatizes Shelley's faith that the individual soul can be shielded from malign influences through proper education. However magical and otherworldly, Ianthe's conducted tour has the force of a serious hypothesis, a controlled experiment in educational psychology. It anticipates the soul's escape, perhaps for the first time in history, from the corrupting influence of established social institutions through the knowledge of its own perfectibility and the validity of its own best instincts. The plan is poetic and visionary. Behind it lies, however, Shelley's scheme for "cultivating" Harriet, his child wife, as the center of a small community of chosen friends who by their reading, discussion, and uninhibited benevolence would preserve a charmed circle sufficient to keep the desecrating influences of the world at bay.

If the framework of *Queen Mab* reflects the optimism of Shelley's plans for educating and protecting Harriet, there are moments in the poem when the logic of perfectibility is undercut by a deeper sense of personal fatality that suggests how much Shelley had been irrevocably changed by his conflict with his father. Here Canto VII—unquestionably the most powerful in the poem—and especially the Ahasuerus episode, so often passed over with little or no comment, are particularly revealing. The canto embodies Shelley's attempt to push through to its conclusion his attack upon religion and, more specially, Christianity. In support of her argument, Mab conjures up the phantom of Ahasuerus to testify before Ianthe. The figure of Ahasuerus, the Wandering Jew, who spurned Christ bearing the cross on the way to Calvary and for this was condemned to wander the earth until Judgment Day, had long exercised a fascination for Shelley and had been the subject of an earlier poem, *The Wandering Jew*, of 1810. In *Queen Mab*, Ahasuerus appears still youthful and defiant, yet singularly subdued.

> His port and mien bore mark of many years,
> And chronicles of untold antientness
> Were legible within his beamless eye:
>   Yet his cheek bore the mark of youth;
> Freshness and vigor knit his manly frame;
> The wisdom of old age was mingled there
>   With youth's primæval dauntlessness;
>   And inexpressible woe,
> Chastened by fearless resignation.   (VII.73–81)

The portrait reminds one of those idealized father figures Shelley habitually was drawn to, the type of the kindly hermit who rescues Laon in Canto III of *The Revolt of Islam*, figures who appear to take much of their identity from Dr. James Lind, the part-time teacher who befriended Shelley at Eton. As opposed to the spirit of timorous conformity, the Jew represents everything vigorous, brave, and forthright that Shelley could identify with. At the same time the Jew seems curiously downcast and despondent.

Ahasuerus is summoned to testify before the spirit of Ianthe in a question-and-answer examination of the problem of evil that anticipates the way Asia interrogates Demogorgon in the second act of *Prometheus Unbound*. "Is there a God?" Mab asks. "Is there a God!—aye, an almighty God," Ahasuerus replies, "And vengeful as almighty!" (VII.83–85). He proceeds to describe a murderous, tyrannical Jehovah who has created a paradise and a tree of good and evil precisely so that man might be tempted and fall. To justify the appalling result, Jehovah resorts to a second act of propagation:

> "One way remains:
> I will beget a son, and he shall bear
> The sins of all the world."   (VII.134–36)

The inconsequence and inhumanity of such a rationalization are central to Shelley's criticism of the Christian ethic. It is curious, however, how Shelley's attack wavers once he turns his attention to the figure of Christ. In his long prose note to the lines last quoted, he characterizes the historical Jesus as a person of good and simple life who was crucified for attempting to redeem the world from barbarous superstition. Yet a footnote to this depiction declares: "Since writing this note I have some reason to suspect that Jesus was an ambitious man, who aspired to the throne of Judea."[21] The same ambivalence pervades the central section of Canto VII. On the one hand we are told of Christ that "humbly he came," a man "scorned by the world" (VII.163,165), compelled by his father to endure his dreadful agony. Yet he comes as "a parish demagogue," teaching "justice, truth, and peace" only "In semblance" (VII.167–69).

This extraordinary ambivalence is nowhere more apparent than in the climactic confrontation between Christ and Ahasuerus on the road to Calvary. The laboring Jesus groans beneath the weight of the cross he bears, but Ahasuerus, mindful only of the greater miseries those sufferings are destined to produce, taunts him with impatience:

> Indignantly I summed
> The massacres and miseries which his name
> Had sanctioned in my country, and I cried,
> "Go! go!" in mockery.
> A smile of godlike malice reillumed
> His fading lineaments.—"I go," he cried,
> "But thou shalt wander o'er the unquiet earth
> Eternally." (VII.176–83)

The scene takes its power from the terrible, unexpected smile of malice that breaks from Christ's features, a smile all the more terrifying by contrast with the traditional expression of long suffering and forgiveness in innumerable depictions in painting and in sculpture. Like the relationship between Shelley and his father, that between Ahasuerus and Christ is complicated by guilt and mutual recrimination. The curse Christ utters is totally un-Christian in its vindictiveness. Yet the scene, as it unfolds, creates the impression that he would never have been moved to utter the malediction were it not for his agony and the gratuitous scorn, however historically justified, heaped upon him by his tormentor. It is out of this complex of anger, guilt, and frustration that the curse descends with the terrible withering effect Ahasuerus immediately proceeds to describe:

upon the stricken Jew is one of the most vividly realized moments in an intellectual and highly abstract work generally unnotable for its sense of lived experience. By contrast there is something extraordinarily tentative about the posture of the attendant Henry as he bends over Ianthe, waiting for her eyes to open. One is reminded curiously of Keats's metaphor of Adam's dream and his later redaction of it when Porphyro kneels by Madeline's bedside in *The Eve of St. Agnes*—an episode in which Keats not so much reaffirms as tests the limits of an earlier metaphor and its truth. At the end of *Queen Mab* Ianthe barely awakens, and the smile which Henry so patiently awaits is intimated but never actually arrives.

The collapse of Shelley's first marriage and the circumstances surrounding it are so well known that they need only the briefest summary. Elizabeth Hitchener, the Sussex schoolteacher whom Shelley hardly knew, yielding at last to the prolonged entreaties of Harriet and Bysshe, threw up her job to join them as a part of their little community in July 1812, when the poet was hard at work on *Queen Mab*. Before the end of the year Shelley's "Sister of my soul" (I,152) had become the "Brown Demon" (I,336). "She built all her hopes on being able to separate me from my dearly beloved Percy, and had the artfulness to say that Percy was really in love with her," Harriet complained (I,331). "She is an artful, superficial, ugly, hermaphroditical beast of a woman," Shelley wrote Hogg in December, "and my astonishment at my fatuity, inconsistency, and bad taste was never so great, as after living four months with her as an inmate" (I,336). Early the following spring he turned violently against his sister-in-law Eliza, who had resided with them almost continuously since shortly after the elopement. "It is a sight which awakens an inexpressible sensation of disgust and horror, to see her caress my poor little Ianthe, in whom I may hereafter find the consolation of sympathy," he wrote to Hogg. "I sometimes feel faint with the fatigue of checking the overflowings of my unbounded abhorrence for this miserable wretch. But she is no more than a blind and loathsome worm, that cannot see to sting" (I,384). These extraordinary reversals of feeling were stages in a process of disillusionment that culminated in his alienation from Harriet herself.

In October 1814, following his abandonment of Harriet and elopement with Mary Godwin, Shelley looked back to the preceding spring when "I suddenly perceived that the entire devotion with which I had resigned all prospects of utility or happiness to the single purpose of cultivating Harriet was a gross & despicable superstition" (I,401). "How wonderfully I am changed!" he went on. "Not a disembodied spirit can have undergone a stranger revolution! . . . I never before felt the integrity of my nature, its various dependencies, & learned to consider myself as an

> The dampness of the grave
> Bathed my imperishable front. I fell,
> And long lay tranced upon the charmed soil.
> When I awoke hell burned within my brain,
> Which staggered on its seat; for all around
> The mouldering relics of my kindred lay,
> Even as the Almighty's ire arrested them,
> And in their various attitudes of death
> My murdered children's mute and eyeless sculls
> Glared ghastily upon me.   (VII.183–92)

The scene is the most powerful and revealing in the whole of *Qu[*
because it conveys the full impact of the curse Shelley brought dow
himself and his future offspring in breaking with his father. Ben
echoes of Satan's awakening on the burning marl, one senses the tr
the rupture as the poet first experienced it. Ahasuerus first reviles,
cursed by the hapless Savior who, however misguided and trea
was compelled to assume a role which he was helpless to esca
complex interplay of guilts and sympathies that links Christ and Ah
reveals the true ambivalence of Shelley's feelings toward a father o
by the greater powers of social evil and conformity to play the
oppressor.

There is a notable contrast within *Queen Mab* between the o
the poem publicly espouses about the inevitable course of human
and the darker sense of personal fatality that covertly emerges f
major episode. The two views are, of course, not necessarily incom
Indeed in a special sense they reinforce each other. It was preci
shock and disorientation of Shelley's break with his father that mad
more imperative the success of his hopes for educating Harriet to
place beside him at the center of a new world of love and securit
work of art, *Queen Mab* rotates on an axis whose emotional p
symbolized by contrasting smiles. The first is intimated in the fram
of the poem, in the poem's opening scene to which its conclusion
us, and the attitude of the expectant Henry as he bends over the s
Ianthe to "catch / Light, life and rapture from her smile" (I.29–30;
11). The other is Christ's perverted smile of godlike malice that d
with such devastating effect upon Ahasuerus. The two moments de
central sources of emotional energy that animate the poem; the
evoke and balance each other. Yet they differ strikingly, not sin
character but in the degree of their realization. The effect of Christ'

whole accurately united rather than an assemblage of inconsistent & discordant portions" (I,403). The imagery is of awakening from a false but paralyzing dream. When they first met at Godwin's house earlier in the year, Shelley and Mary had fallen immediately and rapturously in love. There is no doubt that in winning Mary's affection Shelley gained a woman not only of exceptional physical beauty but ideally suited by birth and education to work beside him toward achieving the highest of his social goals and intellectual ambitions. The poet was hardly the first man to discover the error of his initial choice and then to have to choose between the unhappiness of continuing the marital tie or once and forever breaking it in favor of a fully gratifying and reciprocal attachment. This can hardly exonerate Shelley for his harsh and even brutal treatment of Harriet in effecting their separation. Indeed Shelley's next major work, *Alastor*, takes its origin, as we shall see, from a process of self-scrutiny and recrimination which reveals guilts he was never able to allay. Nevertheless what is most striking is Shelley's need to justify, or rationalize, his new attachment to Mary by idealizing their relationship: "Above all, most sensibly do I perceive the truth of my entire worthlessness but as depending on another. And I am deeply persuaded that thus enobled, I shall become a more true & constant friend, a more useful lover of mankind, a more ardent asserter of truth & virtue—above all more consistent, more intelligible more true" (I,403). The words betray an element of sophistry and rationalization, but it would be wrong to dismiss them as simple dishonesty. Just as the idealized world he had sought to create around Harriet was a replacement for an earlier universe of harmony and love that had been destroyed, so it was impossible for him to reach out to Mary without visualizing her as the nexus of a new reformulation of his own moral and intellectual identity.

As Shelley's first major work, *Queen Mab* proclaims a rational, necessary, universal order. The relationship between that vision and the framework that contains it suggests, however, how conditional and tentative that order actually was. Undoubtedly *Queen Mab* is a "poem of ideas"; but it takes its driving power from the personal relationships that mattered most to the poet. In conceiving his major poems, Shelley habitually sought to epitomize his highest imaginative perceptions by idealizing those relationships that served to connect him with the outer world. When those relationships altered, as indeed they changed throughout the whole of his career, they required new imaginative reformulations in the poetry, visionary structures he was forced to modify repeatedly under the pressures reality brought to bear. The verse struggles to reify and to reflect the

permanence and value of relationships that in reality were forever susceptible to reappraisal and change. There is thus a continuous and vital interplay between the poems and the life, between the apparently self-
contained order of ethical and historical absolutes and the flux of lived
experience that underlies and sustains it. Such an interchange is hardly
surprising; in Shelley, however, where it is often less than obvious, it
assumes particular importance. *Queen Mab* has most to tell us in the partly
concealed connections it reveals that unite the poetry with the life.

two

BROODINGS IN SOLITUDE

Alastor

The myth that dominates *Queen Mab* is that of Pygmalion, the sculptor who falls in love with his own handiwork. The myth that informs *Alastor* is its close correlative, the story of Narcissus and his love for his own reflection. The two tales are intimately related; to trace Shelley's transference from the one to its deeper counterpart is to understand the intellectual and psychological connections between the two fables as well as Shelley's growing preoccupation with the central problems of his experience.[1]

Shelley composed *Alastor* in the autumn and early winter of 1815, after he and Mary settled down in a cottage at Bishopsgate near Windsor Park and the Thames. Shelley spent many hours reading or composing beneath the great trees or drifting with the current of the river in his boat. The poem had been long developing in his imagination and, as Richard Holmes has written, represents "the final point which these [earlier] months of introspection and self-assessment reached, and his own comment, as a poet, on the inner significance of the events of 1814."[2] Most probably Shelley was thinking seriously about the poem, if not actually at work on it, in July when he left Mary in London to spend some weeks at Marlow with Peacock. Although Shelley spent his time ostensibly searching for a house for Mary and himself, the process of introspection and self-assessment was intensified by the fact that he had placed himself under the care of a London physician with the conviction that he was suffering from a serious, perhaps fatal illness.[3] These weeks are marked, as Holmes has written, "by a curious sense of detachment and vacancy, as if suddenly he had seen through life and all it had to offer."[4]

In his self-preoccupation Shelley was reworking in imagination the pattern of events that had led to his current situation: the alienation from his family, the failure of a subsequent network of idealized relationships culminating in the rupture with Harriet, and the force of his new attachment to Mary. In Mary he had gained a new companion, his intellectual equal, with whom he shared a passionate relationship such as he had never known. But he had deserted Harriet, now the mother of his second child and first son, Charles, in a fashion that could only appear both self-serving and unfeeling. Moreover in leaving Harriet he had abandoned an ideal of himself he had invested in her, which he was unable to relinquish. The loss demanded time to work through a process akin to grieving. He needed to come to terms with the origin and magnitude of the failure and in some way to account for it, if only as a necessary consequence of the somber destiny he had come to feel as man and poet. The problem, in all its complexity, weighed upon his spirit and was impossible to ignore. About to settle down with Mary to a more fixed existence, was he fated to resume the familiar pattern of alternating attraction and repulsion, of commitment and loss? Such preoccupations provide the emotional background of *Alastor* and explain its extraordinary psychological complexity and ambivalence.

In its introspective irony and self-questioning, *Alastor* seems light-years away from the confident optimism and broad outlook of *Queen Mab*. At the beginning of her note on the later work Mary remarked on their differences and sought in part to account for them:

> *Alastor* is written in a very different tone from *Queen Mab*. In the latter, Shelley poured out all the cherished speculations of his youth—all the irrepressible emotions of sympathy, censure, and hope, to which the present suffering, and what he considers the proper destiny, of his fellow-creatures, gave birth. *Alastor*, on the contrary, contains an individual interest only. A very few years, with their attendant events, had checked the ardour of Shelley's hopes, though he still thought them well grounded, and that to advance their fulfilment was the noblest task man could achieve.[5]

Mary goes on immediately to touch upon the causes for this change of tone and its mixture of inner withdrawal and disappointment, but she does so with an understandable evasiveness. "This is neither the time nor place," she writes, "to speak of the misfortunes that chequered his life. It will be sufficient to say that, in all he did, he at the time of doing it believed himself justified to his own conscience; while the various ills of poverty and loss of friends brought home to him the sad realities of life."[6] Mary never reveals the nature of those misfortunes that required Shelley to rationalize his behavior to his conscience, nor does she identify the friends whose loss he felt so keenly. At the time of her writing she had been forbidden by Sir Timothy to compose a biography of his son under threat of losing the small sum Timothy contributed to maintain her and her one surviving child, Percy Florence. Even had she not been constrained by that injunction, however, to have touched on such questions would have involved her in the embarrassment of discussing the circumstances that led to her replacing Harriet in Shelley's life and, more distressing yet, precipitated Harriet's suicide. One understands Mary's reticence; nevertheless her comments, however vague or cursory, indicate that *Alastor* takes its origins from some of the most deeply felt and intimate experiences of Shelley's life.

It is sometimes assumed that once he had determined to commit himself to Mary, Shelley abandoned Harriet with relative indifference. Such was not the case. Peacock describes going up to London to meet Shelley during the time of the poet's first attachment to Mary. "Between his old feelings towards Harriet, *from whom he was not then separated*," Peacock wrote with special emphasis, "and his new passion for Mary, he showed in his looks, in his gestures, in his speech, the state of a mind 'suffering, like a little kingdom, the nature of an insurrection.'" Later Peacock wrote that "Harriet's untimely fate occasioned him deep agony of mind, which he felt the more because for a long time he kept the feeling to himself."[7] That Shelley's surviving correspondence does not reveal the strong feelings of remorse and self-recrimination to which Peacock alludes does not prove that Shelley was impervious to them. As Cameron has written of Shelley's separation from Harriet: "The marriage had not deteriorated to a point where the husband hated the wife from whom he wished to be free . . . [Harriet's] sweetness of character, her beauty, her very helplessness must have held great appeal to him. The thought of leaving her must at times have been almost intolerable, and the fact that he suppressed it did not mean that he had killed it."[8]

The failure of his relationship with Harriet brought to the forefront of Shelley's mind the problem of human desire—the drive we would today describe as libido—and the idealization to which it naturally leads. In his fragmentary essay "On Love," Shelley writes of the natural tendency to reify, through an act of imaginative introspection, an image of what is admirable or beautiful—an ideal archetype that thereafter provides, through our search for its earthly counterpart, the vital stimulus for human desire and exertion.

> We dimly see within our intellectual nature a miniature as it
> were of our entire self, yet deprived of all that we condemn or
> despise, the ideal prototype of every thing excellent or lovely

that we are capable of conceiving as belonging to the nature of man . . . a mirror whose surface reflects only the forms of purity and brightness: a soul within our soul . . . To this we eagerly refer all sensations, thirsting that they should resemble or correspond with it.[9]

The essay, which shares many affinities in imagery and tone with *Alastor*, seems to describe the same process as that by which the youth, in the words of the "Preface" to the poem, "images to himself the Being whom he loves" in a "vision in which he embodies his own imaginations" of "all of wonderful, or wise, or beautiful, which the poet, the philosopher, or the lover could depicture."[10] "On Love" has repeatedly been used as a principal gloss for elucidating *Alastor*. Nevertheless the parallel it affords has always puzzled readers because the pursuit that in the essay is represented as an unqualified ideal is in the poem a hopeless quest that leads to the Poet's desolation and death. The discrepancy is only disconcerting, however, so long as we fail to understand that Shelley was capable of examining the same problem from contrary perspectives and that prose argument and poetic composition drew on different levels of his mind and sensibility.

Certainly Shelley had earlier noticed potential drawbacks to his favorite formulation. In 1810 and 1811, acting virtually as a go-between, he had sought to promote a romance between Hogg and his favorite sister Elizabeth (who had never met), through his power to inspire in each an idealized image of the other. Realizing the error of his attempt, Shelley wrote to Hogg who, despite a total lack of encouragement, was reluctant to withdraw: "You loved a being, an idea in your own mind which had no real existence. You concreted this abstract of perfection, you annexed this fictitious quality to the idea presented by a *name,* the being whom that name signified was by no means worthy of this . . . The being whom you loved is not what she was, consequently as love appertains to mind & not body she exists no longer" (I,95).[11] Hence the manifest error of pursuing mere illusions.

Yet on the other hand, was not the habit of idealization an essential, indeed an inescapable, part of all imaginative activity? In August 1815, the very month when he was getting down to *Alastor*, Shelley wrote Hogg:

Yet who is there that will not pursue phantoms, spend his choicest hours in hunting after dreams, and wake only to perceive his error and regret that death is so near? One man there is, and he is a cold and calculating man, who knows better than to waste life, but who alas! cannot enjoy it. (I,429–30)

The totally rational, unimaginative man might know how to escape such errors; but he could hardly experience life to the full. The dilemma lies at the very center of *Alastor*. Moreover it was one of which Shelley was specially mindful as, with Harriet still much in his thoughts, he was about to settle down into a new and intense relationship with Mary. The preceding autumn he had written her:

> Your thoughts alone can waken mine to energy. My mind without yours is dead & cold as the dark midnight river when the moon is down. It seems as if you alone could shield me from impurity & vice. If I were absent from you long I should shudder with horror at myself. My understanding becomes undisciplined without you. I believe I must become in Marys hands what Harriet was in mine—yet how differently disposed how devoted & affectionate: how beyond measure reverencing & adoring the intelligence that governs me.   (I,414)

Despite the manifest differences between the two women and the apparent reversal of his role, was he in danger of idealizing Mary in the same way as he had Harriet? Already Mary had begun to appear to his imagination under the figure of the presiding moon. Yet the implication is that, for all her seeming dominance, her true function was defined by the orbit of the greater planet she served to animate and illumine. Even while Shelley was mindful of the dangers of preformulating, of idealizing his relationships, the habit was one he seemed constitutionally incapable of escaping.

The dilemma is mirrored in the contradictory dialectics of the "Preface" to *Alastor* which have so often puzzled commentators. As frequently pointed out, the first paragraph of the "Preface" presents the hero of the poem as a nobly educated and inspired youth "led forth by an imagination inflamed and purified through familiarity with all that is excellent and majestic." To the surprise of readers, the same youth is promptly condemned at the beginning of the second paragraph for temerity and "self-centred seclusion."[12] As Carlos Baker aptly summed up the problem some years ago: "The real point at issue would seem to be this: when Shelley wrote the poem, did he mean it to be the story of a peerless youth's quest for the ideal maiden of his dreams, or did he mean to imply that the youth was in some way culpable, and that the quest was a punishment?"[13] Is the youth, in all the fervor that drives him forward on his ideal quest, deserving of praise or condemnation?

These questions, which repeatedly emerge throughout the poem, cannot be considered in isolation from the particular view of human existence which the "Preface" proceeds to set forth and which materially conditions them. That view is in good part established by the declaration that although the Poet's temerity was "avenged by the furies of an irresistible passion pursuing him to speedy ruin . . . that [same] Power which strikes the luminaries of the world with sudden darkness and extinction . . . dooms to a slow and poisonous decay those meaner spirits that dare to abjure its dominion." The point is driven home by the lines from Wordsworth's *Excursion* with which the "Preface" ends:

> The good die first,
> And those whose hearts are dry as summer dust,
> Burn to the socket!

The fact is that all men decay; all die; all are consumed by the fire of life within them. The principal question is the degree to which we choose to retard or to accelerate the process. For the "Preface" clearly implies that what hastens the inevitable exhaustion of energy are those same imaginative exertions that make life most valuable—sympathy, friendship, love— the very qualities that Keats, in his reworking of *Alastor* in *Endymion*, placed in ascending order "high / Upon the forehead of humanity" (I.801–2). Thus there are those who, "selfish, blind, and torpid," conserve their powers and extend their lives, "prepar[ing] for their old age a miserable grave."[14] Others, yearning for communion with the soul-companion of their dreams, consume themselves in the ardor of their quest. It is only a matter of choosing which course to follow.

Of course, as Keats was to discover in the process of composing his poem, to pursue the brightest visions of the imagination may not lead to the discovery of the ideal in some attainable human form. That possibility was hardly lost on Shelley. Nevertheless, he had by now come to see that all love required some element of idealization. In order to sympathize it was first necessary to identify imaginatively with another, and such identification was impossible without idealizing certain aspects both of the self and of another being, if only to create the grounds for some conceivable relationship. Idealization was as necessary for love as it was inevitable, and, however dangerous the premise, the higher the love, the greater the idealization. In this connection one warning in the "Preface" stands out: "They who, deluded by no generous error, instigated by no sacred thirst of doubtful knowledge, duped by no illustrious superstition, loving nothing on this earth, and cherishing no hopes beyond, yet keep aloof from sympathies with their kind, rejoicing neither in human joy nor mourning with human grief; these, and such as they, have their apportioned curse." The sentence, the longest and most complicated in the "Preface," partly conceals a form of logic that deserves elucidation. It seems to argue as follows: the greater the error, the more generous the impulse that inspires it; the more doubtful the knowledge, the more sacred the thirst that longs for it; the deeper the superstition that dupes us, the more illustrious its nature. Similarly, the greater the "Power" that attracts us and the more "exquisite" our "perception of its influences," the more "sudden" the "darkness and extinction" that overwhelm us as a consequence.

The two views of the Poet, then, in the "Preface" to *Alastor* are not absolutely contradictory but rather distinct and complementary. Given the implacable logic of the energy-time equation that dominates man's earthly condition, there are only two ways of proceeding. If one course had its "apportioned curse," so certainly had the other. Given the ultimate extinction to which all alike are fated, one could conserve his energies in cold self-restraint. But this was neither Shelley's way nor that of his Poet in *Alastor*. Better to burn quickly and brightly than to smolder dully. Better to aspire grandly even at the cost of sudden exhaustion. Better to imagine greatly, to sympathize intensely even at the risk of crushing disappointment. *Alastor* is a case study of a passionate and radical assent to these latter options. It is a poem that allowed Shelley to rework in imagination the central predicament of his career to date, to recognize its pattern of recurrent failure, yet at the same time to forgive himself. It is a work that enabled him to come to terms, if partly on an unconscious level, with some of the most painful disappointments and miscalculations of his life. Yet it permitted him to reconfirm that ideal of his own integrity, both psychological and moral, so essential to his being.

The force that drives the youth forward on his quest is never made exactly clear. There is an important hint, however, of youthful sorrow and dispossession in the preliminary assertion that "When early youth had past, he left / His cold fireside and alienated home" (75–76). In his search for "Nature's most secret steps" (81), his travels lead him from her milder appearances, with their "claims / To love and wonder" (97–98), to more immoderate climes where "The red volcano overcanopies / Its fields of snow and pinnacles of ice / With burning smoke" (83–85) or where, hidden in caves fed by "springs / Of fire and poison" (88–89), domes of diamond and gold rise upon columns of crystal and chrysolite. The celestial and the subterranean, the beautiful and the noxious combine and even cooperate in unexpected ways, while the natural piety of the Wordsworthian enthusiast resonates uneasily amid the perceptions of a Julian Huxley. From the realm of nature the youth is led on to inspect the remnants of the great civilizations of antiquity. These sites, once the seats of thriving cultures, now only manifest total desolation. Yet the fragments they contain seem to hold frozen in their hieroglyphics the secrets of the world's origins. His struggle to retrieve their meaning is prolonged and painful in its intensity:

> through the long burning day [he]
> Gazed on those speechless shapes, nor, when the moon
> Filled the mysterious halls with floating shades
> Suspended he that task, but ever gazed
> And gazed, till meaning on his vacant mind
> Flashed like strong inspiration, and he saw
> The thrilling secrets of the birth of time.   (122–28)

The passage appears to culminate in a triumphant burst of illumination. However, the nature of the "secrets" the youth intuits is never disclosed. Indeed the ominously gathering shades and the strained, hypnotic quality of the syntax ("ever gazed / And gazed") make us wonder whether we are witnessing an act of archaeological reconstruction or of autosuggestion. For all the excitement of the youth's presumed enlightenment, the passage seems to imply that, given sufficient pressure of the mind's desire in the face of its own vacancy, the imagination necessarily invents its own answers to the intractable questions oppressing it, answers as nebulous as the void from which they issue. Just where it rises to a point of affirmation, Shelley's narrative characteristically complicates and qualifies itself to leave us more than ever in doubt.

Resuming his journey, the youth ventures on, oblivious of the Arab Maiden who follows him to tend upon his slumbers and who serves to dramatize how far removed he is, in his unconscious commitment to the as yet unrealized goal of his wanderings, from the consolations of the simple human love she offers him. The direction of the quest now turns further inward. The youth's travels take him across Arabia and Persia and the mountains of the Hindu Kush to the vale of Kashmir, the supposed site, as Donald Reiman has pointed out, of the birth of civilization, so that the journey takes on more than ever the aura of a search for the origins of the self.[15] He falls asleep within a natural bower and is granted a vision of all he seeks. There is no doubt that when the Veiled Maid appears to him in his dreams, he recognizes her as the prototype of all he longs for. Like a lost, dimly remembered Eurydice, she draws him to her amid the shades that surround her and back into which, at the end of the episode, she flees. Their intercourse dramatizes, as Keats so well understood, the poet's primordial incest, his romance with his muse—the theme Keats appropriated (albeit with his own quite different emphasis) for the allegory of

Endymion, the theme that dominates so much of his later verse. Like Keats's Cynthia, the Veiled Maid incorporates and subsumes all the youth's earlier desires—his love of nature, his desire for secret knowledge, as well as ambitions of an intellectual and humanitarian cast: "Knowledge and truth and virtue were her theme, / And lofty hopes of divine liberty" (158–59). Her frame is kindled with a permeating fire, a potency missing from the opening invocation to its three brother elements, which now enters the poem prominently for the first time.[16] Above all the youth is swayed by her "wild numbers" (163), for she bears a harp and is "Herself a Poet" (161), so that we realize that what we are witnessing in the hero's answering rapture is the initiation of the youth into poethood—the birth of the archetypal bard.

Appropriate to its new intensity, the relationship between the lovers now enters an overtly sexual phase. He is transported:

> Her voice was like the voice of his own soul
> Heard in the calm of thought; its music long,
> Like woven sounds of streams and breezes, held
> His inmost sense suspended in its web
> Of many-coloured woof and shifting hues.   (153–57)

The description brings to mind phrases of the essay "On Love" proclaiming that perception of "a soul within our soul," the discovery of "a frame whose nerves, like the chords of two exquisite lyres strung to the accompaniment of one delightful voice, vibrate with the vibrations of our own."[17] At the same time the verse, in its extraordinary effects of synesthesia, is more subtle and complex.[18] There are overtones of seduction in the way the Poet is held "suspended" in the "web" of her song and hints of instability and change that play around the shifting texture. Like much of *Endymion*, the passage is a flow of vague erotic reverie, shot through, here and there, with reminiscences of lived experience:

> at the sound he turned,
> And saw by the warm light of their own life
> Her glowing limbs beneath the sinuous veil.
> . . . . .
> His strong heart sunk and sickened with excess
> Of love. He reared his shuddering limbs and quelled
> His gasping breath, and spread his arms to meet
> Her panting bosom.   (174–76,181–84)

The powerful alliterative pull of the lines introduces an uncomfortable sense of compulsion. The intensity of aroused desire is the more striking for the way it is conveyed through images of physical illness: "sickened," "shuddering," "gasping," "panting." The transport is too consuming to be long maintained:

> Now blackness veiled his dizzy eyes, and night
> Involved and swallowed up the vision; sleep
> Like a dark flood suspended in its course,
> Rolled back its impulse on his vacant brain.   (188–91)

Like a wave sweeping up the shore of consciousness, one of Shelley's favorite metaphors, sleep obliterates every detail of the experience from memory. Yet the effect of the experience remains, like the desire a dream leaves with us, even though all other recollection of it has fled. Here at the climax of his poem, Shelley represents the object of the archetypal poet's quest, the reenactment in all its primal rapture of the first union with the mother, muse, or anima. It is the deeply buried remembrance of this rapture that the poet is forever driven to seek and to which he compares all other sensations. The logic of the essay "On Love" remains, but united now with a terrible view of the poetic calling and its fatality.

The lines that immediately commence the next verse paragraph I take to be the most beautiful in *Alastor*:

> Roused by the shock he started from his trance—
> The cold white light of morning, the blue moon
> Low in the west, the clear and garish hills,
> The distinct valley and the vacant woods,
> Spread round him where he stood.   (192–96)

It is odd to think of a beauty born of disillusionment. The simplicity of diction and the clarity of outline, extending even to such a note as "garish," contrast with the rapturous, hectic interlude they follow. The landscape appears suddenly cleansed and freed of the fierce intensities that had enveloped it. Such is Shelley's mastery of his stylistic medium that the shift of tone by itself raises implicit questions. Is it possible to enjoy, even love the forms of nature for their own sake, independent of the visionary intimations or consolations with which we are habitually impelled to endow them? If the poem suggests from time to time the desirability of such a modern and emancipated attitude, it more often depicts the difficulty, perhaps impossibility, of actually achieving such psychological or emotional detachment.

We soon realize that the transition of moods represents no genuine catharsis but only a momentary displacement; for the Poet is now pursued by tormenting questions that dramatically reveal his plight:

> Whither have fled
> The hues of heaven that canopied his bower
> Of yesternight? The sounds that soothed his sleep,
> The mystery and the majesty of Earth,
> The joy, the exultation?   (196–200)

With its heightened rhetoric and rhythms, the verse recalls the haunting questions at the end of the first movement of Wordsworth's "Intimations Ode," which Shelley's poem has already echoed: *"Whither is fled* the visionary gleam? / Where is it now, the glory and the dream?" (my italics).[19] The image of the veiled maid has departed. Nevertheless the aura that surrounds her, the hues and harmonies she wakened, remain to testify to a presence felt through absence, a void, a need, a craving that cannot be appeased and renders the Poet desolate:

> His wan eyes
> Gaze on the empty scene as vacantly
> As ocean's moon looks on the moon in heaven.   (200–202)

The imagery of Narcissus that recurs here ironically inverts the customary play of reference. The reflection of the moon within the ocean gazes back unthinkingly at its heavenly begetter, as if it shared the same reality as its source. From one point of view the Visionary Maiden appears the mere projection of the Poet's imagination. Yet we realize from the blank vacancy of his gaze the truth that he owes his identity—his defining quality of pathos—if not to her influence then to her loss. In such a relationship, which is the reality and which the reflection, which the moving stimulus and which the reaction? In Ovid's tale we feel secure in distinguishing between the human features and their shadowy repetition figured in the pool. In *Alastor* we are no longer sure.

It is, of course, just our human need to project beyond ourselves, to imagine a source of responsiveness that corresponds to what we feel within, that sets in motion, almost like the operation of a necessary, impersonal law, the dread "Alastor principle" which now assumes control over

the poem. Oblivious to the charms of the Arab Maiden, the Poet falls prey
to a more compelling, dangerous lure:

> The spirit of sweet human love has sent
> A vision to the sleep of him who spurned
> Her choicest gifts.   (203–5)

With their suggestion of vindictiveness, the lines are the most shocking in
the poem and have always been the most difficult for readers to accept, as
Shelley no doubt intended. Despite the title of the poem and the allusion
in the second paragraph of the "Preface" to the avenging furies, we are
hardly prepared, amid the familiar landscape setting, for the alien, barely
believable figure of avenging justice drawn from an altogether different
literature and culture.[20] In any case our first reaction as readers is to
exclaim, How can the "spirit of *sweet* human *love*" be imagined to dispatch
a punishment at once so alluring and so vengeful? Yet it was just Shelley's
point that our human tendency to anthropomorphize and idealize, once
indulged, can set no limits and that the insights of an older, starker
mythology as to what that tendency may produce offer a necessary correc-
tive to the easy, sentimental neopaganism of his Romantic contemporaries. The lines, too, may make us pause to reflect upon some further
questions. Does not the spirit of love send her vision to the Poet only after
the failure of his search for something adequate to his desires? Would the
Poet really be any happier or more grateful had she withheld her gift?

The Poet is now driven to "overleap the bounds" (207) and to pursue, like Orpheus, the fleeting shade into "the wide pathless desart of dim
sleep" (210), so that the narrator exclaims:

> Alas! alas!
> Were limbs, and breath, and being intertwined
> Thus treacherously?   (207–9)

The lines refer to the fatal sexual embrace of the Poet and the Visionary
Maiden as the origin of the destructive frenzy that now seizes him. At the
same time the passage echoes the biblical account of when God formed
man's limbs from the dust of the ground and infused them with the breath
of His life. Both contexts, together with the process the poem has up to
now described—the upbringing, education, and motivation of the hero—
remind us that we have been witnessing the birth of the archetypal poet.
Introduced by lamenting exclamations, the question the narrator poses
seems to beg our assent to the most ominous and dire view of that genesis.

Such is Shelley's way with interrogations, however, that it is not long before the question turns itself around in our mind as if to ask us whatever men or poets were created for if not to pursue some quest to the utmost of their being.

Here as elsewhere the extraordinary complexity of *Alastor* lies in its perpetual ambivalence; we are puzzled throughout whether to read central passages as positive or negative in their bearing, as straightforward or ironical.[21] At last we come to realize that the narrative invites, indeed demands, us to explore both sets of possibilities and that the effect of the poem as a whole arises from our simultaneous pursuit of different and sometimes contrary implications without relinquishing either.

Like an addict, the Poet is now caught up in an anguish of desire for his "lovely dream" (233). He "Burn[s] with the poison" (229). His seared hair and withered skin betray the inner fire that feeds upon his life in his "autumn of strange suffering" (249). Like Manfred, he appears before a mountaineer, poised like a "spectral form" on the brink of "some dizzy precipice" (258–59). Like the Wandering Jew or Ancient Mariner, he must set forth again upon his endless journey. Before he embarks in the "little shallop" (299) which awaits him, however, we have the beautiful, sad idyll of his encounter with the solitary swan among the reeds which so haunted Yeats's imagination.[22] As the Poet approaches, the bird takes wing, as if to dramatize nature's absolute indifference to his plight. Following the bird with his eye, the Poet meditates:

> "Thou hast a home,
> Beautiful bird; thou voyagest to thine home,
> Where thy sweet mate will twine her downy neck
> With thine, and welcome thy return with eyes
> Bright in the lustre of their own fond joy.
> And what am I that I should linger here,
> With voice far sweeter than thy dying notes,
> Spirit more vast than thine, frame more attuned
> To beauty, wasting these surpassing powers
> In the deaf air, to the blind earth, and heaven
> That echoes not my thoughts?" (280–90)

The passage and its self-questioning are worth pausing to consider if only as a means of countering the sentimental arguments of those who, pointing to the phrases in the "Preface" about the "unfruitful lives" of "those who love not their fellow-beings," seek to condemn the Poet as at bottom a misanthropist. Set off against the happiness of the swan and its mate, the plight of the Poet, so the argument goes, is not that he has abstracted an ideal of beauty but that he has failed to realize that ideal through love for an obtainable fellow-creature like the Arab Maiden, pursuing instead hopeless fictions of his own imagination.[23] This criticism, which Keats worked through to a quite different resolution in *Endymion*, is undeniably relevant to our sense of the problematic nature of the Poet and his quest. Yet one cannot read the passage without realizing that what raises the Poet in dignity and power above the bird and its song is precisely his isolation from the kind of natural community the swan enjoys. The distinguishing quality of the Poet's humanity, his very voice and timbre, are rooted in his solitude, in his unappeasable desire and despair, which find no echo or reflection in the "deaf air" or "blind earth." The passage holds out two implications about the Poet and his quest, the one deploring, the other reconciling. It brings to mind Yeats's dictum that one must choose between perfection of the life and of the work.[24]

Yielding to the impulse that seizes him, the Poet embarks in the little boat floating nearby, a typical Shelleyan vessel, derelict and decrepit. The carelessness with which he abandons himself to the fury of the tempest, to be driven "Like a torn cloud before the hurricane" (315), intimates the desperate logic of his course: only by surrendering himself to the power of the elements that confront him and the emotional and psychological forces they imply can he hope to regain "the light / Of those beloved eyes" (331–32). His voyage seems at first enveloped by the most terrifying perils. Yet the very enormity of the cataracts and whirlpools he encounters, accentuated by the narrator's repeated exclamations, have the effect of convincing us, paradoxically, that for all the horrors that surround him the Poet remains, like "an elemental god" (351), somehow immune and protected— reserved for a different end. Beginning in alarm, the repeated outcries of the narrator as he follows the progress of the boat—"Who shall save? . . . Shall it sink / Down the abyss? . . . Now shall it fall?" (357,394–95,397)— seem to conclude in a note of almost triumphant defiance. As critics have pointed out, the direction of the Poet's boat is at first upstream, against the current.[25] It is only after he discovers the impossibility of pursuing his vision back to and beyond the sources of human consciousness that he redirects his course downstream, in order to resolve the question of the reality or illusion of his dream through death.

The Poet's search for his vision thus draws him back toward the state of primal narcissism from which it derives, in quest of that joyful presence that, as in the "Intimations Ode," suffuses our earliest recollections of the world. In the summer of 1815, the year in which Shelley was at work on *Alastor*, he and Mary, in the company of friends, made a trip up the

Thames to discover its source. They proceeded upstream as far as the water proved navigable and then turned back. Recollections of the journey up and down, together with those of the more turbulent descent of the Rhine that Shelley had made with Mary in the summer of the preceding year, obviously suggested a certain logic as well as much of the background scenery for the voyage in *Alastor*. Throughout the poem, however, the natural description is strongly colored by psychological implications. Carried to the ascending vortex of a whirlpool which threatens to plunge it to the depths, the Poet's boat is miraculously swept aside into a little cove where "yellow flowers"—narcissus—"For ever gaze on their own drooping eyes" (406–7). From here he is conducted through banks over-canopied by "meeting boughs and implicated leaves" where the oak with "knotty arms / Embraces the light beech" (426,432–33) and where parasites like

> gamesome infants' eyes,
> With gentle meanings, and most innocent wiles,
> Fold their beams round the hearts of those that love.
>
> (441–43)

The imagery of maternal protection and enclosure, the secure haunt for the earliest sports of infancy, all suggest that the Poet is approaching his goal, the source and animating spirit of his dreams, "Nature's dearest haunt, some bank, / Her cradle" (429–30).

Where a fountain rises from the "secret springs" (478) which feed a well, the Poet stands to behold his own eyes reflected in the pool. Suddenly

> A Spirit seemed
> To stand beside him—clothed in no bright robes
> Of shadowy silver or enshrining light,
> Borrowed from aught the visible world affords
> Of grace, or majesty, or mystery.   (479–83)

Stripped of all vestments of the natural world, divested even of the luminous mist that envelops Wordsworth's earliest recollections, the apparition in its purity is barely apprehensible, intimated merely in the motion of the leaves or the music of the brook. The Poet seems on the point of communing with the pure indwelling spirit of nature itself. The surrounding shades begin to deepen, as if "for speech assuming" (486), even while the Poet is overcome with the desolating sense that "he and it [the Spirit] / Were all that was" (487–88), as if the external world had disappeared. When at length he raises his glance from the well, he sees only "Two starry eyes" (490) above him in the gloom. Are they, we wonder, truly the eyes of another being or only the vestigial image of his own self-contemplation in the pool? The identity of the Spirit seems at last inseparable from his own, and the effort to penetrate beyond nature to the apprehension of an animating presence collapses beneath the serene but tantalizing gaze of the eyes as they beckon him still further.

"Obedient to the light / That shone within his soul" (492–93), the Poet now follows the rivulet downstream. The alteration in his course appears to spring from the recognition that the source he has been seeking is "inaccessibly profound" (503). Dancing at first, "like childhood laughing as it went" (499), the stream is clearly, as he recognizes, a symbol of his being: "Thou imagest my life" (505). Having failed in the attempt to discover the mystery of existence by returning to the origin of life, he now embraces the only other means possible—to solve the enigma by following the current downward to its termination in death. He precipitates himself forward to this goal with frenetic speed:

> As one
> Roused by some joyous madness from the couch
> Of fever, he did move; yet, not like him,
> Forgetful of the grave.   (517–20)

With the stream's deepening descent, the landscape of flowers and musical groves changes to one of blasted pines and yawning caverns. So too, under the impress of such "wintry speed" (543), the Poet's appearance becomes gaunt and haggard. He seems to welcome the downward rush as expediting death and the ultimate revelation it must hold. Just where the pass expands and the tumultuous river falls at last into the "immeasurable void" (569), a solitary pine clings to the crag and bends before each straining blast. With its "solemn song" (567) all but lost amid the roar of wind and waters, it is the aeolian symbol of the agony of his life.

Characteristically, however, Shelley will permit his hero no such common end as that for which he seems imminently destined: "Yet the grey precipice and solemn pine / And torrent, were not all" (571–72). Despite the Poet's collaboration with the horrendous forces sweeping him to his ruin, his life, poised "Even on the edge of that vast mountain" (573), is prolonged yet again by one more of those perverse quirks of fate that fly in the face of every law of probability. Rather than plunging over the abyss, he is swept into a silent and unviolated cove that seems "to smile / Even in the lap of horror" (577–78). It is here that he is destined to yield up "the colours of that varying check, / That snowy breast, those dark and drooping eyes" (600–601), the beauteous but curiously sexless elements of his being. Leaning against the trunk of the old pine, as if to dramatize his kinship with it, the Poet feels his powers fail him. He gives up his life, however, only gradually and in an expansive setting lit by mysteriously symbolical and Lawrentian images.

The Poet dies facing a great crescent moon that illuminates the scene, and his last sight is of its two horns as they drop beneath the horizon. As long as the moon falls, his blood still "beat[s] in mystic sympathy / With nature's ebb and flow" (652–53); but his life now seems concentered in the orb which as it slowly disappears takes with it the last of his waning forces:

> till the minutest ray
> Was quenched, the pulse yet lingered in his heart.
> It paused—it fluttered.   (657–59)

The image of the disappearing moon, as the dying Poet lies tranquilly smiling up at it, has the climactic logic of one of those geometrical paradoxes so dear to Shelley's heart. For as the tips of the two horns disappear into the darkness, they narrow brilliantly—"two lessening points of light alone / Gleamed through the darkness" (654–55)—in a way that unmistakably suggests "the light / Of those beloved eyes" (331–32) that ever since the Poet's rapturous union with the dream maiden have been the object of his quest, the eyes that seemed momentarily to hang above him at the wellspring of his existence.[26] On the very brink of death, indeed so close to dissolution that the transition between the final ebbing of life and the onset of death seems imperceptible, the Poet is granted one last glimpse of the ideal he has so faithfully pursued.

The complex figure of the setting moon provides the culminating recognition in *Alastor*, even if for readers that recognition remains in large part unconscious. Only through the loss of the dominant moon (and with it the extinction of the Poet's life) can the beloved eyes come into view. The eyes grow out of the matrix image of the sinking moon, but they achieve definition—and then for the briefest instant—only through the obliteration of the orb that underlies them. The logic of the image recalls the sudden disappearance of the dream maiden at the ecstatic summit of her brief romance with the Poet, a disappearance that reawakens within him the underlying recollection of a deeper, earlier, barely memorable rapture, felt now as an unendurable sense of vacancy which leaves him forever craving. The figure of the sinking moon thus dramatizes at the moment of his death the predicament that dominates the Poet's existence. The effort to wrest some human expression, some personal embodiment from the larger nexus of maternal sympathies uniting him with life is doomed to failure. The narrowing and definition required by the effort lead only to the diminution and destruction of the central matrix. The ties of loyalty and dependence that bind the Poet to his earliest and deepest love are incompatible with any human realization of it, though the Poet remains hopelessly committed to both ideals.

Alastor does not end with the Poet's dissolution. The beginning of the narrator's impassioned outburst, "O, for Medea's wondrous alchemy" (672), reminds us, unexpectedly, of his continued presence. The effect within the poem is a splitting of consciousness. Although briefly distinguished from the Poet at the outset, the narrator has continued such a close and sympathetic observer that his character has seemed virtually submerged in that of Shelley's hero.[27] With the culminating demonstration of the Poet's failure and his death, it is as if his alter ego had remained behind to sum up and evaluate, to praise or condemn, perhaps forgive. We come to understand that a poem of quest (or inquest) has begun to modulate toward elegy. The persistence of the narrator as a hidden presence in the poem and his reemergence into our awareness near the conclusion provides the opportunity for a fitting commemoration. We are quick to sense, however, that because of his close identification with the Poet the narrator hardly possesses the detachment required for a dispassionate assessment.

Certainly the grief-stricken opening of his peroration, in which he longs for the Poet's restoration, hardly shows an adequate comprehension. His outcry for some reviving potion like Medea's magic, or the eternizing draught drunk by the Wandering Jew, or the elixir of life caught in the crucible of some decaying alchemist, even granting the possibility of their attainment, must strike us as pointless and cruel. After all the Poet's agonizing travail, when death has finally come as merciful deliverance, any willful renewal of his torment would be an almost unthinkable cruelty. Moreover, as the narrator goes on to point out, the Poet, though departed, continued to the last uncompromised and loyal to the ideal of his quest. In a sense he remains the dedicated spirit of his youth, "The brave, the gentle, and the beautiful, / The child of grace and genius" (689–90), while

> Heartless things
> Are done and said i' the world, and many worms
> And beasts and men live on. (690–92)

Even as we contemplate the idea of the Poet's eternity and the happy logic of his escape, however, the narrator's continuation reverses our perspective. While the earth continues in its ceaseless round, "In vesper low or joyous orison" (694), the Poet can

> no longer know or love the shapes
> Of this phantasmal scene, who have to thee
> Been purest ministers, who are, alas!
> Now thou art not.   (696–99)

The lines bring us round with keen irony to the persistence of a nature that has remained and will continue untouched by the Poet's dreams and aspirations, a nature consistent only in the perpetually shifting play of its appearances.

The same paradox surrounds the narrator's refusal to mourn. "Let no tear / Be shed," he insists, "not even in thought" (702–3). Such restraint is appropriate, however, not, as we at first assume, because the Poet's deliverance from the world in death transcends all cause for human sorrow. On the contrary, it is because his loss is too great, "too 'deep for tears' " (713), defying the powers of verse, painting, or sculpture to commemorate, indeed threatening the arts themselves with extinction. What exactly are we to make of the narrator's rising strain as it alternates between loss and denial, desperation and resignation, grief and repression to conclude in a paradox of Donne-like proportions, that the greatest grief, like trepidation of the spheres, is innocent? As Norman Thurston has aptly written, "The conclusion of *Alastor* is, among other things, an elegy for the dead Poet, and, like all elegies, it seeks to express both grief and consolation. Unlike most elegies, however, it denies itself the possibility of doing either."[28]

The paradox is hardly new; it can be traced as far back as the "Preface." What is extraordinary is the rising pitch of intensity with which it is pursued up to the very conclusion. The persistence of the central paradox to the end is a reflection of the poem's desperate need to have it both ways. *Alastor* traces the failure of the Poet's quest to recover the visionary maiden of his dreams, a pursuit that ultimately costs him his life. Yet even while it recounts that furious and self-destructive passage, the poem invites us to see the quest, through the very confusion of the narrator who remains behind to moralize, as the outgrowth of an imperishable and unassailable ideal. If the Poet is driven, he is forced onward by the power of a fate which he can repudiate only at the cost of denying all that is most vital and ingrained in his existence.[29]

Alastor is the most compulsive of Shelley's longer poems. As I have argued, the compulsions it reflects are those of his life. The experience of writing the poem was a kind of personal catharsis.[30] It was a way of working through a pattern of repeated failure. It brought greater understanding of the habitual erosion and collapse of those ideal images which he sought to invest with the light and fire of all that was most sacred to his being. The composition was a way of reexperiencing that failure. Yet it was also a way of seeing it as preordained, inescapable, and therefore finally venial. In a sense the poem was a way of saying goodbye to Harriet and the hopes he had invested in her. It enabled him to relinquish her from his experience by seeing her as a fleeting embodiment of an imperishable ideal that would never cease to exercise its commanding spell over his life.

The paradox of these complexly divided and competing motives is reflected in the narrator's final tribute to the Poet in the poem's closing lines:

> It is a woe "too deep for tears," when all
> Is reft at once, when some surpassing Spirit,
> Whose light adorned the world around it, leaves
> Those who remain behind, not sobs or groans,
> The passionate tumult of a clinging hope;
> But pale despair and cold tranquillity,
> Nature's vast frame, the web of human things,
> Birth and the grave, that are not as they were. (713–20)

Nature and the course of human life are both totally changed and totally unchanged by the Poet's experience. The universe continues with its ceaseless round, solemn or joyous, oblivious to his passing, while those impoverished or less adventurous souls, conserving their energies to the last, continue to descend ever nearer to the grave. Yet for one brief moment the Poet has cast a brilliant glow over the natural world, irradiating it with the power of his aspirations and his desires. In this sense it can never be the same. Indeed his feat has plunged the world only more deeply in the shadow, for with the end of his life and the hopes that rose with his attempt, all that remains for those who follow are the "pale despair and cold tranquillity" of an absolute hopelessness. One must admire the Poet his "surpassing Spirit"—the limitlessness of his ambition and insatiability of his desire. However, his failure drives the world only deeper into desolation. The paradox remained to haunt Shelley's later years. *Alastor* argues that we cannot live with the poet and we cannot live without him. It is the view of the skeptic who has accepted the impossibility of our discovering any adequate reflection of our highest instincts in the world outside us and yet can conceive of true humanity only in the attempt to do so.

three

THE TRIUMPH OF LOVE

The Revolt of Islam

Shelley's longest poem, *The Revolt of Islam*, composed in 1817, represents in many ways a return to the spirit of *Queen Mab*. The all-consuming inwardness of *Alastor* has vanished. *The Revolt* shares with *Queen Mab* a broadly prophetic character that draws on the poet's sense of his own place and time. (An earlier version, suppressed and revised at the insistence of his publishers, was entitled *Laon and Cythna; or, The Revolution of the Golden City: A Vision of the Nineteenth Century*.) There is, however, one major difference between *Queen Mab* and *The Revolt*. The Fairy Queen's vision of human progress and betterment is unrolled before the passive soul of the sleeping Ianthe. In *The Revolt* Laon and Cythna, Shelley's hero and heroine, cooperate to define an ideal of active service and dedication to humanity. As the two dedications suggest, the first to Harriet, the second to Mary, Shelley had discovered in his second wife not simply a new fund of sympathy but an active feminine intelligence equal and complementary to his own, a new range of sensibility he could draw on for the dramatic and psychological development of his work.

From its outset the "Dedication" to Mary suggests how much Shelley, with her help, had put the mood of *Alastor* behind him. The poet began work on *The Revolt* at about the time he and Mary took up residence in March at Albion House at Marlow.[1] Shelley composed much of the poem, as he had *Queen Mab*, from his boat as it drifted on the Thames, but in a very different mood:

> The toil which stole from thee so many an hour,
>   Is ended,—and the fruit is at thy feet!
> No longer where the woods to frame a bower
>   With interlacèd branches mix and meet,
>   Or where with sound like many voices sweet,

> Waterfalls leap among wild islands green,
>   Which framed for my lone boat a lone retreat
> Of moss-grown trees and weeds, shall I be seen:
> But beside thee, where still my heart has ever been.[2]   (10–18)

The setting recalls *Alastor*; but gone are solitude and its attendant loneliness. Even more important, gone are the driving compulsions of the quest and the need to concenter all ambitions in a single object:

> Alas, that love should be a blight and snare
>   To those who seek all sympathies in one!—
> Such once I sought in vain; then black despair,
>   The shadow of a starless night, was thrown
> Over the world in which I moved alone:—
> Yet never found I one not false to me,
>   Hard hearts, and cold, like weights of icy stone
> Which crushed and withered mine, that could not be
> Aught but a lifeless clod, until revived by thee.   (46–54)

The conclusion of the stanza describes a dark night of the soul through which Shelley has passed together with that freezing and splitting of the ego under the pressure of personal disappointment which was such a recurrent and distressing aspect of his experience. Already under Mary's benign influence there are signs of a reconstellation of energies; Shelley devotes several stanzas to a brief idealized history of his own development from childhood, as if to recapitulate his past in line with the new reorientation his relationship with Mary has made possible. Already "friends return" (74). Moreover Mary, in giving birth to William and Clara, has blessed them with the companionship of a family circle: "from thy side two gentle babes are born / To fill our home with smiles" (77–78). Shelley does not end his "Dedication" before he has praised Mary's parents, Mary Wollstonecraft and William Godwin, as ideal exemplars of the male and female attributes that determined the being of his wife. In William and Mary, Bysshe and Mary, little William and Clara, the "Dedication" suggests an ideal genealogy, a pattern of continuity and evolution perpetuated by the sexes in their separation and recombination. The living ideal was powerfully to influence the development of Shelley's heroes, Laon and Cythna, in their growth and progress through their various incarnations.

Although it alternately draws on and illuminates so much of Shelley's life, *The Revolt of Islam* remains the most neglected of his major works.[3] Reasons for this neglect are not hard to find. The poem is sprawling and amorphous, a difficult and often confusing intermixture of epic, allegory, and romance. Despite Shelley's assertion that, with the exception of the first canto and a part of the last, *The Revolt* "is narrative, not didactic,"[4] his poem, like *Queen Mab*, dramatizes a host of reasoned conclusions on such subjects as human progress and the course of historical evolution, liberty, equality, nonviolence, and even vegetarianism. Fundamental to its composition was Shelley's desire, stated in his "Preface," to account for the failure of the French Revolution and indeed for the possibility of future setbacks, and yet at the same time to rebuke the revulsion and despair of his contemporaries by reaffirming the imaginative ideals of millennial fulfillment—essentially the same task Coleridge had urged Wordsworth to undertake in composing *The Recluse*. In order to achieve the complicated perspective such a goal required, Shelley composed what Carlos Baker has described as "two poems, one within the other."[5] By far the longer segment, the second through the eleventh cantos and the first sixteen stanzas of the twelfth, is a narrative account of the labors of Laon and Cythna for human enfranchisement, leading in the end to their martyrdom and immolation at the hands of the tyrant Othman and his Iberian priesthood. Yet this story of human tragedy and unfulfilled ambitions is dominated by the Temple of the Spirit from which the lovers proceed in the first canto and to which they return following their deaths in the last, the ageless structure that provides a vantage point for their struggle and its significance.[6]

The deliberate ambivalence of the poem's framework and the divided perspective it creates were essential to Shelley's aim of arbitrating between optimism and pessimism, historical progress and mere oscillation, the realm of the imaginative and ideal and that of human actuality. The lovers may fail in their aim to reform the world; they do not, however, perish but are in the end reunited in a kingdom where their vision is reflected in the eternal artifice of the heavenly city. They cannot escape the toils of the tyrants of the world, but the end of their travail is not simple annihilation. The evolution of the poem makes us feel that they have preserved and augmented the ideal of virtue they have for a time embodied. In their reunion they are drawn back into the stronghold of the heavenly city as if into the recesses of power, and we are led to view their adventure as one of a succession of attempts; others will follow to extend their achievements and accomplish what they have failed to realize.

The framework Shelley establishes for the narrative action of *The Revolt* thus permits him to anticipate repeated defeats for the Spirit of the Good within the world and yet to argue the illogic of despair. The design of the poem and its mythology depict the eternal return and self-perpetuation of the living Spirit and the way its powers are transformed and extended through its repeated conflict with evil. The plan reflects Shelley's intellectual development and the convictions he deliberately built into the design of his work. Yet the practice of reading the poem strictly for its metaphysical implications has obscured the perception that Shelley's vision of possible perfection is directly conveyed in his lovers' ordeals and the development they together undergo. Aware of the abstract features of his conception, Shelley was repeatedly at pains to claim for the poem a strong human interest, a work vitalized by "the common & elementary emotions of the human heart" and filled with "pictures of friendship & love & natural affections."[7] Throughout the poem, in fact, Shelley appears to be looking not so much forward into the millennial future as backward on his own past. Much of the poem's narrative power derives from recollections of the poet's childhood and adolescence, recollections often tinged by a strong element of fantasy.[8] Laon and Cythna awaken from death in the realm of the eternal as if they had emerged from a dark dream to the pure light of reality. The sudden transition obscures the truth that they both, and more especially Laon, have changed and grown in the course of their earthly experiences and that such development is crucial to their ultimate transcendence. In his story of the lovers' upbringing, separation, trials, and final reunion, Shelley succeeds in dramatizing a moving and psychologically profound relationship between the sexes that draws on his community with Mary. It is just here, in our sense that Laon's evolution is in many ways a reflection of Shelley's own, that the public and private aspects of the poem's symbolism can be seen to interpenetrate and reinforce each other. For all its weaknesses, no other major work has so much to tell us about the poet himself or is more characteristically his own.

The image that dominates the poem from its outset is that of the eagle and the serpent "wreathed in fight" (193) which the narrator beholds on arising from his dreams of despair at the failure of the French Revolution and which the beautiful woman who becomes his companion interprets to him. She relates how the Spirit of Good had appeared to her in dreams as the Morning Star, her declared lover, but had subsequently been transformed into the loathed snake by his eternal foe, the evil principle. Scholars have often pointed out that the image of the eagle and the serpent was essential to Shelley as a representation of the continuous struggle between the powers of good and evil, which he had come to see as characteristic of human life and against which his poem was nevertheless to urge hope and practical exertion.[9] This interpretation of the image and its

Manichaean implications, however justified, has nevertheless obscured an understanding of how the image actually introduces the all-important episode in Shelley's first canto. What has been neglected is the way the opening image changes and develops, the way it both initiates and is subsumed by a larger structure of symbolical events that deepens its significance.

Among the various sources of Shelley's conception of the image of the eagle and the serpent is the story of the creation of Hermaphroditus in Book IV of Ovid's *Metamorphoses*.[10] The nymph Salmacis becomes inflamed with desire for the son of Hermes and Cythera as he bathes in her pool. When he resists her advances, Ovid describes how

> She winds herself about him, as entwines
> The serpent which the royal bird on high
> Holds in his talons;—as it hangs, it coils
> In sinuous folds around the eagle's feet;—
> Then twists its coils around his head and wings.[11]

The gods at length favor Salmacis's entreaties, and she and the youth she desires are transformed into a single being, neither man nor woman but a form compounded of both sexes. What Shelley has depicted at the outset of *The Revolt* is just the opposite of this unification: not simply conflict but division. As they first appear to the narrator in an opening space of blue calm framed by the warring whirlwinds of the clouds, the eagle and serpent appear at first a single "wingèd Form" (186). There seem no grounds for distinguishing between the warring combatants, either on the basis of good or evil or by way of relative advantage. The conflict continues until

> Hung high that mighty Serpent, and at last
> Fell to the sea, while o'er the continent,
> With clang of wings and scream the Eagle passed,
> Heavily borne away on the exhausted blast.   (249–52)

Unlike the tale in Ovid, the conflict ends not in resolution but in separation.

Following his drop into the sea, the serpent, in answer to the Lady's mysterious calls, swims to her to be enfolded in her breast. The narrator's momentary terror and perhaps our own trepidation prove groundless, for the serpent's homing instinct effects a kind of propagation: out of the reunion between the Lady and the serpent everything else in the canto, and indeed the poem itself, is to proceed. Shelley's image of the eagle and the serpent locked in even and unyielding fight may suggest a radical Manichaeism at the heart of his vision of human destiny. His subsequent elaboration of the image, however, points to a larger pattern of a fall from unity into division and then a reformulation into further unity. Indeed these two patterns of historical relationship—the one unchanging and repetitive, the other self-integrating and evolving—control the structure of the poem and its significance.

Our sense of an overall design, admittedly imperfect throughout the varied scenes of the first canto and their complex symbolism, is extended by the extraordinary events that take place once the bark bearing the Lady, the serpent, and the narrator reaches the Temple of the Spirit and they enter its hall, enriched by painting and statuary of the departed great. Above them looms a vacant seat, "a throne, / Reared on a pyramid like sculptured flame" (613–14). As she advances, the Lady suddenly shrieks the Spirit's name and falls, disappearing into darkness, from which there emerge two lights, revolving hypnotically like "Small serpent eyes" (624) until they dilate, "commingling into one,"

> One clear and mighty planet hanging o'er
> A cloud of deepest shadow, which was thrown
> Athwart the glowing steps and the crystalline throne.   (628–30)

The planet ascends to irradiate a cloud that divides to reveal a figure seated on a throne who, sitting, with "limbs rose-like and warm . . . Majestic, yet most mild—calm, yet compassionate" (634,639), moves the speaker with strange wonder. The first critic of Shelley's poem, his friend and sponsor Leigh Hunt, suggested in the initial installment of his review in the *Examiner* (1 February 1818) a significant interpretation for this mysterious metamorphosis and its aftermath:

> A magic and obscure circumstance then takes place, the result
> of which is, that the woman and serpent are seen no more, but
> that a cloud opens asunder, and a bright and beautiful shape,
> *which seems compounded of both,* is beheld sitting on a throne,—a
> circumstance apparently imitated from Milton.[12]

Hunt's remarks clearly imply that the Lady and the serpent, following their disappearance from view, are integrated into a single being, and that the figure who emerges from the planet that contains them to hold majestic sway over the scene is to be understood as an androgynous ideal, a perfect union of the male and female sexes.[13] A voice rouses the narrator and declares that "two mighty Spirits now return, / Like birds of calm, from the world's raging sea" (645–46), concerning whom he must prepare to "list and learn" (648). Straightaway two glorious figures appear, one a man, the other "like his shadow" but "far lovelier" (660–61). They are, indeed, Laon and Cythna, restored to the Temple of the Spirit following their immolation in the last canto (for the poem has at its beginning come full circle, although we are not yet aware of it) to preside over the account of their struggles and martyrdom that immediately commences.

Admittedly the symbolism of Shelley's first canto is both complex and elusive, but it seems to set forth a hierarchy presided over by a union of the sexes and embracing beneath it ideals of the male and female form and character. Laon and Cythna step forth as if begotten by the figure on the throne. Yet this hierarchy, in its elaboration, is not rigid or fixed; the androgynous ideal, compounded of the union of the Lady and the serpent and fostering the rebirth of Laon and Cythna, is continually divided into and reconstituted from its sustaining parts. Such a formulation allows for both an ideal of permanence and a conception of historical progress and development, for there is already the idea that in their return Laon and Cythna have been changed, as individuals and as representatives of their sexes, by the struggles they have separately and together pursued.

It deserves to be noted in passing how strenuously Shelley resisted the changes his publishers, the Olliers, obliged him to carry out in the text of his poem—the principal of which was directed toward disguising the work's overtly incestuous nature. John Taylor Coleridge, the reviewer for the *Quarterly*, who affected to be thoroughly scandalized by the poem, pointed out that such changes as the redesignation of Cythna from Laon's "sister" in the original version (a copy of which unfortunately came into his hands before it was withdrawn from publication) to "orphan" in the later retitled version were merely nominal.[14] Shelley did all he could to preserve the kindred relationship of his hero and heroine and to evade the demands that he alter or conceal it. His determined recalcitrance, far from any desire to flaunt conventional morality, suggests how seriously he regarded the incest motif as integral to the effect and meaning of the whole work.

From the first stanza of Canto II and the opening of the narrative section, the poem sketches for us an idyllic, harmonious, maternal world as a background for Laon's youth and the development of his "spirit's folded powers" (675):

> The starlight smile of children, the sweet looks
>   Of women, the fair breast from which I fed,
> The murmur of the unreposing brooks . . .   (667–69)

This pristine world is overrun by tyranny, and Laon, like the *Alastor* poet, finds himself wandering amid "broken tombs and columns riven" (754). Unlike the despairing wanderer of the earlier poem, however, he is able to read these remains as "scrolls of mortal mystery" (765) which bear testimony to a lost ideal of greatness and to everything mankind may yet become. In the belief that "we all were sons of one great mother" (817), Laon seeks the companionship of a single friend, "my own heart's brother" (812), only to find him treacherous and false (a misunderstanding that is corrected later in the poem).[15] Disappointed in this first attempt at emotional community with one of his own sex, Laon finds his need for sympathy fulfilled by the orphan child raised by his parents, Cythna, to whom he grows so closely attached that she becomes like his "own shadow . . . / A second self, [but] far dearer" (874–75).

The bond that develops between the two could hardly be closer. At night they sleep locked in each other's arms. By day they exchange their hopes and plans for the betterment of humanity. It is she who encourages his interpretation of those memorials of the past which teach how man may become "Ay, wiser, greater, gentler" (767) than the best who have gone before. It is she, too, who encourages him to forge from "a mine of magic store" of hidden knowledge the "adamantine armour" of his heroic calling, the "Words which were weapons" (841–43) for his poetic war against the tyrants of mankind. All the while "Unconscious of [her] power" (967), she fosters his vision with her smiles and tears, until "all things became / Slaves to my holy and heroic verse" (933–34). One is reminded again of the atmosphere of Shelley's childhood at Field Place, the community of sympathy the poet sought to create for himself and his imaginative creations in the audience composed of his four younger sisters, especially Elizabeth, his intimate companion and poetical collaborator. Shelley's second canto depicts the harmony of an ideal relationship, sheltered from the troubles of the external world. Differences of temperament or sex are abrogated in the incestuous love of Laon and Cythna.

At the same time it is important to observe how, as the canto draws toward its conclusion, significant differences between the two lovers begin to emerge. Laon from the first is dedicated to the cause of human liberation from all forms of slavery, while Cythna, in enthusiastic response to his plans, is to undertake the task of feminine emancipation. Of course the two will cooperate in the joint cause of liberty and equality,[16] and Cythna rejoices at the prospect of leading "a happy female train / To meet thee over the rejoicing plain" (1003–4) of the Golden City in Shelley's "*beau ideal*" of the French Revolution.[17] Nevertheless, the recognition grows that they must for a time work asunder, a prospect Cythna greets, near the end of the canto, with some disquietude: " 'Thou wilt depart, and I with tears shall stand / Watching thy dim sail skirt the ocean gray; / . . . I shall remain alone' " (1064–67). As later events unfold, Cythna's expectations are reversed: it is Laon who, bound on his tower, watches the sails of her captors sink beneath the horizon.

Cythna has reached early adolescence (885), and it is not surprising that, simultaneous with the recognition of their need to separate in order to fulfill their different social goals, the two companions undergo a change in the temper of their emotional relationship toward the close of the canto. Cythna is the first to voice the shock of recognition: " 'We part!—O Laon, I must dare nor tremble / To meet those looks no more!—Oh, heavy stroke!' " (1081–82)—whereupon, as Laon recounts it,

> sudden she woke
> As one awakes from sleep, and wildly pressed
> My bosom, her whole frame impetuously possessed.
> (1087–89)

The lines mark the first approach to sexual passion in the poem. Nevertheless the conclusion of the scene, which ends the canto, finds the lovers returning speechlessly in a strangely suppressed mood toward their abode where "Each from the other sought refuge in solitude" (1107).

Such is the suggestive chain of events that provides the prologue to Canto III, the most phantasmagoric in the poem and the one in which Shelley's subconscious fantasy seems most intensely engaged. It begins with Laon's account of his all-consuming dream, which in its strange and powerful fluctuations of feeling leaves him "Sometimes for rapture sick, sometimes for pain aghast" (1116). In a vision he perceives himself together with his lover:

> Methought, upon the threshold of a cave
> I sate with Cythna; drooping briony, pearled
> With dew from the wild streamlet's shattered wave,
> Hung, where we sate to taste the joys which Nature gave.
> (1122–25)

The scene is lighted by "Intenser hues" (1129) and Cythna is displayed in a new radiancy so that Laon declares, "if I loved before, now love was agony" (1134). The strange irradiation of the scene and the compulsive alternation between desire and aversion in Laon's feelings remind one of the dream-maiden episode in *Alastor* and suggest the growth of sexual passion. The onset of evening and its moon together with the calm of the lovers' talk appear conducive to what throughout much of Shelley's verse is a predictable conclusion.[18]

Suddenly "a nameless sense of fear" (1138) besets them, and Laon seems to hear shrieks from the depths of a cave behind. The scene changes, and Laon imagines that he is speeding "Through the air and over the sea" while once more "Cythna in my sheltering bosom lay" (1145–46). Their flight, however, is impeded by a host of noisome shapes which arise from the darkness like snakes and menace them:

> the gaping earth then vomited
> Legions of foul and ghastly shapes, which hung
>   Upon my flight; and ever, as we fled,
> They plucked at Cythna.   (1148–51)

Aspects of the scene remind one of the image from the first canto of the eagle and the serpent wreathed in fight.

What is the meaning of this violent anticlimax? A setting and a mood leading the pair to a harmonious consummation of their love have been unexpectedly subverted by feelings of terror culminating in Laon's strange fantasy. Behind the incident one senses the adolescent boy's experience of facing the full implications of sexual maturity and divergence from the opposite sex and his guilt at feelings such as lust. Overtones of certain images (the contrast, for example, between the drooping briony that hangs about the lovers and the foul, hanging shapes that pluck at Cythna) particularly suggest a boy's growing but partly unconscious awareness that he has been hung with genitals.

The notion that the narrative events draw much of their logic from Shelley's insight into the psychology of sexual development, perceptions deriving from his own experience, is confirmed by the actions that immediately follow in Canto III. Laon awakens abruptly from his dream to find himself surrounded by armed men "whose glittering swords were bare" (1160). He hears Cythna cry out and sees her about to be borne off into captivity. Despite her calm smile and her plea that he withdraw without interfering, he grasps his own weapon, "a small knife" (1166), and with the cry of "death or liberty" slays three of her captors before being struck down and subdued. Critics have pointed to Laon's unthinking recourse to powers that he must learn to forswear as the dramatization of Shelley's advocacy of nonviolence. More striking, however, is the way the moral theme emerges from the crisis in Laon's sexual development, dramatized by the overtly phallic character of the imagery—Laon's small knife against the warriors' swords. Logically the episode argues, with an incisiveness that reveals Shelley's intuitive understanding of the human psyche, that aggression is the inevitable outgrowth of masculinity. That Shelley is able to suggest such a conclusion, altogether alien to his ethical belief, is a tribute to the complexity and tempering power of the poem's continuation.

Laon's resort to violence and the scenes giving rise to it are vital to the structure of the remaining narrative, for his loss of self-control comes as the prelude to the lovers' separation, their quite different trials, and their reunion founded on a newly gained maturity.[19] The design of the poem thus corresponds to the typical pattern of a fall from naive or unthinking innocence, atonement, and restoration to a higher conception of integrity that is so familiar to students of Romanticism.[20] The work must be understood as portraying an initiation into a proper ideal of adulthood; much of what follows comes not simply by way of dramatic and imaginative reparation for Laon's single act of violence but through a reordering of the pattern of psychological instability that underlies it.

With its fantastic and macabre apparitions, the fit of madness that now overtakes Laon in Canto III is, if possible, even more lurid than the events leading up to it. He remembers or imagines that he is conveyed by soldiers to a cavern in a hill beneath a mighty column, where he is stripped and then led up a winding stairway to the dizzy summit to be chained and abandoned. The situation brings to mind, of course, the painful isolation of Prometheus; but the imagery conveys at the same time a somewhat special implication. The mighty column and its capital serve to support no structure but rather, "sculptured in the sky" (1208), stand out in relief to the surrounding sea and countryside, a beacon

> Which to the wanderers o'er the solitude
>   Of distant seas, from ages long gone by,
>   Had made a landmark. (1209–11)

One thinks of the columns erected or appropriated during the French Revolution and its aftermath, on which statues of liberty were raised, sometimes displacing the images of kings or tyrants hurled down to make way for them. One recalls, too, the Temple of the Spirit and its "Ten thousand columns" (595), the home of the "mighty Senate" of the departed great; for it was Shelley's idea that the true heroes of the past were immortalized as living sculptures, like Yeats's "sages standing in God's holy fire,"[21] creative presences incorporated within the eternal structure. The column, then, and Laon's chained position aloft it emblemize ironically both his failure and the challenges of his heroic undertaking for which he is not yet prepared, which he realizes as he ashamedly recalls his impulse to break his chains in order to destroy himself:

> O Liberty! forgive the base endeavour,
>   Forgive me, if, reserved for victory,
>   The Champion of thy faith e'er sought to fly.   (1272–74)

More lurid is Laon's recollection or dream of how his captors return conveying four corpses "And from the frieze to the four winds of Heaven / Hung them on high by the entangled hair" (1326–27). Three of the forms are "Swarthy," the corpses of the soldiers he has slain.[22] The fourth is "very fair" (1328), a figure that he only gradually makes out as Cythna's:

> A woman's shape, now lank and cold and blue,
>   The dwelling of the many-coloured worm,
> Hung there; the white and hollow cheek I drew
>   To my dry lips—what radiance did inform
>   Those horny eyes? whose was that withered form?
> Alas, alas! it seemed that Cythna's ghost
>   Laughed in those looks, and that the flesh was warm
> Within my teeth!   (1333–40)

Projections as phantasmagoric as these raise problems of interpretation. One can say, however, that to the three corpses, the symbols of his crime, is now added the phantasm of Cythna, whose boat he has watched as it bears her away below the horizon to captivity following his murderous attack. In slaying the soldiers, he has also destroyed Cythna, at least as an imaginative ideal, which accounts for her strangely withered apparition. The burning sun, his raging thirst, the sense of guilt and isolation are reminiscent of the Ancient Mariner, whose lonely ordeal provides the closest analogue to Laon's experience.[23] At the same time his surrender to the cannibalistic impulse to consume her physically, a reversion to infantile behavior, suggests the strength of his dependence on identification, a psychological function crucial to the course of his development.[24]

Our sense that in dramatizing the trauma that overtakes Laon, Shelley was drawing not only on Coleridge's poem but also on a deep level of his own psychological experience is reinforced by the second "vision" (1316) of his hero. The appointed champion of liberty, Laon remembers how the revered and kindly hermit comes to remove his chains and free him from imprisonment. Here there is important relevant biographical information; Mary Shelley in her note to the poem asserted that the character of the old man was founded on that of Dr. James Lind, who befriended Shelley at Eton. She further testified, as recorded in Thomas Jefferson Hogg's life of Shelley, how the poet revealed to her his debt to Lind, significantly on the night when he first opened his heart and professed his full love for her:

> "This man," [Shelley] has often said, "is exactly what an old man ought to be. Free, calm-spirited, full of benevolence, and even of youthful ardour; his eye seemed to burn with supernatural spirit beneath his brow, shaded by his venerable white locks; he was tall, vigorous, and healthy in his body; tempered, as it had ever been, by his amiable mind. I owe to that man far, ah! far more than I owe to my father; he loved me, and I shall never forget our long talks, where he breathed the spirit of the kindest tolerance and the purest wisdom. Once, when I was very ill during the holidays, as I was recovering from a fever which had attacked my brain, a servant overheard my father consult about sending me to a private madhouse. I was a favourite among all our servants, so this fellow came and told me as I lay sick in bed. My horror was beyond words, and I might soon have been mad indeed, if they had proceeded in their iniquitous plan. I had one hope. I was master of three pounds in money, and, with the servant's help, I contrived to send an express to Dr. Lind. He came, and I shall never forget his manner on that occasion. His profession gave him authority; his love for me ardour. He dared my father to execute his purpose, and his menaces had the desired effect."[25]

What is significant about this fantastic account is not that it was in every respect true but that it held for Shelley, who told the story repeatedly, a strong psychological reality. Shelley was reworking in imagination the still vivid recollections of his youthful illness and delirium as the materials for the fantasies Laon undergoes in his imprisonment.[26] The nature of the disorder the poet suffered is unknown. Yet the time of his illness—during one of his boyhood vacations from Eton—together with his father's threats, whether real or imagined, of eviction and confinement point to a trauma of an obviously Oedipal character.[27] Following his resort to violence in obedience to a false idea of masculinity, Laon is rescued from his guilt and punishment by the kindly savior who stands in contrast to the treacherous and oppressive father of the poet's boyhood recollection.[28] The effect of Laon's hallucination is to distill a just ideal of manhood and maturity with whom the hero can identify.

Although mighty of limb, the Hermit is gentle, embodying a quiet power the very opposite of the aggressiveness by which Laon had been earlier provoked and overcome. When Laon first awakens in the old man's boat bearing him away from captivity, he suspects that he is being abducted by some fiend; like the Ancient Mariner on his homeward journey, he fears to look behind him lest he find "some Spirit, fell and dark" (1376). Such initial confusion and distrust, traces of the fear of the betraying father of the poet's recollection, are rapidly dispelled, for the old man is as gracious as Coleridge's hermit, his undoubted model, and tends his charge "even as some sick mother seems / To hang in hope over a dying child" (1402–3). The root of Laon's disorder, the threatening onset of his masculinity, is hinted at in the imagery of burning and in the nature of the Hermit's ministrations:

> my scorchèd limbs he wound
> In linen moist and balmy, and as cold
> As dew to drooping leaves. (1365–67)

Despite his first apprehensiveness, Laon draws new power from a virtually physical identification with the old man's vigorous form, a power he can accept precisely because it is tempered by benevolence:

> the pillow
> For my light head was hollowed in his lap,
> And my bare limbs his mantle did enwrap. (1380–82)

When the two reach the old man's dwelling beside a lake, in Canto IV, Laon's madness returns, but in a milder form, prompted by the fear that his recollection of Cythna may be no more than a dream. The Hermit renews his careful tending, mingling "soft looks of pity" with glances "keen as is the lightning's stroke" (1465–66). During the seven years in which he is nurtured back to health by the Hermit's instruction in "Kind thoughts, and mighty hopes, and gentle deeds" (1540), Laon does not so much learn what is new as regain a knowledge and composure he had lost:

"Thus slowly from my brain the darkness rolled, / My thoughts their due array did re-assume" (1468–69). The Hermit does not so much enlighten his pupil as "relume / The lamp of Hope" (1472–73), for from long study the old man is a repository of the knowledge of those deeds of past greatness that Laon has, with Cythna's help and encouragement, already taken to heart. The fact that, prior to Laon's appearance, the old man has lost faith in the possibility of revolution should not be held against him, for it was Shelley's understanding that inevitably "custom maketh blind and obdurate / The loftiest hearts" (1486–87). It is only the young, in their innocence and courage, who can pick up the banner that their elders, after so many setbacks, have abandoned. The Hermit's declaration, "For I have been thy passive instrument" (1549), shows how much he comprehends his proper role.

With his reports of the success of a gentle maiden teaching "equal laws and justice" (1594) in the Golden City, the Hermit inspires Laon to join Cythna in the struggle for freedom. The climax of the canto comes at the end of the old man's lengthy exhortation when, in one of those beautiful turns with which the poem repeatedly surprises us, Laon casts down his eyes to see his own reflection in the lake:

> I saw my countenance reflected there;—
>   And then my youth fell on me like a wind
> Descending on still waters.   (1666–68)

Beneath the prematurely gray hair and lined features of his suffering he recognizes, in a remarkable act of introspection, the enduring strength of his youthful attributes: "A subtle mind and strong within a frame thus weak" (1674), the peculiar power of his poetic gift and calling. It is as if, during the interval of years, he "had gone from the world's scene, / And left it vacant" (1679–80), in order to renew himself. He rediscovers in his own reflection Cythna's features: " 'twas her lover's face" (1680). In the central episode of the early cantos of the narrative Laon resolves a remarkable crisis of identity by liberating himself from a harsh and intimidating ideal of masculinity and, with the help of his guiding foster father, recovering a strength founded in gentleness that is the counterpart to the feminine benignity and grace of Cythna, whom he feared he had lost or destroyed. The allegory of *The Revolt* projects a program of revolutionary ideology; but the poem derives its power of emotion from a condensation of the history of Shelley's own imaginative effort to recover ideals that, in the struggle for adulthood, had become obscured.

Early in the next canto, the fifth, Laon, having journeyed to the

Golden City to take up the struggle, falls into conversation with a name-less soldier, "An armèd youth" (1744). As they exchange their thoughts and hopes, Laon suddenly recognizes and embraces the seemingly false but actually strangely slandered friend of his early childhood. Critics have often, with some reason, associated the episode with Shelley's rupture and later reconciliation with Hogg after the latter tried to seduce Mary in the days just following her marriage. As the event takes place in the poem, however—"Then, suddenly, I knew it was the youth / In whom its earliest hopes my spirit found" (1756–57)—it is almost as if Laon has rediscovered part of himself, the unspoiled image of his own masculine identity re-trieved from childhood.

If Laon's experiences in the first half of the poem can be thought of as a necessary part of his initiation, the trials Cythna undergoes in Canto VII offer, as Donald Reiman among others have noted, a parallel to her lover's ordeal.[29] The watery cave with its narrow opening to the heavens where she is imprisoned contrasts in its inwardness to the soaring column where Laon is bound. Both lovers endure fits of madness during which they are unable to separate dream from reality. He discovers himself eating her flesh; she imagines the eagle who provides her food is bearing Laon's mangled limbs. Through a daring exercise of imaginative sympathy, Shel-ley portrays a trial appropriate to test the spirit of womankind in the extreme way he has just tested his hero's spirit and at the same time to dramatize comparable but different kinds of catharsis and deliverance.[30] Shelley characteristically concentrates on those aspects in which a woman is most susceptible, the vulnerability of her sexual and maternal instincts, in a way that anticipates some of his later work, most notably *The Cenci*.

The ordeal Cythna must undergo is double. First she is raped by the tyrant Othman, who flees away in guilt when daylight unveils the throes of his victim's anguish. The Ethiopian diver who plunges with her, entwin-ing his strong limbs around her own, abandons her to the strange sea prison that seems to represent the all-consuming madness that overcomes her as a result of her violation. Like Shelley's later heroine, Beatrice Cenci, Cythna finds her consciousness radically altered by her injury:

> Thus all things were
> Transformed into the agony which I wore
> Even as a poisoned robe around my bosom's core. (2962–64)

Such is not all she must endure, however, for she recollects—or seems to, for her state of mind does not permit her to be certain—how, after a given term, she gives birth to a child, a little girl, only to dream that the Ethiopian diver returns to take it away by night. Waking to find her little companion gone, she comes to doubt her remembrance. She thus undergoes the worst spoliation a woman can endure: separation from her proper lover, the loss of her virginity to the hateful tyrant, and the deprivation of the darling child who is born to her, leaving her to question its very existence.

If Shelley reworked aspects of his own emotional history in dramatizing Laon's ordeal, he was drawing as well on his new relationship with Mary in his conception of Cythna's trial. Here again there are relevant biographical data. Kenneth Cameron has pointed out that one detail of Cythna's recollection after she awakes to the loss of her child—" 'I was no longer mad, and yet methought / My breasts were swoln and changed' " (3037–38)—points to a major shock Mary suffered.[31] On 22 February 1815, Mary delivered her first child, prematurely at seven months, precipitated possibly by the exhausting confusion of her early days with Shelley and a removal to a larger accommodation in Hans Place earlier the same month. The baby, a girl, was not expected to live, but its health improved. Then on March 6, only a few days following yet another change of lodging, Mary woke to find the baby dead. The admirably restrained, pathetic note she wrote to Hogg the same day requires full quotation:

> My dearest Hogg my baby is dead—will you come to me as soon as you can—I wish to see you—It was perfectly well when I went to bed—I awoke in the night to give it suck it appeared to be *sleeping* so quietly that I would not awake it—it was dead then but we did not find *that* out till morning—from its appearance it evidently died of convulsions—
>
> Will you come—you are so calm a creature & Shelley is afraid of a fever from the milk—for I am no longer a mother now
>
> Mary[32]

As her journal reveals, Mary was not easily reconciled to her loss. On March 9 she wrote, "still think about my little baby—'tis hard indeed for a mother to loose [sic] a child." Again, on March 13, when Bysshe and Claire went off to bury the child: "stay at home net & think of my little dead baby—this is foolish I suppose yet whenever I am left alone to my own thoughts & do not read to divert them they always come back to the same point—that I was a mother & am so no longer." Then, on March 19: "Dream that my little baby came to life again—that it had only been cold & that we rubbed it by the fire and it lived—I awake & find no baby—I think about the little thing all day." And on the following day: "Dream again about my baby."[33] It seems clear that in his imaginative depiction of the travail of his heroine, Shelley was drawing on his knowledge of the real anguish Mary had only recently undergone. Indeed, in his perception of Mary's chief vulnerability, Shelley was disconcertingly prescient. The later losses of Clara and William in Italy were to try the limits of Mary's endurance.

I have argued that Shelley invented the trials of Laon and Cythna not as exercises in sadomasochism but as a revelation of the resources of the human spirit in accordance with the intention of his "Preface" and its belief that "There is a reflux in the tide of human things which bears the shipwrecked hopes of men into a secure haven after the storms are past. Methinks, those who now live have survived an age of despair."[34] Like Laon, Cythna recovers her sanity through a period of psychological and spiritual recuperation, though her experience is more difficult to interpret than her lover's. Unlike him, she has no need of the fatherly Hermit. Her regeneration comes about, rather, through the very introspection at first associated with her madness, so that her cave is gradually transformed from prison to a revelation, through its ever-changing waves, rocks, and sands, of universal truths hidden below the tide of everyday awareness— "Clear, elemental shapes, whose smallest change / A subtler language within language wrought" (3111–12). As she tells Laon later in the poem, the greatest truths lie written in the universal heart of men: " 'In their own hearts the earnest of the hope / Which made them great, the good will ever find' " (3703–4). Such understanding has its origin in her ordeal of suffering and the subtle way in which the cave as prison becomes transmuted to an image of the sustaining powers of human consciousness:

> "My mind became the book through which I grew
>   Wise in all human wisdom, and its cave,
> Which like a mine I rifled through and through,
>   To me the keeping of its secrets gave—
>   One mind, the type of all, the moveless wave
> Whose calm reflects all moving things that are,
>   Necessity, and love, and life, the grave,
>   And sympathy, fountains of hope and fear;
> Justice, and truth, and time, and the world's natural sphere."
>
> (3100–3108)

Like Laon, she gains the ability to read the universal human mind and the truths hidden there, and even an intimation of "One mind, the type of all," and the kind of hope it promises.

Such is the general character of Cythna's recovery. Yet Shelley's treatment of this development is more exact, employing an imagery that connects it with other major sections of the poem and ultimately with its resolution. Shortly after having regained her sanity, Cythna continues to bemoan her fate, searching her cave and its store of shapes for "Some smile, some look, some gesture which had blessed / Me heretofore" (3052–53)—some reassuring recollection of the baby daughter she had lost. Time passes and she pines with grief

> "until, one even,
> A Nautilus upon the fountain played,
> Spreading his azure sail where breath of Heaven
> Descended not, among the waves and whirlpools driven."
>
> (3060–63)

The eagle which has brought her food seems prepared to attack the creature; but at Cythna's anxiety for "that lovely thing, / Oaring with rosy feet its silver boat" (3064–65), the bird relents and soars above, leaving it in peace. The mysterious event seems a crucial turning point in Cythna's recovery, for as she declares,

> "This wakened me, it gave me human strength;
> And hope, I know not whence or wherefore, rose,
> But I resumed my ancient powers at length." (3073–75)

She is now able to ask herself, "what was this cave?" (3078), and to pursue the course of her self-enlightenment until the moment when, her term completed, her prison is shaken by an earthquake and she is released to pursue her ministry once more within the world. One might almost say that until the time of her release she exists like a little nautilus in the shell that is her cave.

The image of the nautilus held strong personal associations for Shelley.[35] Some years later, in April 1821, one finds him writing to Claire of a boat Henry Reveley was fitting up for him: "she will be a very nice little shell, for the Nautilus your friend" (II,288). The term assumed the character of a favored nickname. As a natural vessel the little mollusk appealed to Shelley's love of boating, especially those times when he let his bark drift aimlessly with the current as he sat composing or lay back gazing at the cloud formations above. The nautilus came to emblemize a way of life, not just the peripatetic existence that he, Mary, and Claire pursued in England and on the Continent, but also a willingness to trust to natural impulse and providence for their guide. It was as if Shelley had adopted the precept of Pope—"Learn of the little Nautilus to sail / Spread the thin oar, and catch the driving gale"[36]—or the advice of Johnson's Imlac to "commit yourself again to the current of the world," advice echoed at the conclusion of *Rasselas* when the philosopher and the astronomer remain "contented to be driven along the stream of life without directing their course to any particular port."[37] In its very frailty and delicacy, its disregard for the most dangerous currents, the creature was an emblem of hope itself, "un bateau frêle comme un papillon de mai,"[38] like those air balloons and paper boats Shelley was forever launching, sometimes charged with the weight of his writing. More than anything else, *The Revolt of Islam* was intended to preserve and transmit this sacred message of hope.

Together with the eagle and the serpent, the nautilus is a governing image in Shelley's poem. In the sixth canto, where Laon and Cythna at last consummate their love for each other following her rescue of him from the army of the treacherous tyrant, the hero declares to her:

> We know not where we go, *or what sweet dream*
>   *May pilot us* through caverns strange and fair
> Of far and pathless passion, while the stream
>   Of life, our bark doth on its whirlpools bear,
>   Spreading swift wings as sails to the dim air;
> Nor should we seek to know, so the devotion
>   Of love and gentle thoughts be heard still there
> Louder and louder from the utmost Ocean
> Of universal life, attuning its commotion.   (2587–95; my emphasis)

In its affirmation of hope and perseverance, the stanza makes implicit use of the imagery of the nautilus. This imagery and the patterns of hope it involves are fully developed in the resolution of the poem in the final canto.

Following their fiery immolation on the pyre prepared for them by the tyrant's Iberian priesthood, the two lovers awaken and are reunited in the afterlife. After their first amazement has passed, they see something approaching:

> As we sate gazing in a trance of wonder,
>   A boat approached, borne by the musical air
> Along the waves which sung and sparkled under
>   Its rapid keel—a wingèd shape sate there,
>   A child with silver-shining wings, so fair,

That as her bark did through the waters glide,
   The shadow of the lingering waves did wear
Light, as from starry beams; from side to side,
While veering to the wind her plumes the bark did guide.

The boat was one curved shell of hollow pearl,
   Almost translucent with the light divine
Of her within; the prow and stern did curl
   Hornèd on high, like the young moon supine,
   When o'er dim twilight mountains dark with pine,
It floats upon the sunset's sea of beams.   (4621–35)

Seeing the approaching boat and its child, Cythna exclaims:

   "Ay, this is Paradise
And not a dream, and we are all united!
   Lo, that is mine own child, who in the guise
Of madness came . . ."   (4643–46)

The "sweet dream" that yet "May pilot us," which Laon proposed to Cythna in Canto VI as an unknown possibility, is fulfilled in Canto XII. The nautilus—the hollow shell with the winged child propelling it— returns to convey the lovers to their home in the Temple of the Spirit. Shelley's governing impulse for his conclusion is to fulfill Mary's dream that her dead baby had come to life again. Despite Laon's initial qualification to the hope he raises—"We know not" (2587)—it is almost as if Shelley were suggesting to Mary through his allegory the possibility that her lost child might someday be restored to her. Given the balance between skepticism and optimism the poem maintains throughout its survey of the perpetual uncertainty of human destiny, who can say that the power of hope is not finally determining? In *The Revolt of Islam* the nautilus is Shelley's image of that hope.

A further reason for reading the allegory of the poem on such a personal level is what Newman White has called the "strange and almost incredible situation"[39] that was developing between Shelley, Mary, and Hogg at the time Mary was carrying her first baby. Her correspondence with Hogg can leave no doubt that late in 1814 and early the next year she was being led, reluctantly but with Bysshe's knowledge and encouragement, to accept Hogg as her lover. In the spring Shelley wrote Hogg: "I shall be very happy to see you again, & to give you your share of our common treasure of which you have been cheated for several days. The

Maie knows how highly you prize this exquisite possession . . . We will not again be deprived of this participated pleasure" (I,426). There are grounds for relating this situation to some principal aspects of Shelley's allegory in *The Revolt*. In a witty and valuable essay E. B. Murray has pointed out that Laon must fail to qualify as the infant's biological father because the child is born after Cythna's rape by the tyrant and before she and Laon consummate their love.[40] As we have seen, the lovers' relationship in Canto II is interrupted by Laon's guilty dream and its violent aftermath in Canto III. Nevertheless Cythna recalls from her fantasy of motherhood, or its reality, that her babe possesses Laon's features. Following his psychological regeneration and triumphant role in bringing about the revolution in the Golden City, Laon comes upon a lovely child attending on the downcast and abandoned tyrant as his sole companion. He seems to recognize Cythna in the child's smile and greets her "with a father's kiss" (1934), taking her from the sultan's arms as if he were accepting his own daughter. Murray goes on to argue that if the child is not Laon and Cythna's natural offspring, it must nevertheless be theirs by a psychological and spiritual principle that, borrowing from Goethe, he characterizes as "elective affinity."

Now it is most unlikely that Hogg fathered either Mary's first child (she was pregnant before the fall of 1814) or William, her second child, born in January 1816. Nor is it necessary to assume that a sexual liaison ever took place between them to see a connection with *The Revolt*. In encouraging Mary to accept Hogg as her lover, possibly as the counterpart to his relationship with Claire, Shelley could argue, as he does in his poem, that the question of a child's paternity is secondary to the higher principle of love. In the working out of the allegory of his poem, even the lust of a tyrant leads to the conception of good. In line with Laon's declaration to Cythna that "To the pure all things are pure!" (2596), *The Revolt* advances on one level of its allegory an argument in favor of free love.

As before, Shelley's method for dramatizing this ideal is to expose the falsity of the different kinds of shame opposing it. Early in the narrative we see the lovers' (especially Laon's) reluctance to confront their growing sexual differences and their need for a new reunification based on recognition of sexual maturity. Laon passes through the crisis, with its threats of regression, to the recovery of a true ideal of masculinity. Later Cythna's trials are intended in good part to bear home the message that, as Shelley was to affirm in the preface of a later work, "Undoubtedly, no person can be truly dishonoured by the act of another."[41] In Canto XII, after Cythna recognizes her daughter, the child turns to Laon to confess the momentary shame—perhaps the reflection of his own—that she felt at their first meeting in the palace of the tyrant:

> Then the bright child, the plumèd Seraph came,
>   And fixed its blue and beaming eyes on mine,
> And said, "I was disturbed by tremulous shame
>   When once we met, yet knew that I was thine
>   From the same hour in which thy lips divine
> Kindled a clinging dream within my brain,
>   Which ever waked when I might sleep, to twine
> Thine image with *her* memory dear—again
> We meet; exempted now from mortal fear or pain."   (4657–65)

It is as if Laon had overwhelmed any question of the child's paternity by making her his own with a father's kiss. No doubt Shelley's thinking in such matters was well in advance of his time; but it differs little from that of those modern parents who willingly adopt other children without discrimination into their own families. Laon, Cythna, and their daughter are in the end reunited by love, free from the "shame," the "fear or pain" of their earlier hesitations and setbacks. One cannot avoid the conclusion that the radical and ideal principles Shelley advances in his allegory of hope drew their power not only from his sympathy for Mary in the distress of her aborted motherhood but from his attitude toward her, Hogg, and Claire and the relationship they shared with one another.

The view of history represented by the emblem of the eagle and the serpent wreathed in fight, the sense of a perpetual and indecisive conflict between the powers of good and evil waged throughout history, in the end prevails in Shelley's poem. Like the French Revolution, the revolt within the Golden City fails, suppressed by the resurgent forces of reaction, and Laon and Cythna are put to death by their heartless captors. It should be clear by now, however, that such a summary does scant justice to the power and complexity of Shelley's allegory of hope. Laon and Cythna may be defeated in their earthly endeavors, but they are reborn and reunited with their child in Shelley's paradise, with the clear implication that others will follow them into the world to pursue their goals, perhaps in the end to succeed where they have failed. In the way it circles back upon itself, returning to the end of the first canto, where we first see the reunited lovers after their fiery immolation, the poem seems to commemorate the eternal return and conservation of the spirit of the good. Such a view, however, cannot blind one to the way Laon and Cythna change and grow as a result of their earthly trials. The lovers may emerge, or reemerge, beneath the benign gaze of the presiding figure whose mildness suggests, as we have seen, the ideal of a superior hermaphroditism. Nevertheless the earthly consummation of their love, shortly before their deaths, comes about only after appropriate trials that force them to rediscover their sexual identities as man and woman.

Thus the vision of perfection the work projects should not be confused, as it increasingly is today, with androgyny or unisexuality.[42] Reminiscent of Blake's Beulah, the bland, reposeful state Shelley depicts in the early cantos, centered on the complete identification between Laon and Cythna, proves inadequate to the strains it must undergo. As in Blake, those tensions emerge through the challenge of generation: the need to confront the inevitable onset of adolescence and sexual differentiation in order to attack the particular evils of the world more effectively. Through their separate trials Laon and Cythna are prepared, in quite different ways, for their reunion in a deeper relationship free from guilt and fear and founded in self-knowledge and acceptance.

In his metaphoric interweaving of the biological and historical, the personal and archetypal, Shelley achieves a complex perspective faithful to his vindication of the French Revolution and its place in history. Earthly warfare, with its victories and defeats, will continue; but each new onset in the cause of the good brings mankind closer to the still unobtained perfection. Only by first losing its achieved integrity in the disorder and apparent defeat of earthly struggle can the spirit of the good achieve those transformations of its nature that purify it ever further. In The Revolt of Islam Shelley's imagination discovered a delicate balance between the vision of possible perfection and a steady awareness of the innumerable struggles, together with their attendant setbacks, necessary to its realization.

four

THE HUMAN SITUATION

Prometheus Unbound, Act I

Shelley regarded *Prometheus Unbound* as his masterpiece, and it is the most deliberately composed of all his major works. Begun in the autumn of 1818, it occupied him for over a year at the height of his career. He carefully revised and added to the whole of the drama when, in the winter of 1819–20, he extended the play with a fourth and final act. The drama is a work of great intellectual and psychological subtlety that has much to say about the mind of its author. Shelley, however, did not intend it as self-revelation but as a profound investigation of the mind and spirit of humanity. Although one can read the play as a reflection of his unconscious drives and fantasies, serious study demands that we start with his conscious aims and intentions, beginning with his "Preface" to the work.

Like the "Preface" to *The Revolt,* which was published the same year *Prometheus* was begun, Shelley's "Preface" to the later work is both detailed and condensed and expresses a wealth of diverse concerns—social, historical, and aesthetic—that forbids any easy summary. Critics will, of course, differ in what they choose to emphasize; but in many respects Shelley's most illuminating declaration comes near the end, shortly after he has confessed to "a passion for reforming the world" and then gone on, rather paradoxically, to assert that "Didactic poetry is my abhorrence." "My purpose," he continues, in what has been one of his most derided declarations, "has hitherto been simply to familiarise the highly refined imagination of the more select classes of poetical readers with beautiful idealisms of moral excellence; aware that until the mind can love, and admire, and trust, and hope, and endure, reasoned principles of moral conduct are seeds cast upon the highway of life which the unconscious passenger tramples into dust, although they would bear the harvest of his happiness."[1]

The words isolate both the genuine originality and the difficulty of his intention. Shelley had arrived at that point in his career where he had come to see the necessity of taking a large step forward in order to dramatize a grand visionary hypothesis, a task that, as he wrote to Peacock afterward, involved him "with characters & mechanism of a kind yet unattempted" (II,94). For some time he had been committed not just to complete social and political reform but to the ideal of the millennium to which such a thoroughgoing change might lead. But what would it be like to experience such a state as an emotional reality? Granted that men might be reasoned into such a condition, was it not first necessary to appeal to or reanimate those feelings of desire and hope and admiration that are primary to the success of any logical persuasion? Poets might claim to be "the unacknowledged legislators of the World";[2] but they were visionaries full of the wonders of a possible future, and the propositions they advanced drew their authority from the unrecorded testimony of the human heart rather than demonstrated laws. How was it possible to begin to move men rationally without first recovering the elemental sympathy and trust from which all rational conduct must necessarily proceed?

In the most interesting section of her note on *Prometheus Unbound*, Mary Shelley declared:

> The prominent feature of Shelley's theory of the destiny of the human species was that evil is not inherent in the system of the creation, but an accident that might be expelled. This also forms a portion of Christianity: God made earth and man perfect, till he, by his fall, "Brought death into the world and all our woe." Shelley believed that mankind had only to will that there should be no evil, and there would be none. It is not my part in these Notes to notice the arguments that have been urged against this opinion, but to mention the fact that he entertained it, and was indeed attached to it with fervent enthusiasm.[3]

It has been increasingly common in recent years to discount Mary's statement as gross oversimplification. Her words, nevertheless, contain a vital element of truth, which it is important to separate from the half-truths in her declaration. Shelley believed that men were susceptible to impulses of both good and evil. The elimination of evil through a simple act of will does not lie, however, in the power of any person or group of people for the reason that individuals are circumscribed and conditioned by their time, their age, and their state of cultural and social evolution. At the same time Shelley believed, contrary to the doctrine of original sin, that evil enjoys no necessary authority or substance and that it would inevitably give way once the superior attractions of virtue were realized. Indeed evil for Shelley possesses no positive attributes of its own but rather derives its reality from the denial or repression of man's virtuous instincts. Shelley characteristically views evil in terms of such negations as discord, disaffection, imperception, injustice, unmercifulness, indifference, disappointment. Even such active forms of evil as hate and fear arise from the rejection of love and trust. As Earl Wasserman has argued, Shelley's basic idea of evil is crystallized in the notion of self-contempt: man's repudiation of all that is best in his true nature.[4]

Mary Shelley might on occasion simplify her husband's thinking. At the same time she perceived what for him were certain fundamental moral truths that later critics, partly from an esoteric concern with the sources and ramifications of his philosophic thinking and partly from embarrassment with such intense idealism, have unhappily discounted. Shelley believed that human beings were created to love, to trust, to admire, to sympathize, to contribute, to assist, to rejoice, that they were, in short, intended to fulfill their best potential. Why then do we find a world in which these impulses, if not altogether rejected, are nevertheless perpetually inhibited and deprived of a fulfillment which is forever made out to seem impracticable or naive? Shelley saw that the fault lay in an ingrained cynicism, thick with the incrustations of time, which maintained the unshakable hegemony of human fear and self-interest and the unwisdom of ever imagining the triumph of our higher impulses. A keen student of history, Shelley well knew the repeated cycles of victory and backsliding, of anticipation and disappointment, that marked the annals of the past. The ever-present example of the French Revolution weighed heavily; and Shelley was familiar with the arguments of Burke and others that such ill-judged experiments in idealism only unleashed man's true destructiveness and, by breaking down whatever fabric of civilized restraints they countered, created a situation more horrific than any they set out to redress. Despite such shining examples as Periclean Athens, one might argue that the accumulated examples of history confirmed a pessimistic fatalism.

History appeared to condemn man to repeat the endless cycle of past errors, for the kind of lessons it taught, based on hindsight never available in the turmoil and complexity of actual situations, were pragmatic and discouraged the possibility of a fundamental change in human nature. Yet, the record of history notwithstanding, if one stepped back to look at humankind with scientific detachment, free from bias and superstition, one had to agree with Godwin that there was no apparent cause why our reason, or reasonableness, should not ultimately prevail to free us from our trammels and direct us toward an ultimate perfectibility. Godwin and his followers argued that the proper course to take lay through quiet fireside discussion, through argument and persuasion, and then through legislation, a slow and gradual process that could be accelerated only with grave danger. Shelley knew, however, that if the change were ever to come, it would come as an emotional realization, spreading like a chain reaction, allowing individuals to recognize in the eyes of their fellows the knowledge avowed by their own hearts. It would be like a mask suddenly fallen to reveal human beings free of the suffocating weight of aspersion that all the pessimisms and cynicisms of the earth had inflicted on them. That Shelley composed a major tract, "A Philosophical View of Reform," advocating peaceable and gradual change, that throughout his life he urged the necessity of particular reforms, that he heralded signs of political change in Britain and in other countries as portents of the future, qualifies but in no way contradicts his true radicalism. The dedicated idealist welcomes every straw in the wind even while he knows that nothing short of a total transformation of society will be satisfactory and that, moreover, once it is achieved, people will wonder why they were so slow in accepting a recognition that now seems inevitable.

Social reformers and legislators, Shelley among them, might argue about the feasibility of such a change and the best means of its accomplishment; but was it not preeminently the role of the poet, using the faculty of imagination, actually to prefigure it, to anticipate its distinctive qualities, to adumbrate its joy and liberation? One could hardly imagine an undertaking at once more daring, serviceable, and urgent. When poets prophesy, they perceive the future; but they also create what they foresee, if only by rendering that future more proximate and accessible. They help bring into being what they descry. They know in part and they prophesy in part. In letters and poems, especially in "Mont Blanc," which is in many ways a preliminary sketch for *Prometheus*, Shelley had revolved in his imagination the metaphor of the alpine landslide as an image of such a change. The figure had obvious advantages, suggesting a weighty incrustation of chilling heresies dramatically giving way to the silent working of a multitude of imperceptible forces. Yet the figure also presented certain difficulties. For one thing it implied the immense and indiscriminate destructiveness revolutions only too frequently bring in their train. For another, it suggested a continuous process of accretion and collapse without defining any bedrock of stability or truth. These connotations, far from being merely fortuitous, represented real concerns that would have to be resolved in any thoroughgoing attempt of the kind he was now determined to make to approximate the remote and familiarize the wonderful—to endow the millennium with a living reality.

Prometheus Unbound has been most often read, and increasingly so in recent years, as the elaboration of a philosophical system prefigured in Shelley's earlier letters, essays, and poems like "Mont Blanc." The work undoubtedly reflects a wealth of keen philosophical as well as scientific interest; but to emphasize these elements above all others is to strip away from the poem what, as its title suggests, is more fundamental. *Prometheus Unbound*: the title itself implies not so much the binding or unbinding of Prometheus or the method of his release, though the play in fact deals with all these questions. Taken by itself the title phrase suggests more simply the state or condition of being unbound: how can one imagine such an experience, what does it feel like, how can one describe the sense of change? These questions, seemingly naive, actually take one to the heart of what is at once most original and problematic in Shelley's poem.

Partly from a sense of misplaced embarrassment, partly from the desire to rescue Shelley from the charge of mindless rhapsodist, scholars generally have tended to minimize the broadly lyrical character and purpose of his play (it is subtitled "A Lyrical Drama"). Kenneth Cameron, for example, who has interpreted Shelley convincingly but in places too narrowly within the terms and programs of revolutionary social thinkers of the Enlightenment, has warned that in *Prometheus* "Shelley, in essence, is depicting not a psychological miracle but a transformation resulting from social change."[5] Better balanced is Timothy Webb's assertion that "it is wrong to see *Prometheus Unbound* simply as a poem which enacts a political revolution; likewise it is wrong to see it simply as a poem which readjusts the mental equilibrium. It does both of these things together and each readjustment or revolution implies and necessitates the other."[6] At the risk of unsettling such a reasonable and balanced judgment, I want, nevertheless, to urge the primacy of the psychological, imaginative, and transformational elements in Shelley's work, because they point to what is both most innovative and difficult in it. The play throughout reverberates with such questions as "Canst thou speak?" "Hast thou beheld?" "Hearest thou not?" "Feelest thou not?"—questions that betray a continual struggle for a revisualization of reality. From the time of its first appearance the play has been understood by the common reader not primarily as the elaboration of a philosophic system or a program of deliberate social reform but as the projection of a vast millennial vision of possible perfection. One early, anonymous reviewer of the work could avow his sympathy for Shelley's ethical, historical, scientific, legislative, social, and (in the broadest sense) Christian concerns and yet turn to protest:

But when he would attempt to realize in an instant his glorious visions; when he would treat men as though they are now the fit inhabitants of an earthly paradise; when he would cast down all restraint and authority as enormous evils; and would leave mankind to the guidance of passions yet unsubdued, and of desires yet unregulated, we must protest against his wishes, as tending fearfully to retard the good which he would precipitate.[7]

In its mixture of astonishment and apprehensiveness, the reaction helps us comprehend the drama at once for what it is: with the possible exception of some of Blake's prophecies, the most ambitious attempt at visionary creation in literature, even in the light of Dante and Milton.

Some sense of Shelley's daring and originality can be gleaned in recognizing his determination to reverse the priorities expressed by Wordsworth who, in a famous passage in *The Prelude*, recalled the transport of those early days of revolutionary fervor in France when intellectuals and "schemers more mild"

> Were called upon to exercise their skill,
> Not in Utopia,—subterranean fields,—
> Or some secreted island, Heaven knows where!
> But in the very world, which is the world
> Of all of us,—the place where, in the end,
> We find our happiness, or not at all![8]

Wordsworth set his heart upon the earthly realization of the aims of the revolution in France, and when the revolution failed, he lost faith in its ideals or, rather, as M. H. Abrams has seen it, transferred his humanitarian ambitions to a more conventional, private, and Christian sphere of endeavor.[9] For Shelley, however, it remains utopia that matters most, which explains his determination, both in *The Revolt of Islam* and in *Prometheus*, to reaffirm the validity of revolutionary and imaginative ideals even in the wake of the disaster on the Continent. None of this is to argue that Shelley was either heartless or unmindful of worldly developments and their significance. Poets are and must remain, he would assert, politically active and socially concerned. Yet if in their role as poets they are, in the resounding phrases that conclude the *Defence of Poetry*, "the hierophants of an unapprehended inspiration, the mirrors of the gigantic shadows which futurity casts upon the present, the words which express what they understand not,"[10] then their primary allegiance is by definition not to the things of this world but to what may become, and their eye is not on the earthly object but on the imaginative and ideal.

Such priorities, unusual as they are, may be rapidly set down; but they immediately suggest difficulties of realization that the more astute of Shelley's early critics were quick to recognize. Even granted the ultimate perfectibility of man and the need to represent it as an achievable ideal, was it really possible to depict—convincingly and movingly—such an unfamiliar state of being? If the millennium brings the eradication of every last trace of human envy, greed, intemperance, and the like, how can one celebrate such a state of perfection without making it appear anticlimactic, childish, or jejeune? It was all very well to argue the necessity for an imaginative example of attained perfection to extend the range of human hopes and possibilities. What inducement, however, could it hold out to a humankind whose happiness seemed to depend, as moralists like Johnson powerfully declared, on existing perpetually in a state of "Effort, and expectation, and desire, / And something evermore about to be"?[11]

The sister arts to poetry, painting and music, depended by their nature on the principle of contrast, a sense of light and shade, of reality and depth built up through an interplay of different tonalities and harmonic modulations. How could one invent a palette of sufficient intensity to convey the sublimity of the ideal world in all its brilliance without undercutting the very means on which art relies for achieving its effects? To take merely one aspect of the problem, if the poet conceives of evil, like Shelley, as nothing essentially vital or real in its own right but rather the darkness and fear that collect within the void created by the absence of the good, how was it possible to develop a compelling sense of conflict and struggle on which great drama traditionally relies? How could one adopt the means of tragedy while at the same time dispensing not only with all sense of tragic grief and loss but also with any full and meaningful sense of opposition? Beyond this there was the challenge of justifying the claim to authority and vision concealed within the most astonishing part of the declaration (made in the *Defence of Poetry* but applicable above all to *Prometheus*) that "Poets are . . . the words which express what they understand not," the contention that poets are only the intimators of a message so sacred and mysterious that they themselves can never comprehend its full significance. Such problems and imperatives would have been sufficient to intimidate any poet less aspiring than Shelley. In obeying his conviction that the time had come, both in his career and in the larger tide of human events, for advancing a vision of a daring and apocalyptic scope, he was acting on a faith of the only kind he could ever truly countenance. He was acting on the convictions of his own heart and the belief that they were ones that united him most closely to his fellow beings.

For some time Shelley had been closing in on the figure of Prometheus as the hero of his drama. The example of Christ had been appropriated and distorted irrevocably by the apologists of religious orthodoxy. Moreover Milton had already taken up the Christian savior as the hero of his *Paradise Regained*, a poem that, however different, bore important similarities to Shelley's intention. For his resolute defiance in the face of overwhelming tyranny, the character of Satan possessed remarkable attractions. At the same time it was flawed, as Shelley observed in his "Preface" to *Prometheus*, by "taints of ambition, envy, revenge, and a desire for personal aggrandisement"[12]—if only from the ineradicable power of Milton's characterization. However brave and resourceful, Satan lacked those gentler traits of long suffering and self-sacrifice that belonged to the Christian savior, with which Shelley fully sympathized. As a mean between Christ and Satan, Prometheus represented the difficult if not contradictory balance between militancy and submission, self-assertion and dedication to others that Shelley was struggling to project. Prometheus, of course, brought with him the admirable but also intimidating example of *Prometheus Bound*, the sole survivor, except for some scattered fragments, of the lost trilogy of Aeschylus. Here Shelley felt on firmer ground, for, however magisterial the Aeschylean drama, his own ingrained extremism could never permit him to sympathize with the political moderation and compromise of the older dramatist's resolution, in which the competing claims of Jupiter and Prometheus were finally reconciled.

More important, he had come to see through Aeschylus's play to certain deeper implications of the myth itself, the kind of reinterpretation that any significant reworking of the heroic legend would require. Not only could he proudly claim at the outset of his "Preface" the right to redact the ancient story for his own quite different purpose, but he could even insert as an epigraph for the finished play the words "Audisne hæc Amphiarae, sub terram abdite?" (Do you hear this, Amphiaraus, buried beneath the earth?)—a partly playful, partly exultant taunt at the older dramatist.

Byron, Mary, and Shelley had discussed the Titan during the summer they spent together on Lake Geneva in 1816, when Mary had begun her own *Frankenstein; or The Modern Prometheus*. Reacting to this stimulus, Byron, who had been haunted by the Promethean figure from the time he adapted into English a chorus from Aeschylus as one of his earliest poetical exercises while a schoolboy at Harrow, had produced his own "Prometheus," one of the most powerful of his lyrics. As usual the force of the older poet's example was intimidating to Shelley. However he could hardly agree with Byron's depiction of the hero as a symbol of man's "funereal destiny," a hero who can find his purpose and identity only in the act of defying his tormentor.

As he mulled over these paradoxes and problems, Shelley began to see a major analogy between the enduring human predicament and what began to define itself in his imagination as the Promethean situation. As we have seen, he had come to view the human position on earth as a striking anomaly. On the one hand there existed no real impediment to our responding at any given moment to the urges of our true and better nature and joining our fellow creatures to overthrow misrule, oppression, and injustice and, short of dispensing with mutability and death, the givens of the human condition, summoning in a new golden age on earth. On the other hand, so heavy was the pall of fear, mistrust, and self-concern that it seemed impossible for any reformer or movement to break through the barrier of false counsel and apparent self-interest protecting the status quo and to capture people's imaginations and hearts. One could empha-size either side of the paradox. One could stress the ever-present availabil-ity, even the imminence of the millennium if humankind could only once see its way through to a just and full realization of its own potential. Or one could fall back in despair at the evidence of the way our best desires and intentions had repeatedly been suborned by the tenacity and deceit of those established powers that ruled the world together with the legion of cohorts they seduced into serving them. Either extreme was perilous, for to emphasize the one view was only in the end to accentuate the other. The danger lay in seesawing wildly back and forth between them both. This had proved to be the lesson of the French Revolution; the initial outburst of triumphant optimism, once disappointed, had given way in the case of intellectuals like Wordsworth to dismay and self-withdrawal and a loss of faith not only in the cause of political radicalism but also in human nature itself. How could one remain faithful to one's most radical convictions without abandoning the balance that a dialectical view of the human situation required?

It was just here that Shelley's reinterpretation of the Prometheus legend assumed major relevance. At the center of the myth was the image of Zeus (or his Roman counterpart, Jupiter) and Prometheus locked in an all-out struggle of wills in which the tyrant sought, by means of the most dreadful torments, to break the resistance of his adversary. Yet in this struggle Prometheus possessed an all-important resource, one that Aes-chylus, in his concern for reconciliation, had seriously minimized. Pro-metheus foresaw Zeus's fatal marriage to Thetis and the offspring destined to depose him, a secret that, once rendered up, would establish the monarch and his reign forever. Zeus's intent, therefore, was to break

Prometheus's will, to force him to yield up his secret, even while the Titan's task was to summon the perseverance necessary to hold out against the most dire punishments. Judged by any standard the hero's position seemed desperate indeed. Yet looked at another way it was, paradoxically, invincible. In one sense Prometheus's victory was assured; in one sense Jupiter was already in his power. All he need do was maintain the fortitude to continue his resistance and to await the arrival of the promised hour hidden, in Shelley's phrase, in that "far goal of Time" (III.iii.174). Given his continued resistance and the unquestionable truth of the prophecies, he could not fail. Indeed there was a sense in which victory was already in his grasp.[13]

Yet look at the Titan's position from the opposite perspective: how long must he, how long could he be expected to endure? The isolation and exposure of Prometheus together with the horrors of the bird's dismembering attack compose one of the most terrifying prospects envisioned by the human imagination, a sight too terrible to be endured. How was it possible for Prometheus to hold on? One had only to project oneself imaginatively into his place upon the rock, to anticipate those dawning streaks of light and the flutter of bird's wings to foresee one's own capitulation. Beyond the threat of whatever new punishments Jupiter might bring to bear was the terrifying element of uncertainty. While the *end* of Prometheus's travail was fixed, its *extent* was by no means certain. Aeschylus' hero had declared that the term of his suffering was ten thousand years; and later he told Io that he would be rescued by Hercules, the offspring of the thirteenth generation of her descendants. For Shelley, however, who had come to understand the knife-edge terror of the predicament the myth conveyed, there could not be even this kind of distant fixity. Although the truth of the prophecies was unchallengeable, they were often riddles whose fulfillment sometimes broke the very hearts to which they seemed to minister. Endowed with his gift of imagination and poetic foresight, the poet could envision the promised end virtually at hand. Yet to return from that leap of the imagination to the realm of actual human experience, a series of repeated postponements that began to assume the span of infinity would be the cruelest disillusionment imaginable and might extinguish hope altogether. For how could one continue living without desire and expectation, since hope was the only thing that made life endurable? How could Prometheus as the champion of human hope, having once conveyed the sacred flame to man, be conceived of allowing it to expire? The possibility of failure, indeed of anything less than victory, was virtually unthinkable. For Aeschylus, who visualized the drama as a struggle between the legitimate claims of vested authority and the demands of innovation or dissent, some resolution in the form of compromise was possible. For Shelley, however, who visualized the evil embodied in Jupiter as residing in the mere absence of the true and good, any compromise was inconceivable because it would lead to the ultimate perversity, the recognition and confirmation of the unreal and inessential.

Shelley's choice of Prometheus as his hero, then, was hardly casual. What lay behind the choice was a thoroughgoing reassimilation of the myth as a major revelation of the perennial human situation, a situation that had come to assume for Shelley contemporary significance. The problem facing any extended dramatic treatment was, of course, that the legend lent itself to such different emphases. It could be adapted as the vehicle for an unqualified millennial optimism. Or it could portray the long suffering of a humanity fated to undergo seemingly indefinite hardship and injustice, a humanity that, as for Byron, must support itself through defiance rooted in the recognition of its own despair. For Shelley, on the contrary, the way forward lay in the strengthening and extending of human hope. Whatever dangers it might involve, only the vision of an achieved perfection could provide humans not simply with the courage or the desire but more basically with the ability to sense and grasp the potential for virtue and happiness that lay within themselves, a potential they had to feel and recognize before they could be reasoned into any systematic implementation. For those dwelling in darkness, the main need was a great light. As Shelley proceeded he knew he would find it necessary to reveal the dark underside of his legend, its potential for false confidence and self-deception. In order for his poem to serve as the ideal prototype he felt so vitally necessary, however, its primary thrust would have to be affirmative, in harmony with his conviction of the ultimate perfectibility of humankind. In seeking to open people's eyes, to make them see and feel and acknowledge a quality of being that poets of the highest sensibility could themselves but barely apprehend, he was committing himself to a visionary work that strained the very limits of poetical conception, a work that was arguably more daring and original than any other poet had yet attempted.

Shelley's perception of the ambivalence at the root of the Promethean situation, his realization of its potential for either hope or despair, in great part explains a question that has always hung over the play. From the outset of the first act and Prometheus's long opening speech, we are aware that we are beholding the Titan's transformation and release. Yet that change is at first so imperceptible, so inexplicable and seemingly unmotivated, that we must wonder how and why, after so many years of suffering, it is now coming about. So gradual is the change, latent even in

the authority of Prometheus's opening declarations, that it might almost
be imagined to have begun, as some critics have suggested, offstage, before the play has commenced.[14]

From Shelley's own day through the Victorian period down to our
own, no contention about the play has been more common than that it
dramatizes man's ability to transform himself and his world in the light of
imaginative ideals. With differing emphases, this is still the major assumption under which the play is introduced in critical studies and anthologies.
If, however, Shelley intended his first act to dramatize man's powers of
self-regeneration through inward recognition, repentance, and reform,
why did he do his work so badly? Granted that the act describes the hero's
change of heart, from hatred toward love, why is that movement so halt-
ing and unfocused? We first see Prometheus unrepentant, "eyeless in hate"
(I.9), though a closer look at the passage suggests that the phrase actually
pertains to the Titan's vision of his former self and is therefore already a
thing of the past. The first emphatic indication of a change comes, oddly,
through his anticipation of his foe's disastrous downfall, when

> these pale feet . . . might trample thee
> If they disdained not such a prostrate slave.
> Disdain? Ah no! I pity thee.   (I.51–53)

Pity, one may argue, is only a first, imperfect approach to the higher love
Prometheus can never achieve until his reunion with Asia. Still, it is curious to find a love born out of its opposite, contempt. Moreover, the larger
change, revealed almost immediately thereafter, comes with all the terse-
ness of an imperial declaration:

> I speak in grief,
> Not exultation, for I hate no more,
> As then, ere misery made me wise.—The Curse
> Once breathed on thee I would recall.   (I.56–59)

The lines are, to say the least, perfunctory. Nor are they illuminated by the
hero's assertion, a few lines later, that "I am changed so that aught evil
wish / Is dead within" (I.70–71). If the first three hundred lines of the play
are meant to describe a distinct process of moral rehabilitation, why is that
process so spasmodic and inscrutable? Why does it not more fully illuminate the grounds for change within Prometheus himself?

Critics who have pointed to the opening of Shelley's play as a pattern
of deliberate moral self-reformation have always brushed aside the difficulties opposing such a view. Nevertheless, as one reader has justly observed,

"Prometheus cannot be said actually to will his pity. Rather, he seems to discover it, almost as a sign of grace, within himself."[15] In this respect the opening of the play resembles the turning point of Coleridge's great ballad, when the Ancient Mariner experiences a sudden, inexplicable upsurge of love for the watersnakes:

> A spring of love gushed from my heart
> And I blessed them *unaware:*
> Sure my kind saint took pity on me,
> And I blessed them *unaware.*   (284–87; my emphasis)

Mary Shelley's assertion in her note on *Prometheus* that her husband "believed that mankind had only to will that there should be no evil, and there would be none," although justified within a general context, seems inadequate and misleading when narrowly applied to the first act of the drama.

Why did Shelley not take greater pains to dramatize effectively the source and growth of his hero's reclamation, for how can one conceive of genuine moral reformation that arises unaccountably, that is prepared for by no process of conscious recognition or convincing renewal of the emotions? The answer lies in several different aspects of the problem. From the first it was Shelley's intention, as we have seen, to press forward with a radically visionary and transforming work, a work above all exemplary in intention and effect, as the only way of breaking through the dilemma constraining humankind. In character and effect the play shares important analogies with the art of classical sculpture. A major part of its dramatic (as opposed to its poetic) power was to reside, as Shelley conceived it, in the sculptural simplicity of the central image of the liberated Titan, in its shock value (an aspect of the sublime he was deliberately seeking) as an infinitely suggestive prototype of human perfection. To begin by prescribing the steps by which such a transformation must come about would not only detract from the classical simplicity of his model but also restrict its power of suggestiveness. More important, Shelley was unwilling, setting aside the limitations of his own knowledge, to specify when or under what conditions the longed-for change might come about. Most of all, however, he was unable to conceive of the change as the result of any simple act of human will. The notion that, shortly after completing *Queen Mab*, Shelley rapidly abandoned the necessitarian ideas that pervade his early thinking for a philosophy of uninhibited activity, free will, and love has gained influential support in recent years. The truth seems to be, however, that Shelley retained the concept of necessity as one of a number of often conflicting premises within his later thought.[16]

The point can be reaffirmed by citation from the prose work of Shelley's, composed shortly after *Prometheus*, that bears the closest relationship to his drama of any of his essays. In his *Defence of Poetry* Shelley writes:

> Poetry is not like reasoning, a power to be exerted according to the determination of the will. A man cannot say, "I will compose poetry." The greatest poet even cannot say it: for the mind in creation is as a fading coal which some invisible influence, like an inconstant wind, awakens to transitory brightness: this power arises from within, like the colour of a flower which fades and changes as it is developed, and the conscious portions of our natures are unprophetic either of its approach or its departure.[17]

For Shelley the act of poetic creation was more than the happy discovery of the proper metaphor or cadence to convey the emotional effect of an intellectual and preconceived design. The power of inspiration was not only aesthetic but also profoundly moral, controlling the work from its first inception, its germ of idea, to its last subtleties of implication. However intermittent, the wind of inspiration was compelling and pervasive, directing the course of the work from beginning to end, so that its organic character, its integrity as a completed whole, was nothing less than a divine mystery. It is not necessary to insist, with Carlyle, on the hero's identity with the poet to see that as the artist cannot say "I will compose," so the hero cannot say, "I will liberate, I will transform myself." Both acts or states of intuition are equally moral, and both take their direction from an inspiration that moves beyond them in a way they cannot fully comprehend. Prometheus is not the instigator of his own transformation but rather the first manifestation of a larger change working throughout the entire universe.

What is this larger change that pervades Shelley's drama and how can one account for it? The answer to these questions is suggested above all by the vernal spirit of the play, a force that distills the essence of the spring season as powerfully as any verse in English and to which Shelley attributed the inspiration of his drama:

> This Poem was chiefly written upon the mountainous ruins of the Baths of Caracalla, among the flowery glades, and thickets of odoriferous blossoming trees which are extended in ever winding labyrinths upon its immense platforms and dizzy

arches suspended in the air. The bright blue sky of Rome, and
the effect of the vigorous awakening of spring in that divinest
climate, and the new life with which it drenches the spirits even
to intoxication, were the inspiration of this drama.[18]

Very simply, the change that *Prometheus* from its beginning dramatizes is
the reflection of Shelley's hope, a hope assuming in its pertinacity the
strength of faith, that spring will follow winter, that the reign of mercy
and peace will some day succeed the dominion of hatred and oppression.
Shelley trusted that, if only through the laws of probability operating in
the immensity of time, the golden years must at length return—that, in the
words of a motto on a ring he cherished, "Il buon tempo verra," the good
time will come.[19]

For several reasons it was important to Shelley to concentrate on the
nature of the change that overcomes his hero rather than its determining
conditions. Nevertheless there was still the need for some poetic mechanism to reflect the character of the transformation, if only to provide the
means for assessing the difference between the "then" of an earlier Prometheus and the "now" of his liberation. In Prometheus's first speech in
the play, immediately after his anticipation of Jupiter's coming downfall,
the Titan determines to retrieve the curse he had so many years before
uttered upon his persecutor: "The Curse / Once breathed on thee I would
recall" (I.58–59). In response to his declaration the voices of the natural
elements describe the blighting effect of the imprecation. They are followed by Prometheus's mother, the Earth, who, refusing to repeat the
curse in the accents of the living for fear of further punishments the tyrant
may yet call down upon her, entreats her son to summon up the phantasm
of Jupiter to repeat the awful words.

The appearance of the phantasm and his repetition of the curse then
sets the stage for the remainder of Act I: the apparition of Mercury and the
Furies and their temptation of the hero, followed by the chorus of celestial
spirits who comfort him after his ordeal. Indeed, Carlos Baker has likened
everything that follows in the drama to the operation of a great machine
set in motion by Prometheus's change of heart.[20] The dispatch of Panthea
to Asia, the latter's transformation, her descent to the cave of Demogorgon, his ascent to the throne of Jupiter, the tyrant's futile resistance and
downfall, the unbinding of Prometheus, and so on—all follow from the
hero's initial reformation. It is no wonder that critics have seen Prometheus's determination to recall the curse as the one crucial act in the
course of the entire play and that many of them have interpreted the
retraction as a required act of moral recognition and repentance.

Yet the more one contemplates the initial expression of Prometheus's impulse—"The Curse / Once breathed . . . I would recall"—the more one comes to question the soul-searching and contrition older critics claim to see. For one thing, it has been pointed out that Shelley most often uses the verb "recall" to mean "recollect," that he never once in his verse clearly uses it to mean "revoke."[21] The two senses of the word are, of course, hardly contradictory; and one might argue logically that calling back to mind the language of the curse is a necessary preliminary to recanting it. As G. M. Matthews has reasoned wittily in this connection, " 'Three thousand years of sleep-unsheltered hours' were naturally hard on the memory."[22] Yet if Prometheus experiences difficulty in recollecting the language of the curse, what prompts him to do so? If after so long an interval he cannot recall his own words, how can he remember having cursed Jupiter at all?

If Prometheus's recalling of the curse does not represent an act of deliberate self-recognition and repentance, what are its significance and function in the drama? This question, the most difficult in the play, has psychological roots of a depth not easy to explore. There seems little doubt, however, that the change has to do with what Leon Waldoff, in a perceptive essay about the psychology of the father-son conflict in the background of the drama, has called "the subtlest transformation of feeling in the entire play." That transformation has to do with "a passing of the Oedipus complex," a source of energy that informs, as every reader has in some way felt, so much of Shelley's drama.[23] The transformation, partly unconscious and partly conscious, of those energies in Shelley's life, and its relationship, through sublimation, to the design and significance of his ideal vision are matters that can never completely be brought to light. Nevertheless it is in just this context that the curse and its recalling emerge as our principal and most revealing clues. Psychologically the function of the curse, or of the hero's need to recollect it, is to provide some means of connecting an all but buried past with a present, a then with a now.

When Prometheus hears the curse repeated by the phantasm of Jupiter, he sees as in a mirror the powerful working of emotions written on features that closely resemble his own:

> I see the curse on gestures proud and cold,
> And looks of firm defiance, and calm hate,
> And such despair as mocks itself with smiles. (I.258–60)

He recognizes both his own features and those of the father, Jupiter. What is reborn within him is an earlier emotional state, one he has repressed or forgotten, a state that once existed "ere misery made me wise" (I.58). In his first impatience to hear the curse repeated, Prometheus is impelled by "an awful whisper [that] rises up" (I.132). Like Oedipus, he is called back in imagination in quest of some past experience that holds the key to his present situation, something more primitive even than the pain in his limbs, the pain of his binding:

> Obscurely through my brain like shadows dim
> Sweep awful thoughts, rapid and thick.—I feel
> Faint, like one mingled in entwining love,
> Yet 'tis not pleasure.   (I.146–49)

The repetition of the curse is the literal means of recalling the experience that underlies it—as with Oedipus, the terrible, perverse pleasure-pain of wrestling with the father, the intermingled joy and guilt of the son's rebellion and defiance. At the beginning of his fine study of Shelley's politics, P. M. S. Dawson recalls a passage in Hogg's account of Shelley's youth, which Dawson finds "curious that commentators have not adduced . . . in discussing the Curse motif in *Prometheus Unbound*":

> Two or three Eton boys called another day, and begged their former schoolfellow to curse his father and the king, as he used occasionally to do at school. Shelley refused, and for some time persisted in his refusal, saying that he had left it off; but as they continued to urge him, by reason of their importunity he suddenly broke out, and delivered, with vehemence and animation, a string of execrations, greatly resembling in its absurdity a papal anathema; the fulmination soon terminated in a hearty laugh, in which we all joined.[24]

Despite Shelley's avowal that "he had left it off," one can sense beneath the dissipating energies of his schoolfellows' laughter the power of deeply repressed resentments working toward recognition and release. Prometheus's recollection of the curse makes manifest what has all the while been latent, reintegrating the hero with his own past self. The reintegration is necessary not only to measure the distance between "then" and "now" but also to connect the hero consciously with a part of himself essential to his present mastery. The impulse or the power to recall the curse operates like the final stage of a long psychological healing process, culminating with a realization the patient is at last superinduced to effect for himself.

The necessary reintegration is not merely psychological but also moral, and vital to the effect of Shelley's drama. From his first speech in the play Prometheus looks forward to that one among the "wingless, crawling Hours" (I.48) destined to bring his foe's downfall; there is no indication that he ever relents in his anticipation of his enemy's ultimate destruction. As we have seen, defiance and resistance are the *sine qua non* of the Promethean hero's nature and role. As traditional critics of the play are quick to point out, however, it is also incumbent on Prometheus to forgive. Indeed both imperatives are clearly stated near the end of Demogorgon's concluding speech in the last act of the play, an adjuration that comes as the moral capstone to the drama:

> To suffer woes which Hope thinks infinite;
> To forgive wrongs darker than Death or Night;
> To defy Power which seems Omnipotent.   (IV.570–72)

To forgive and to defy: the double imperative is clearly stated. Yet how is it possible to imagine a defiance winnowed and purified of any trace of personal animus? The distinction, so easy to make in the abstract, so difficult to realize in human experience, takes us once again to the knife-edge of the Promethean situation and to the extraordinarily difficult reconciliation of qualities Shelley was seeking.

In dramatizing his hero's apotheosis and transfiguration it was not Shelley's purpose to repudiate the past. The rational reformer, the advocate of justice and mercy, grows directly out of the Eton schoolboy who so violently cursed his father and thereafter suffered the blighting consequences of his own self-hatred. The first act of *Prometheus Unbound* explores the way in which the Promethean spark, the enduring flame of self-assertion and self-respect, can retain a vital power after the fires of hatred and resentment that kindled it have consumed themselves. Hence the hero's words on hearing the repetition of the curse, words that have been taken as the major *peripeteia*, have always seemed anticlimactic:

> It doth repent me: words are quick and vain;
> Grief for awhile is blind, and so was mine.
> I wish no living thing to suffer pain.   (I.303–5)

So often cited as the moral turning point of the drama, Prometheus's declaration has the force of a quiet afterthought, a recognition of a change already effected, rather than the power of a transforming insight. "It doth repent me" seems only the formal acknowledgment of blindness and grief that have now run their course. "Revenge, retaliation, atonement, are pernicious mistakes," Shelley declared in the "Preface" to *The Cenci*;[25] and to the list of proscriptions one might add repentance. Such a logical extension of Shelley's ethic is what Demogorgon means in his closing lines to the final act:

> Neither to change nor falter *nor repent:*
> This, like thy glory, Titan! is to be
> Good, great and joyous, beautiful and free;
> This is alone Life, Joy, Empire and Victory.
> (IV.575–78; my emphasis)

In the recalling of the curse it was not Shelley's purpose to represent his hero's instant self-transcendence through rejection of the past. The power of necessity that dominates the drama, the force that decrees that Prometheus must patiently await the coming of the promised hour, involves a profound element of historical and psychological fatalism. However different from its Aeschylean model, Shelley's *Prometheus* shares with it and with ancient drama generally certain fundamental premises. The play seems to insist that although tyranny and hatred must at length yield to freedom and enlightenment, it is only from suffering over time that the necessary wisdom springs.

A major irony of Shelley's drama is that Prometheus's recalling of his curse only sets the stage for the principal ordeal he must undergo. Mercury and the band of Furies who first taunt, then tempt the hero, and the chorus of "subtle and fair spirits" (I.658) who then console him, represent, like Blake's experience and innocence, the two contrary states of the human soul. The comparison is, however, misleading; for Blake's innocence, in its quality of naiveté, is unsatisfactory and continuously implies the evil it denies, while the two conditions point forward to a synthesis that draws upon the powers of each. By contrast, the visions of the Furies and the prophecies of the consoling spirits are irreconcilably opposed. Together they dramatize radically different possibilities for the development of the human mind and soul.

Shelley's adaptation of Mercury and the Furies from Aeschylus plays brilliantly upon the irony of their collaboration. The band of loathsome and rapacious harpies are conducted by the sublime figure Shelley knew from ancient statuary, descending

> With golden-sandalled feet, that glow
> Under plumes of purple dye
> Like rose-ensanguined ivory.   (I.319–21)

Blood and gold, the colors of tyranny, are harmonized within the divine beauty of the figure to suggest a grace and cultivation dependent on barbaric forces of oppression, powers that, as Mercury laments, he is loath to employ and by which he is in fact enslaved. Prolific and prodigious, the teeming Furies cut off the light with their wings. Representing the tide of human hatred and mistrust, they are a perfect metaphor for Shelley's conception of evil because, for all the horror they inspire, they take their reality from the fear and terror of their victims, being essentially parasitic, empty, and "hollow underneath, like death" (I.442). Mercury begins by protesting his reluctance to deliver Prometheus up to the more brutal torments of his servitors and attempts to win him over by means of the intellectual arguments he prefers to employ:

> O that we might be spared—I to inflict
> And thou to suffer! Once more answer me:
> Thou knowest not the period of Jove's power? (I.410–12)

To Prometheus's answer, "I know but this, that it must come," the god continues:

> Yet pause, and plunge
> Into Eternity, where recorded time,
> Even all that we imagine, age on age,
> Seems but a point, and the reluctant mind
> Flags wearily in its unending flight
> Till it sink, dizzy, blind, lost, shelterless;
> Perchance it has not numbered the slow years
> Which thou must spend in torture, unreprieved. (I.416–23)

Mercury's question pierces to the very heart of the Promethean dilemma. His argument adapts the design of the asymptote, or Zeno's paradox, in which time and eternity, though theoretically distinct, appear inseparable. Of what use to Prometheus is the promise of an end if he has not the means of anticipating it, of actually visualizing it? Lacking such he must, surely, fall into despair, into *dolor* and *amor mortis*. As Kerenyi has written in his classic study of the Prometheus legend, "The prophecies lose their value if [Prometheus] would rather die at once than await their fulfillment."[26] Mercury's speech distills the abiding doubt and terror of mankind's situation, a terror that accounts for the compulsion Shelley felt to envision an end to the ordeal with the composition of his drama.

The Titan's resolution to endure the passage of the years and hours—"Perchance no thought can count them—yet they pass" (I.424)—

leaves Mercury no choice. The impatience of his master, Jupiter, is mani-
fested in the bolt of lightning that cleaves a huge cedar. The beauty and
pathos of Mercury's departure as perceived through the eyes of the wistful
Panthea—"See where the child of Heaven, with winged feet, / Runs down
the slanted sunlight of the dawn" (I.437–38)—emphasizes by contrast the
terror of the execrable black shapes that now rise up, like a cloud of doubts
and misgivings, to besiege the hero in his isolation:

> We are the ministers of pain and fear
> And disappointment and mistrust and hate
> And clinging crime; and as lean dogs pursue
> Through wood and lake some struck and sobbing fawn,
> We track all things that weep and bleed and live
> When the great King betrays them to our will. (I.452–57)

The terrifying dialectic ingeniously readapts one of Shelley's favorite
myths, that of Actaeon. The love of merciless destruction, the Fury urges,
is just as ingrained in the human soul as the thirst inspired by beauty. The
two impulses are precisely reciprocal in strength. The Furies flaunt their
own deformity as if it were an attraction akin to beauty, exulting in their
powers of fascination with a psychological penetration that corroborates
their claims.

> The beauty of delight makes lovers glad,
> Gazing on one another—so are we.
> As from the rose which the pale priestess kneels
> To gather for her festal crown of flowers
> The aerial crimson falls, flushing her cheek—
> So from our victim's destined agony
> The shade which is our form invests us round,
> Else are we shapeless as our Mother Night. (I.465–72)

Perhaps no other passage of Romantic poetry expresses such a profound realization of the nature of sexual perversion. In his "Discourse on
the Manners of the Antient Greeks Relative to the Subject of Love,"
Shelley recognizes that the highest gratification of sexual intercourse arises
less from physical stimulation than from lovers' psychological involvement
in each other, in the mirroring and multiplication of each other's delight, a
pleasure that transcends the act of physical possession. Yet, as the Furies
proceed to argue, the same phenomena are at work—as Shelley was
shortly to explore in *The Cenci*—in the pleasure a tormentor finds in the
fear of his victim, in the loss of self-possession he induces with his threats

and intimidations. Though divided from each other as the natural and the diseased, the two kinds of pleasure arise from comparable effects and can, moreover, pass into each other with unnerving swiftness.

The perception that the Furies, like harpies, derive their real identity from the consternation of their victims might seem to deprive them of reality. The irony is that they possess such vitality and animation:

> we will be dread thought beneath thy brain
> And foul desire round thine astonished heart
> And blood within thy labyrinthine veins
> Crawling like agony.   (I.488–91)

The very susceptibility that accounts for man's ever-present responsiveness to good renders him equally open to evil impulses which, far from being simply external, enjoy a primordial latency, a kind of "animal life" within the constitution of his very being. Taunted by the Furies, Prometheus cannot deny this human vulnerability. He can only claim to rule the conflicting impulses within him, as the "king over myself" (I.492). His triumphant rejoinder is the closest Shelley comes within the play to an assertion of a personal doctrine of free will.

Having failed to overcome the Titan with the psychological evidence of their perpetual immanence, the Furies now seek to crush his spirit by moving from the individual to the social realm. Collecting themselves into a chorus, they present him with several historical tableaux, adding taunts that claim for the spirit of evil the same invincibility that Shelley was wont to claim for the good. Beneath the devastation of ruined cities

> Fire is left for future burning,—
> It will burst in bloodier flashes
> When ye stir it, soon returning.   (I.507–9)

The lines are an infernal parody of the Promethean spark of hope, the ashes of the "unextinguished hearth" of Shelley's great lyric of self-dedication, "Ode to the West Wind," published in the same volume as *Prometheus*. If the winds of spring are full of vernal promise, so the Furies claim the invincibility of their own prophecies—

> Hell's secrets half-unchanted
> To the maniac dreamer: cruel
> More than ye can be with hate,
>   Is he with fear.   (I.513–16)

Cruelty and fear, the two great principles of the Furies, multiply and augment each other as rapidly as love and beauty. Self-infatuated, the daemons revel in the power of their spells until restrained ("Speak not—whisper not!" [I.533]) lest they spoil by anticipation the full effect of the two spectacles they are about to unfold before the Titan.

The examples of Christ and the French Revolution that break upon Prometheus when the Furies tear the veil that separates the past from the present and future validate a dreadful lesson:

> Behold, an emblem—those who do endure
> Deep wrongs for man, and scorn and chains, but heap
> Thousand-fold torment on themselves and him.   (I.594–96)

Worse than merely useless, dedication to the cause of relieving the ignorance and suffering of humanity only exacerbates the evils it would remove. Reified in language and institutionalized as faith, Christ's message and intent have been converted to tyranny and superstition. The Savior's very name is now a curse. In the depiction of the Titan's fascinated gaze upon the agonized Christ one senses something of the Protestant's instinctive revulsion:

> Fix, fix those tortured orbs in peace and death
> So thy sick throes shake not that crucifix,
> So those pale fingers play not with thy gore.—
> O horrible!   (I.600–603)

As Shelley's pupil Swinburne was to dramatize, the gentle lesson of mercy and forbearance has been converted by orthodox Christianity to the morbid worship of the lurid horrors of suffering. In a similar way the enthusiasm and dedication of the French revolutionaries only ensure a more oppressive tyranny when the ensuing reaction sets in.

The two historical perspectives the Furies present make their mark upon Prometheus. Yet Ione observes his struggle for self-control:

> Hark, sister! what a low yet dreadful groan
> Quite unsuppressed is tearing up the heart
> Of the good Titan.   (I.578–80)

The contrast with the gory convulsions of Christ's throes suggests how much, despite Shelley's admiration for the biblical Jesus, in his eyes the true exemplary power of the Savior had been perverted by Christian ritual and the worship of sorrow.

Having reinforced their analysis of the human psyche with the examples of history, the Furies now sum up their lesson in terrible maxims, which took on for Yeats the power of a nightmare:[27]

> The good want power, but to weep barren tears.
> The powerful goodness want: worse need for them.
> The wise want love, and those who love want wisdom;
> And all best things are thus confused to ill.   (I.625–28)

The Furies need not deny the prevalence of wisdom and love; they deny only that they can ever free man for long from the fear and custom that oppress him. Nor does Prometheus in his final rejoinder deny their assertion: "Thy words are like a cloud of winged snakes / And yet, I pity those they torture not" (I.632–33). The words hardly constitute a triumphant rebuttal. Yet they surely mark a turning point within the play. The Fury's final line, "Thou pitiest them? I speak no more!" (I.634) together with the stage direction, "Vanishes," suggest that the voices of despair and darkness have attained the limits of their power. Deprived of all ground for confidence, Prometheus is reduced to compassion. It is just Shelley's point, however, that pity, the last residuum of desire and hope, affirmation in its most primitive form, is sufficient, like the Promethean spark, to rekindle the rehabilitating energies that now enter the drama.

The opening of Prometheus's first speech following the disappearance of the Furies, "Ah woe! / Ah woe! Alas! pain, pain ever, forever!" (I.634–35) echoes a portion of his first speech in the play (I.23) to suggest how little his actual condition has changed. In forcing the hero to recognize the grim truths of historical awareness, Jupiter has taken a "dread revenge" (I.641). Nevertheless the words Prometheus addresses to his tormentor testify that the effect of the ordeal on him is different from what one might suppose:

> This is defeat, fierce King, not victory.
> The sights with which thou torturest gird my soul
> With new endurance, till the hour arrives
> When they shall be no types of things which are.   (I.642–45)

Again we are reminded, now in an affirmative way, of the extraordinary ambivalence of the Promethean situation. If the hero's premonition of the torments he must endure before the destined hour arrives threatens to crush his spirit, the knowledge can also, paradoxically, fortify his resolve to hold out to the end of his ordeal. Prometheus's willingness to summarize for Panthea the essence of the deadly truths of the Furies by itself suggests a kind of mastery:

> Names are there, Nature's sacred watchwords—they
> Were borne aloft in bright emblazonry.
> The nations thronged around, and cried aloud
> As with one voice, "Truth, liberty and love!"
> Suddenly fierce confusion fell from Heaven
> Among them—there was strife, deceit and fear;
> Tyrants rushed in, and did divide the spoil.
> This was the shadow of the truth I saw.   (I.648–55)

The sad perversion to which the good is so habitually susceptible is figured as a travesty of Pentecost. The bright ideals the nations hail "As with one voice" are suddenly obliterated in the confusion that falls from heaven. The appropriation of the sacred watchwords into various tongues and modes of understanding is the first step in the process by which their meaning is wrenched and misapplied by self-serving tyrants, a process the Furies have depicted as the endlessly recurring pattern of history.

To console the hero in the face of this stark fatalism, the Earth summons up "those subtle and fair spirits / Whose homes are the dim caves of human thought" (I.658–59). Closely associated with the spring, these spirits are the antithesis of the Furies, for "As the birds within the wind, / As the fish within the wave" (I.683–84), they represent the virtuous instincts that exist spontaneously and seemingly indestructibly in human consciousness. Following the opening chorus, individual spirits console Prometheus with a more constructive view of human destiny, drawing evidence from an instinctive sense of the enduring strengths of man's nature rather than the dogmas of Christian eschatology. The First Spirit recounts those scenes of war and devastation the first chorus of Furies had gleefully rehearsed, in the same pulsing, frenetic rhythms: "On a battle-trumpet's blast / I fled hither, fast, fast, fast" (I.694–95). Now, however, is the time not for the destruction of free nations but for the overthrowing of tyrannical "creeds outworn" (I.697). Revolution can work for good as well as evil. And now the various ascending outcries—"Freedom! Hope! Death! Victory!"—do not break out into confusion but are reconciled with a single ground bass:

And one sound, above, around,
One sound beneath, around, above,
Was moving; 'twas the soul of love.   (I.703-5)

The strophe dramatizes love not only as the necessary culmination of successful revolution but also as the primary impulse of the human soul.

The spirits' examples of the endurance of the good proceed from the most humble toward the esoteric and refined. The Second Spirit cites the instance of a common seaman cast adrift amid the tumult of a naval battle who abandons his plank to an enemy, then plunges to die. The Third Spirit sings of the dreaming sage, like a figure out of Blake or Samuel Palmer, nodding over the book that has inspired his dream of "Pity, eloquence and woe" (I.730). Next the Fourth Spirit sings of the poet in the act of creation and how he takes his inspiration from "shapes that haunt thought's wildernesses":

He will watch from dawn to gloom
The lake-reflected sun illume
The yellow bees i' the ivy-bloom.   (I.742,743-45)

The poet minutely studies each event in nature only to ascend above a consciousness of all natural observation:

Nor heed nor see, what things they be;
But from these create he can
Forms more real than living man,
Nurslings of immortality!   (I.746-49)

The poet necessarily depends on nature and its images for the materials of his analogies. Yet the lines also proclaim the poet's complete independence of the natural world, for he draws his inspiration not from nature but from thought. The passage, so often quoted in isolation, is central to the larger visionary context of the drama. For the play itself springs at its inception from commitment to the imagination as a moral agent and from the conviction that whatever man can desire or imagine must possess, for good or evil, potential reality. Keats was never closer to his brother-poet than when, early in his career, he wrote: "I am certain of nothing but of the holiness of the Heart's affections and the truth of Imagination—What the imagination seizes as Beauty must be truth—*whether it existed before or not*" (my emphasis).[28]

Ione announces the appearance of the last spirits, the fifth and sixth, who arrive "from the East and West" (I.752). Descending together like "two doves to one beloved nest" (I.753), they symbolize the unification and synthesis of the prophecies of the Occident and Orient and hence anticipate the marriage of Prometheus and Asia. The description reminds one of the culmination of the first canto of *The Revolt of Islam* when "two mighty Spirits now return, / Like birds of calm, from the world's raging sea" (645–46) and Laon and Cythna emerge for the first time to assume their places before the androgynous figure enthroned above them. Both scenes dramatize the eternal return and rebirth of the spirit of good under the aegis of love. Hence the logic of the question the chorus of spirits addresses to the recent arrivals: "Hast thou beheld the form of Love?" (I.763).

The songs of the fifth and sixth spirits are closely juxtaposed. In answer to the question of the chorus, the Fifth Spirit recounts her vision of a "planet-crested Shape" whose footsteps leave the world "paved . . . with light" (I.765,767). Yet the traces soon fade, exposing beneath them emptiness and ruin and "Great Sages bound in madness / And headless patriots and pale youths who perished unupbraiding" (I.768–69). The half-sketched figures, Tiepolo-like in their exaggerated attitudes, create a sense of epic monotony and repetition. Time and again throughout history love and hope raise expectations that leave emptiness and despondency behind them when they fade. The moral is driven home by the Sixth Spirit in her answering verses, "Ah, sister! Desolation is a delicate thing" (I.772). True despair, she asserts, is known only by the "best and gentlest" who, indulging "tender hopes," dream visions of ideal bliss only to wake to the reality of love's dark underlying shadow, pain (I.775–79). It is remarkable that the message of the spirits who console our hero and prophesy his coming triumph also stress the extraordinary dangers of the hope that makes that victory possible. If man's fate is so delicately balanced between such radically different possibilities, what can he rely on for positive assurance? It is hardly any wonder that Prometheus's final words to the spirits in the face of their affirmative predictions take the form of an overwhelming question: "Spirits! how know ye this shall be?" (I.789).

In their departing chorus the spirits point to the signs "the wandering herdsmen know" (I.794) of coming spring; their voices fade away as Prometheus, Panthea, and Ione strain to retain them. We are left to intuit the importance of the first act above all from the mood in which it leaves the hero:

> How fair these air-born shapes! and yet I feel
> Most vain all hope but love . . .
>   alas! how heavily

This quiet morning weighs upon my heart;
Though I should dream, I could even sleep with grief
If slumber were denied not . . . I would fain
Be what it is my destiny to be,
The saviour and the strength of suffering man,
Or sink into the original gulph of things . . .
There is no agony and no solace left;
Earth can console, Heaven can torment no more.

(I.807–8,812–20)

Prometheus's mood is one of complete submission, growing out of emotional exhaustion. His words leave us with a sense that, with all the evidence for both sides fully offered, there is nothing more that we or the hero can learn of the potential for either human good or human evil in the world. The conflicting claims have been made and the rival positions argued, and there is in the end no clearly rational basis for choosing between the two opposite visions of human destiny. Faced with this ultimate indeterminacy, Prometheus falls back on his resolution to remain faithful to his hopes for suffering man, to "Be what it is my destiny to be." There is an intermarriage here between the willing intelligence and an unknown, predestined, but potentially benign order of things in which the one can fulfill itself only with the help of the other. Given the violently conflicting evidence for either hope or skepticism, given the radically different prospects for the future of mankind, the only course Prometheus can accept is to hold out in expectation of the best, in the conviction that it would be better, like Jupiter later in the drama, to "sink into the original gulph of things" than to abandon the potential victory of the good. Such determination springs from resignation. It is a quality best conveyed by Ione in her characterization of the blending voices of the two last returning spirits: " 'tis despair / Mingled with love, and then dissolved in sound" (I.756–57).

The first act of *Prometheus Unbound* serves as prelude to the unbinding of the hero and his reunion with Asia in the acts that follow, but it also serves as self-justification, even apology. The act prepares the way for nothing so simple as the inevitable triumph of human wisdom and virtue over negation and despair, but rather for a vision of a possible perfection so tenuous and insecure that it must be fostered and promoted in every way conceivable. The first act of *Prometheus Unbound* is Shelley's justification for writing a drama that he knew might prove worse than futile, even dangerous, but that nevertheless embodied, as he saw it and in spite of the views of his leading contemporaries, the only practical hope for mankind.

five

HOPE AND NECESSITY

Prometheus Unbound, Act II

The conclusion of the first act of *Prometheus* leaves us carefully balanced between the competing claims of good and evil, optimism and despair. The mood of the hero as we leave him, far from anticipatory exhilaration, is quiet resignation, a state that at best looks forward to the mood heralded by his lover, Asia, who at the beginning of the second act hails those "beatings [that] haunt the desolated heart / Which should have learnt repose" (II.i.4–5). It was Shelley's determination from the first to write a millennial drama representing the reunion of Prometheus, the unsubdued champion of human freedom, and Asia, his bride, the enduring spirit of love. But how was he to represent their all-important transformation and reunion, which the first act had introduced by way of uncertainty and warning?

Shelley's response to this need for a quantum leap forward in the visionary dimensions of his drama is simply to make it. In the last speech in Act I Panthea had clairvoyantly discerned that Asia's vale, once frozen and desolate, was already "haunted by sweet airs and sounds" (I.830). At the opening of the second act, the spring, the acknowledged "inspiration" of Shelley's drama, has arrived. Asia greets it:

> thou hast descended
> Cradled in tempests; thou dost wake, O Spring!
> O child of many winds! As suddenly
> Thou comest as the memory of a dream
> Which now is sad because it hath been sweet;
> Like genius, or like joy . . .   (II.i.5–10)

The resurgence of the spring seems like "the memory of a dream," a dream that is momentarily sad because the sweetness it recalls had seemed so distant, lost, and irretrievable. There is no explanation for the sudden alteration for the better other than the renewal of the year, an event thoroughly rooted in our experience of the natural order of things that yet never ceases to strike us with wonder and surprise. Shelley's analogies convey a sense of the miraculous in the most common elements of our experience.

Asia greets the returning spring with words full of portent: "This is the season, this the day, the hour" (II.i.13). The full meaning of her exclamation is apparent: this is the day, the very hour of Prometheus's deliverance. She goes on to exclaim, "How like death-worms the wingless moments crawl!" (II.i.16), as if she were watching the last minutes of the term of his endurance expire. Her depiction of the beautiful prospect unfolding before her deepens in significance like the colors of the dawning. In the closing speech in Act I, Panthea had observed that "the Eastern star looks white" (I.825). Now Asia, as she traces the gradual expansion of the sunrise, notes its effect on the fading planet:

> The point of one white star is quivering still
> Deep in the orange light of widening morn
> Beyond the purple mountains; through a chasm
> Of wind-divided mist the darker lake
> Reflects it—now it wanes—it gleams again
> As the waves fade, and as the burning threads
> Of woven cloud unravel in pale air . . .
> 'Tis lost! and through yon peaks of cloudlike snow
> The roseate sunlight quivers.   (II.i.17–25)

Employing a device we have seen him use before, Shelley marks a spiritual or psychological transformation by analogy with a familiar diurnal occurrence. The development of the description and the logic of its placement suggest that Prometheus's term expires just at the moment the morning star is lost to Asia's view, or as it is subsumed by the greater radiance of the sunrise that gradually envelops it. Prometheus's release takes place with the exactness of an astronomical conjunction.

Does Asia from her prospect of the vernal sunrise intuit the long-preordained moment of her lover's release? Or does Prometheus, through his courage and long suffering, permit the destined moment to fulfill itself? As before, the logic of Shelley's poem seems to favor both implications. The promised hour arrives with the precision of an astronomical event determined by the succession of the seasons. Yet emotionally the scene does not impress us as the result of the operation of the laws of an unqualified necessity. For one thing, we observe the spring dawn and achieve a sense of its significance only through Asia's eyes, as if her sympathy and understanding were a necessary "greeting of the Spirit" (in Keats's phrase),[1] a condition essential for its full realization.[2] For another, there is the emotional suggestiveness of the increasing pallor of the morning star as if, "pale for weariness"[3] from the long night through which it has kept watch, it had held out long enough to herald the sunrise into which it blends. Shelley seems to defeat, or to evade, the old philosophical conundrum by suggesting a universal necessity that can fulfill itself only with the cooperation of the human will and spirit.

The division between Prometheus and Asia, dramatized by their physical isolation from each other at the outset of the second act, represents Shelley's view of the fallen state of humankind. The division can be analyzed in many ways. Stuart Curran, for example, has emphasized the contrast between the intellectual propensities of the hero and Asia's more emotional, intuitive way of understanding.[4] In articulating such distinctions to anticipate the perfect union of the sexes in the marriage of Prometheus and Asia, Shelley was not simply falling back on easy sexual stereotypes. Yet Prometheus's heroic endurance and his defiance of the father figure Jupiter suggest a role Asia is not qualified to play. Prometheus alone undergoes the strains of the Oedipal compulsion. Indeed it is only by transcending those strains that Prometheus can free himself for the mature love Asia represents. In working out his allegory of the salvation of the human soul, Shelley was respecting what he saw as certain fundamental and inalienable differences between the sexes, differences writ large in his own experience.

The transformation of Prometheus and his reunion with Asia are hardly simple or direct but depend on a complex intermediation involving Asia's younger sisters, Panthea and Ione. Both of them have remained with Prometheus during his ordeal. Shortly after the commencement of the second act, Panthea journeys to Asia to relate, as a portent of the change, her experience of two dreams. Panthea describes to Asia the one dream she can recall, her vision of the transformed Titan. She was sleeping at the feet of the bound Titan, embracing her younger sister, with

> Our young Ione's soft and milky arms
> Locked . . . behind my dark moist hair
> While my shut eyes and cheek were pressed within
> The folded depth of her life-breathing bosom.   (II.i.46–49)

Like much Pre-Raphaelite art, the description combines the richly sensuous and the innocent. In its interlocking self-containment, the embrace of the two sisters has almost incestuous overtones. Panthea goes on to relate the troubled feelings Ione describes on awakening from her sleep in the arms of her sister:

> Ione wakened then, and said to me:
> "Canst thou divine what troubles me tonight?
> I always knew what I desired before
> Nor ever found delight to wish in vain.
> But now I cannot tell thee what I seek;
> I know not—something sweet since it is sweet
> Even to desire—it is thy sport, false sister!
> Thou has discovered some inchantment old
> Whose spells have stolen my spirit as I slept
> And mingled it with thine . . ."   (II.i.93–102)

The scene is illuminated by Coleridge's *Christabel*; however different Christabel's traumatic slumber in the arms of Geraldine, the two scenes are linked by a common interest in the awakening of latent sexual desire. Ione's words convey the surfacing of longings that can no longer find contentment in sisterly warmth and companionship.

The cause of this change in Ione is clearly attributable to the dream Panthea experiences while the two are slumbering together, the dream she remembers and describes to Asia. In her dream of the transformed Titan

>   his pale, wound-worn limbs
> Fell from Prometheus, and the azure night
> Grew radiant with the glory of that form
> Which lives unchanged within, and his voice fell
> Like music which makes giddy the dim brain
> Faint with intoxication of keen joy.   (II.i.62–67)

The pale, suffering Christ of the crucifixion is here subsumed by the triumphant figure of the risen Savior. Or, more exactly perhaps, the worn and agonized features of the Christian martyr fall away to reveal the figure they have long concealed—the joyous pagan god fit to take his place beside Asia, whose chief archetype is Aphrodite, the goddess borne in from the sea on her shell at the birth of spring and love.[5]

Critics such as Curran who emphasize Shelley's fusion of classical and Christian imagery and themes may favor the doctrinal reading. Shelley's vision of renewal, however, also links him with Swinburne, D. H. Lawrence, and the Richard Strauss of *Ariadne auf Naxos*. Certainly Panthea's subsequent description of being alternately absorbed and condensed by Prometheus, the risen sun, a passage Tennyson drew upon in his "Tithonus," is overtly sexual in its rapture:

> I saw not—heard not—moved not—only felt
> His presence flow and mingle through my blood
> Till it became his life and his grew mine
> And I was thus absorbed—until it past
> And like the vapours when the sun sinks down,
> . . . . .
> My being was condensed.   (II.i.79–83,86)

As Desmond King-Hele has pointed out, the passage makes remarkable use of the chemical imagery of evaporation and condensation to convey the intensity of sexual congress, "the first of many sublimations of sexual feeling into scientific form" within the poem.[6]

It was only natural that Shelley should portray the effects of Prometheus's transformation through the renewal and expansion of physical desire. Like Lawrence, he believed, as the first act of his play demonstrates, that the repression or perversion of the sexual drives is one of the surest indications of social evil. He also saw that these same drives are paradoxically the most ingrained and tenacious. Like the unextinguished spark of hope, they preserve the flame of higher human renewal. Panthea's journey to Asia dramatizes love as a rejuvenating impulse, growing from its roots in sisterly affection to the mature sexual responsiveness that Asia embodies.[7]

At the same time aspects of the episode, among the most peculiarly Shelleyan in the drama, remain mysterious. Asia does not merely receive from Panthea an account of the Titan's change. She actually reads in her sister's eyes an image of the transformed god. The vision appears to originate with Panthea's own first glimpse from the feet of the glorified Prometheus, when he commands her, "Sister . . . lift thine eyes on me!" (II.i.68,70). It is this image that Panthea transmits to her sister. Yet as Asia stares into Panthea's eyes, "dark, far, measureless,— / Orb within orb, and line through line inwoven" (II.i.116–17), she seems not so much to read the vision as actually to bring it into focus with the power of her gaze: "There is a change . . . / I see a shade—a shape—'tis He, arrayed / In the soft light of his own smiles" (II.i.119–21). This mirroring effect, in conjunction with the agency of smiles, occurs as early as *Queen Mab*, and its recurrence at this moment in the drama of *Prometheus* seems to point to some more deeply seated traits of Shelley's character. One cannot help being reminded of Jacques Lacan's well-known postulation of the "mirror phase," in which the helpless and uncoordinated infant exultantly acquires a sense of his own coming bodily mastery by identifying with his own reflection.[8] Asia's eyes seem to provide the necessary medium to reflect the image of the renovated god. One senses that Shelley was drawing on deeply buried memories of the helplessness and fragmentation of his own infancy and of the reassuring power of his mother's smile.

As Asia discovers in Panthea's eyes the shape of her lover and the change that has overcome him, she sees another shape, rude and quick, whom Panthea immediately recognizes as the dream she has been unable to remember. It is, in fact, the shape of the hour that is shortly to bring about the fall of Jupiter. As they exchange impressions, the two sisters seem to piece out each other's fragmentary recollections, like traces of a common dream of lost experience. With its refrain of "Follow, follow!" the chorus of echoes awakened by their talk leads them downward to their ultimate destination, the throne of Demogorgon. They are impelled as if by a "wind / Which drives them on their path" (II.ii.53–54). Yet "they / Believe their own swift wings and feet / The sweet desires within obey" (II.ii.54–56). The distinction between free will and necessity has become all but imperceptible. They pass through thickets of cedar, pine, and yew so dense as to seem impenetrable, never illuminated save

> when some star of many a one
> That climbs and wanders through steep night,
> Has found the cleft through which alone
> Beams fall from high those depths upon,
> Ere it is borne away, away,
> By the swift Heavens that cannot stay—
> It scatters drops of golden light
> Like lines of rain that ne'er unite.   (II.ii.14–21)

The passage sheds special light on Shelley's sense of the operation of necessity by adumbrating the all but endless years that must elapse for a given star to achieve the precise position in the heavens from which it can illuminate the pathway of Asia and Panthea through the forest. Given the infinitely complex design and movements of the heavens, how infrequent the enabling conditions! Yet in view of the endless course of time, the passage also suggests the inevitability of their ultimate recurrence. Curiously anticipating the thinking of certain contemporary physicists and philosophers of science, he proposes a case of low probabilities that become high through the immensity of available time.[9] The same principle of necessity that governs the release of Prometheus also conditions the movements of Asia and Panthea at this point in the drama.

The opening of Scene iii finds Asia and Panthea where the chorus of echoes has led them, at the rocky portal leading down to Demogorgon's cave. The most difficult and obscure figure in Shelley's allegory, Demogorgon has often been identified with the principle of necessity. He is, however, more properly Shelley's image of infinite potentiality, a power limited only by the laws of nature, beginning with those of physical existence, and by the force of love.[10] He is the final repository of the forces and events that have shaped the universe, and contains the potential for all that may occur in future. When she first perceives him, Panthea describes him as hidden in darkness, "Ungazed upon and shapeless" (II.iv.5); and it is appropriate that before the entrance to his cave there streams up "the oracular vapour" (II.iii.4) that is the source of all the dreams and prophecies, and with them all the hopes, ambitions, and designs that have ever inspired and driven mankind. Such vapor is of course the source of poetry, and of Shelley's own *Prometheus Unbound* in particular. Indeed it is the transporting, inspiring ether that "lonely men," above all poets,

> drink wandering in their youth
> And call truth, virtue, love, genius or joy—
> That maddening wine of life, whose dregs they drain
> To deep intoxication, and uplift
> Like Mænads who cry loud, Evoe! Evoe!
> The voice which is contagion to the world.   (II.iii.5–10)

One critic has likened the vapor to the enthusiasm that misleads "men, like the misguided young idealist in *Alastor,* [to] dissipate their energies in a vain frenzy that can be as dangerous to true inspiration as was the Maenads' madness to Orpheus."[11] However, the power Shelley is describing is amoral, a force without which no significant change can come about. The vapor can prove a force for good or evil, the inspiration of millennial change or a desolating pestilence depending on its use and application.[12] It is no wonder that, as an image of "a mighty Darkness" (II.iv.2), Demogorgon is so intimidating and inscrutable. As a power he is akin to a principle of conservation by which the energies of the universe are withdrawn and held under restraint but ever ready to burst out into new eruptions.

Moved to admiration by the magnificence of the scene before her and the rude but mighty power it reflects, Asia is momentarily impelled to "fall down and worship that and thee" (II.iii.16), but is restrained by recognition of the manifest signs of imperfection. Shelley was always aware of the human tendency to anthropomorphize and worship the power behind the natural universe and its eternal process of creation and destroying. Like Manfred before the Witch of the Alps or the throne of Arimanes, Asia refuses to bow down and adore a might that, for all its sublimity, she recognizes as inhuman and amoral. Yet the oracular vapor proceeds to accomplish its effects. As Asia and Panthea talk, a tide of mist rises about and "islands" them (II.iii.23) and the peak where they stand, breaking like a sea at their feet. They hear the distant crash of the avalanche, Shelley's image of revolutionary change, and the mist of vapor envelops them. Asia's hair is disentwined like a maenad's by the wind, and, as her brain grows dizzy, she sees shapes in the mist. Enveloped by the cloud of pure potentiality, she is disoriented and inspired with a sense of new expectations.

The song of the spirits which guides Asia through her initiation and reorientation, "To the Deep, to the Deep, / Down, down!" (II.iii.54–55), is both incantatory and seductive. The direction is down because Demogorgon's cave is situated at the *omphalos* or navel of the world, the source of all experience. The effect is dizzying, like being drawn steadily deeper into a vortex:

> While the sound, whirls around,
>   Down, down!
> As the fawn draws the hound,
> As the lightning the vapour,
> As a weak moth the taper;
> Death, Despair; Love, Sorrow;
> Time both; to-day, to-morrow;
> As steel obeys the Spirit of the stone,
>   Down, down!   (II.iii.63–71)

The lines accelerate the sense of dislocation. Yet it is worth pausing for a moment to examine some of their subtler effects. Ellsworth Barnard, among other editors, may be right that the fourth and fifth lines invert the normal grammatical order.[13] The fact remains, however, that it is impossible to read them initially except in the order that the preceding syntax has established: As the lightning [draws] the vapour, / As a weak moth [draws] the taper. Shelley was fond of inverting our customary sense of cause and effect; but the confusion here is relevant to the disorienting effect of the passage as a whole. Was it not, after all, possible for Shelley to intuit that within the rational mechanics of Newton's universe such processes as time and motion are not unidirectional but reversible? The idea of a unidirectional causality, like the idea of a time that can move in one direction only, derives from our ingrained habits of consciousness and memory. Yet within the realm of pure physics, the laws that govern time and motion are not irreversible but symmetrical. To take only one example, it can be argued that "the laws of optics are entirely symmetrical with respect to the emission and absorption of light. If time is imagined as reversed, emitting and absorbing objects exchange roles but the optical laws are unchanged."[14] It may be difficult to accept the notion that Shelley anticipated the attack of modern physics upon the conception of "time's arrow."[15] Yet the inversion of our commonly accepted notion of causality, and with it the reversibility of time, seem to be exactly what Shelley is suggesting through the logic (or illogic) of his poetic figures.

Within the larger context of his play, Shelley saw that the conviction of a unidirectional time brought with it a commitment to irreversible process, the idea, as in *Paradise Lost,* of some original sin setting in motion a process of degeneration that could be redeemed only by suffering and expiation or by the intervention of a God and his providence or both. This general notion to some degree pervades the first act of his play. Yet it was Shelley's purpose in the more visionary acts that follow to adumbrate the possibility of a totally different human alteration. The dizzying disorientation that Asia, and with her the reader, undergoes represents Shelley's attempt to loosen the grasp of some of our most commonly held assumptions concerning the nature of life and human development, as the necessary initiation into a new awareness of human potential. Indeed, what we discover at the climax of the act is Asia's journey back through time toward the source of potentiality. The symbolism of Asia's journey conveys the most startling and original aspects of Shelley's vision.

With the arrival of the two sisters before Demogorgon's throne in Scene iv, the stage is set for Asia's celebrated confrontation of the awesome power. Her tide of passionate and impatient questions, demanding some explanation for the existence of evil in the world, is of course futile. Indeed its pointlessness is Shelley's point. There is no use in seeking ontological explanations from a universe of physical energies. The processes of nature can neither justify themselves nor testify to any creator or first cause. With her questions Asia seeks to invade a realm impervious to interrogation, a conclusion driven home by Demogorgon's declaration that "the deep truth is imageless" (II.iv.116). Asia acknowledges this by the quiet resignation of her reply, as if she had already intuited for herself the truth of Demogorgon's answer: "So much I asked before, and my heart gave / The response thou hast given" (II.iv.121–22). Asia's confrontation with Demogorgon dramatizes Shelley's atheistical conception of a universe of physical energies blindly indifferent to man, a universe in which, nevertheless, he was intent to disclose the possibilities for human regeneration.

Even as Demogorgon's words drive home the futility of seeking any divine purpose or justification for the dread forces he controls and symbolizes, he holds out at last the kind of promise Asia seeks:

> what would it avail to bid thee gaze
> On the revolving world? what to bid speak
> Fate, Time, Occasion, Chance and Change? To these
> All things are subject but eternal Love. (II.iv.117–20)

Two elements, distinct but potentially cooperating, give force to Demogorgon's affirmation. The first is the idea of necessity implicit in "Fate, Time, Occasion, Chance and Change." The phrase suggests a principle substantially different from that Shelley had so confidently proclaimed in *Queen Mab*. The necessity Demogorgon's words imply is nothing akin to an immanent will working itself out in the creation or even to an inherent general propensity toward progress and the good. The idea of necessity his words suggest is starker, an idea, close to certain modern studies of the laws of probability, that given the infinity of change within the physical universe together with the endlessness of time, the conditions favoring human renewal and fulfillment are bound ultimately to come about and, if wasted, to recur. The other element, the one constant in Demogorgon's pronouncement, is the eternity of love, which, as Donald Reiman and Sharon Powers have asserted, must here be understood as eros or desire.[16] The possibilities for human change that time and chance occasion can fulfill themselves only through the endurance of hope, through the fortitude of Prometheus and the longing and responsiveness of Asia. Demogorgon's words ring forth like an eternal pledge. But Asia's impatience will brook no delay, and the all-important question rises to her lips: "When shall the destined hour arrive?" He replies only "Behold!" (II.iv.128). It is almost as if she had precipitated the emergence of the promised hour through the force of her desire.

The multitude of cars she now beholds through the cleft in the rocks before her, each driven by a wild-eyed charioteer urging his flight with impetuous speed, is, as Demogorgon explains, the host of the immortal hours. They represent Shelley's attempt to reconcile necessity with a universe of infinite potentiality. Each hour impatiently seeks to realize the destiny it contains. Yet each can achieve its desire only in turn and by an order that remains inscrutable. Within the infinitude of possibilities they collectively represent, who could assume, in response to Asia's question, that the dark hour of destruction and the bright hour of love are just now ready to emerge, in proper conjunction? Yet, as Demogorgon has indicated, the miracle is at hand. He rises from his throne, a "terrible shadow," to mount a dark car of terrifying power, the power necessary to dethrone Jupiter. At the same time Panthea observes the appearance of an altogether different chariot:

> See, near the verge another chariot stays;
> An ivory shell inlaid with crimson fire
> Which comes and goes within its sculptured rim
> Of delicate strange tracery—the young Spirit
> That guides it, has the dovelike eyes of hope.   (II.iv.156–60)

The conveyance that bears Asia upward to reunion with Prometheus is the shell traditionally associated with the sea-born Venus, the goddess of love. Yet it also calls to mind the little nautilus, Shelley's favorite image for the persistence of human hope. It is necessary for Asia to follow rapidly in Demogorgon's path, for, as Kenneth Cameron has written in a discussion of the political dimensions of Shelley's allegory, "unless love arrives quickly, the revolution may degenerate into violence and anarchy."[17] Within the design of Shelley's allegory, the precise concurrence of the two hours, the dark and the bright, must strike us as an extraordinary combination of the miraculous and the inevitable.

Having ascended the second car with her sister, Asia tells the Spirit of the Hour who guides its steeds: "Thou breathest on their nostrils—but my breath / Would give them swifter speed" (II.v.6–7). Asia's mild reproach is that her desire, being greater than his, would bear the car forward more swiftly. The simplicity of his reply, "Alas, it could not" (II.v.7), has often been interpreted to mean "your desire could not exceed mine." However, Shelley's meaning lies deeper: Asia's desire, however great, cannot by itself hasten her reunion with Prometheus.[18] She must await the arrival of the destined hours. In distinguishing between the two cars, Shelley was seeking to distinguish between different powers and roles, symbolizing different hours or revolutionary phases. Yet his treatment of the myth up to now has encouraged us to think of the climax of his drama as arriving with a single promised hour, a single instant of time. Panthea observes that "the sun is yet unrisen" and the Spirit who conducts them reports that "The sun will rise not until noon" (II.v.9–10), as if, from the moment of Asia's observation of the morning star just fading into the light of dawn in her speech at the opening of the act, time had been suspended and the events that follow take place in a temporal vacuum.

The act comes to its termination with two songs that describe Asia's transfiguration. "Life of Life!" is sung by a spirit in the air who observes her; the second, "My soul is an enchanted Boat," is sung by Asia herself. The two lyrics have been acclaimed by Shelley's admirers as the summit of his achievement as a lyric poet, lyrics that dramatize the major turning point in his drama of regeneration. For other, less sympathetic readers, like the New Critics in Britain and America, the lyrics illustrate the characteristic weaknesses of Shelley's verse. Thus the dazzling contrasts of light and shade, the failure to realize forms concretely, testify for F. R. Leavis, the most formidable of Shelley's detractors, to the poet's "weak grasp upon the actual." There is no attempt made, Leavis complains, to create feelings in ways that sharpen our apprehension of the external world and its familiar objects. Instead the verse exhibits Shelley's habit of "surrendering to a kind of hypnotic rote of favourite images, associations and words." What the verse represents is a poetry of incantation or intoxication, a poetry that "offers the emotion in itself, unattached, in the void."[19]

To account for such differing assessments one must turn to the lyrics themselves. The first celebrates Asia's new and all but intolerable radiance as the source of a power that has just achieved release. She is the "Life of Life," a universal energy; the "Child of Light," the Platonic soul behind the form; the sun newly risen in heaven. She both attracts and repels because of her eclipsing luminosity. She both exhilarates and awes. She is a universal presence but invisible to sight. She both illuminates and blinds with her dazzling, unaccustomed radiance so that the new shapes she brings to view are only dimly outlined. She both sharpens the senses and overwhelms them.

> Lamp of Earth! where'er thou movest
>   Its dim shapes are clad with brightness
> And the souls of whom thou lovest
>   Walk upon the winds with lightness
> Till they fail, as I am failing,
> Dizzy, lost . . . yet unbewailing!   (II.v.66–71)

It is hardly surprising that the verse is lacking in concreteness, because its purpose is to epitomize that sense of dislocation from everyday perception that has characterized the development of the act as a whole.

The first song conducts us away from all sense of present reality to a source of abstract potentiality, newly released and bringing into experience a universe of new and unrealized possibilities; Asia's song, which ends the act, draws us backward in time from age, through manhood and youth, to infancy and birth and what lies beyond:

> We have past Age's icy caves,
> And Manhood's dark and tossing waves
> And Youth's smooth ocean, smiling to betray;
>   Beyond the glassy gulphs we flee
>   Of shadow-peopled Infancy,
> Through Death and Birth to a diviner day,
>   A Paradise of vaulted bowers
>   Lit by downward-gazing flowers
>   And watery paths that wind between
>   Wildernesses calm and green,
> Peopled by shapes too bright to see,
> And rest, having beheld—somewhat like thee,
> Which walk upon the sea, and chaunt melodiously!
>   (II.v.98–110)

For Shelley nothing less could be satisfactory than a total reversal of time, an unraveling of history back to the pure potential of the unborn child. The two songs, then, are correlative. The first seeks to withdraw us from all sense of present objects to an awareness of a potential that is primary to experience. The second seeks to draw us backward out of time and history to the innocence of our origins.[20] It seems odd to attack Shelley for being "peculiarly weak in his hold on objects—peculiarly unable to realize them as existing in their own natures and their own right"[21] when it is exactly our common grasp of the world of familiar forms and appearances he is seeking to dissolve and dissipate. We appear to be examining a failure of critical appreciation founded in part upon a misunderstanding of means and ends.

A comparison between Shelley and Wordsworth may prove useful. As certain critics have observed, the germ of inspiration for Shelley's two songs, as indeed for much of his verse, lies in Wordsworth's greatest lyric, the "Intimations Ode." Shelley looks back, however, not so much to the ode as a whole as to its first four strophes and the crisis they precipitated. It was there that the older poet so feelingly developed his extraordinary sense of loss of those "intimations" that once surrounded his childhood, vestiges of a glory and a power buried in his earliest reminiscences of life. Wordsworth tells us that at least two years passed between his writing of those four strophes with the troubling questions they pose and his continuation, an interval that seems to mark an intellectual and emotional breakdown rather than a simple suspension of composition.[22] He resumed work on the poem only with the help of a Platonic theory of prenatal experience that celebrated the infant child, in what for some of his admirers are among the most questionable lines he ever penned, as "best

Philosopher," "Eye among the blind," "Mighty Prophet! Seer blest!" (111–12,115), verses that Coleridge cited as instances of "mental bombast."[23]

Wordsworth later felt it necessary to apologize for adapting the Platonic idea of pre-existence in a poem he intended as Christian orthodoxy.[24] In fact the closing stanzas of the ode, with their emphasis on the reconciling power of time and human suffering, on the value of aging and maturity, contradict the impulses from which the poem springs in a way that adumbrates Wordsworth's later career. For Shelley all that was valuable in the ode lay in its earlier sections, in its depiction of the luminous cloud of glory surrounding the infant child and its recollections of primal splendor. During its composition, the visionary focus of the poem had become reversed; Wordsworth concluded by looking to the end of life when he should have remained looking toward its beginning. Indeed, the construction of the poem revealed, more clearly than any other work of Wordsworth, how the inspired insights of genius could, through the pressure of conformity and custom, betray themselves and testify to the very opposite of what they affirmed. The apostasy was of a kind Shelley had clearly exposed in the first act of his drama. Like *The Revolt of Islam* before it, *Prometheus Unbound* finds its origin in Shelley's desire to remain faithful to Wordsworth's vital impression of "the fountain light of all our day" and "that imperial palace whence [we] came" (152,85) even if the older poet could not.

Most modern criticism is dedicated to an ideal of a literary tradition progressively built up by writers struggling to articulate ever more complex states of feeling in the effort to render accurately a sense of their own time and culture. Yet the major thrust of Shelley's visionary impulse is not to heighten our sense of the actual world and its present evil but to repeal the claims of forces he viewed as essentially nugatory and void. His ultimate intent is not to sharpen the modern consciousness (with its pervasive sense of misery) but to return to earlier states of awareness that have been defaced or obscured and yet remain always with us, like recollections of a half-forgotten dream. His impulse is not forward, toward the more precise definition of the modern world and its states of feeling, but rather backward to a sense of those "shapes too bright to see," images that are necessarily indistinct because they return us to our birthright and to a realization of a human potential that life once held out and has never, despite history, abandoned. Much of the violent modern antipathy to Shelley springs from the recognition of the regressive character of his genius, which stands in sharp contrast to the governing ideals of our own society and culture.[25]

Asia's transformation and the songs depicting it mark the real climax of Shelley's drama, not the later and somewhat anticlimactic deposition of the tyrant Jupiter. The two lyrics together distill what is most powerful and original in his vision. To say as much, of course, is hardly to disarm the skepticism or the repugnance of Shelley's critics or the questions that immediately rise to their lips. Even if we desired to, how can we give up our hold on the present and, for all our fears and dissatisfactions, the growth and accomplishment we connect with it? Is it really possible in any practical sense to reverse the momentum of the present and to return to our past, and how can we be sure that the alluring shapes that beckon us back to a bright world of undifferentiated possibilities will in the end prove any more congenial or fulfilling than our present situation? Shelley was as aware of the pressing relevance of such questions as his critics. That he could largely discount them in order to project a vision which flies in the face of so many ingrained assumptions with the audacious simplicity of Demogorgon's "Behold!" is owing, more than anything else, to a sense of desperation. Shelley had become convinced that humankind was bent upon a path that led only to its own destruction and from which it could be recalled only by the most radical of appeals. In working to reopen channels of feeling and perception all but lost in the unhesitating forward march of intellect of his time, he was seeking to project a vision of a possible beatitude from which humanity, with a kind of Promethean irony, was ever moving further but could never be altogether alienated. It remained a vision humankind would one day have to rediscover in order to be saved.

six

THE TRANSFORMING HARMONY

Prometheus Unbound, Acts III and IV

Shelley's need to compose a third act for his drama raised special problems in a play already rife with difficulties. To begin with, he had already represented virtually all the elements essential to his vision. In Act I he had dramatized his own sense of the irony of man's Promethean situation, beset by the rival claims of both evil and good but with the ever-present possibility, indeed the inevitability, of his ultimate liberation from tyranny. In Act II, in the interview between Asia and Demogorgon, he had outlined his view of a world destiny governed by the principles of a scientific necessity yet susceptible to, indeed in certain respects dependent for fulfillment on, the powers of endurance and love represented by his hero and heroine. With Asia's reawakening he had dramatized the entry of the life-renewing energies into his poem, and with her transformation he had achieved the climax of his drama. Yet there remained elements of his myth he could hardly ignore: the dethronement of Jupiter, the unbinding of his hero, and the reunion of Prometheus with Asia.

Given Shelley's dedication to nonviolence, and that Jupiter and the evil he represented were mere negations, the possibilities for dramatic confrontation in the deposition scene were limited. Hercules might appear at the unbinding, but it would have to be Demogorgon, acting as the force of a larger destiny, rather than any individual who overthrew the tyrant. Following the greater change already traced within the drama, the mere freeing of Prometheus from his chains must seem anticlimactic. On the other hand, the need to dramatize the hero's long-awaited reunion with Asia was positively intimidating. For how could one characterize the realization of pure potentiality into which they were to emerge? To particularize was of necessity to define and therefore to limit what was unapprehended, perhaps inapprehensible. Shelley had reached that point in his poem few poets ever reach, where the visionary imagination outruns the means for its expression.

Shelley's handling of the deposition scene draws its particular effectiveness from the powerful sense of hubris it creates. The effect derives in great part from Jupiter's presumption that Demogorgon's car of the promised hour bears the child destined to succeed him and will confirm the eternal triumph of his reign. Unlike Aeschylus, Shelley allows the Prometheus legend and its prophecy to run their course so that the fatal child prophesied to overthrow its father is actually presented to Jupiter. Because misunderstanding is close to the root of Shelley's conception of evil, it is only fitting that Jupiter altogether misconceives the significance of the approaching car, misinterpreting the dire revolutionary thunder that surrounds it as the portent of his own victory. The scene has the aura of one of Shelley's triumphal occasions—run in reverse. Jupiter exults to Thetis about the child they have together produced: "Two mighty spirits, mingling, made a third / Mightier than either" (III.i.43–44). The scene stirs recollections of the moment when Laon and Cythna, "two mighty Spirits" (645), are reunited at the end of the first canto of Shelley's earlier poem beneath the benevolent gaze of the androgynous figure from which they seem to emerge.

When Jupiter, at last realizing his peril, attempts to launch his dreaded thunderbolt, he finds to his dismay (the nightmare of all atomic powers) that his deterrent has been neutralized. As he falls from his pinnacle of power, the tyrant takes Demogorgon with him into the abyss:

> Sink with me then—
> We two will sink in the wide waves of ruin
> Even as a vulture and a snake outspent
> Drop, twisted in inextricable fight,
> Into a shoreless sea.   (III.i.70–74)

The process intimated here seems just the opposite of that at the outset of the first canto of *The Revolt*, in which the eagle and the serpent "wreathed in fight" (193) at length separate, allowing the serpent to transform and repropagate himself as Laon and Cythna, who then enter the world to carry forward the work of human renewal. Describing Jupiter's fall to the god Ocean in the following scene, Apollo likens him to a storm-encompassed eagle sunk down "to the abyss," "to the dark void" (III.ii.10). Jupiter seems in his fall to be subsumed back into the eternity that Demogorgon represents, an aspect of potentiality that is now dispossessed but that may at some future time reemerge to dominate and tyrannize anew.

Following his release by Hercules at the opening of Scene iii, Prometheus is reunited with Asia and the two withdraw toward the embrasure of a cave "All overgrown with trailing odorous plants" (III.iii.11). The vines "curtain out" the light of day while a fountain provides with its perpetual play an ever-changing panoply of shifting sounds, lights, and textures. As the apotheosis of Shelley's drama, Prometheus's withdrawal with Asia to the cave has drawn fire from hostile critics. Edward Bostetter, for example, has written that at this point Shelley's play "ceases to be a dramatic allegory and becomes a Shelleyan daydream." Shelley, he declares, "leap[s] over the hard labor, the intellectual discipline of showing man in process of transformation, to the dazzlingly simple dream of the achieved perfection." Bostetter goes on to write of Shelley's "tendency to reduce Utopia to a kind of sexless second childhood," of a "terrible coziness of . . . conception," and of "an unhealthiness of perspective, an emotional immaturity, a kind of infantilism which is prominent in much of Shelley's early writing."[1] Critics writing in defense of Shelley have usually found it convenient to ignore Bostetter's comments altogether or to dismiss them as unsympathetic. His objections, however, summarize commonly held antagonisms which may prove impossible to appease but which crystallize the major issues at stake.

Bostetter's protests concern two interrelated aspects of Shelley's conception: first, the precipitancy of Prometheus's and Asia's withdrawal and second, the adequacy of their retreat within the cave as a symbol of their apotheosis. The first objection has already been largely dealt with in the earlier part of this discussion. As a political writer and thinker, Shelley throughout his career advocated the importance of gradual reform. Yet it was also vital to him to believe that nothing separated humanity from immediate perfection if it could once free itself from the toils of custom and misapprehension. Indeed, it was the poet's duty to prefigure that possible perfection as a model of aspiration for his fellow man. The reformer who addressed himself in prose to specific political evils and the visionary poet straining to realize the nature and scope of human perfectibility had quite different methods and intentions. The two roles, however, ultimately reinforce each other. To confuse them is to simplify Shelley's complexity and sophistication. His recognition of the practical necessity of gradualism as a political reformer did not preclude retaining the everpresent imminence of the millennium as a permanent and essential element of his poetry. Following the immolation that terminates their struggles to reform the human world, Laon and Cythna reawaken to their reunion in the Temple of the Spirit with astonishing abruptness.

The second and more serious charge concerns the adequacy of the cave as a metaphor for apotheosis. Wasserman seems best to portray the

significance of the scene when he writes that the retirement of Prometheus
and Asia to their cave is "a withdrawal from the mutable actuality of space
and time into the containment of potentiality."[2] What disturbs critics like
Bostetter is the aura of self-absorption and childishness of the retreat,
where the two lovers

> will entangle buds and flowers, and beams
> Which twinkle on the fountain's brim, and make
> Strange combinations out of common things
> Like human babes in their brief innocence.   (III.iii.30–33)

If Shelley's drama is intended to describe a meaningful regeneration,
surely it must provide one more responsive to the reality of our human
condition. However, in *Prometheus* Shelley does not look forward to the
amelioration of our present condition in any commonly accepted sense.
His poem envisions, rather, the repudiation of our present nature and a
return to one that is earlier and pristine. Later in the scene Prometheus
bids the Spirit of the Hour blow from his "many-folded Shell" (III.iii.80)
the music of the universal renovation. Earth is rejuvenated by a quickening
spasm of joy that unwithers all her life:

> all plants,
> And creeping forms, and insects rainbow-winged
> And birds and beasts and fish and human shapes
> Which drew disease and pain from my wan bosom,
> . . . become like sister-antelopes
> By one fair dam.   (III.iii.91–94,97–98)

Earth's rejuvenation suggests the reversal of natural evolution, so that the
various species that have grown painfully asunder through differentiation
and opposition are drawn back toward the harmony of a common genesis.
In the same way Asia and Prometheus, as they retreat into their cave, are
subsumed into their principal archetypes, Adam and Eve, unfallen and in
the state of grace, to preside over the original garden of humankind.

It is, of course, our difficulty in imagining anything like the practical
realization of such a vision that explains the hostility of so many of Shelley's critics. Prometheus and Asia appear to retreat into a state of contemplation close to pure passivity. So conditioned are we by the notion of
original sin and the nineteenth-century ideal of struggle, progress, and
evolution that it is all but impossible to conceive of any approach to
human salvation that does not allow for them. The objections to Shelley's

vision can be rapidly summarized. How is it possible to imagine a human-kind defecated of every trace of evil? Looking within ourselves, we recognize traits like acquisitiveness and envy as natural and inalienable propensities. Such characteristics not only are ingrained but even serve a necessary purpose. Without some initial germ of emulation, for example, how could individuals develop aspiration and ambition, the drives necessary to the carrying through of any higher social purpose? The evil and self-serving instincts of our nature cannot be abrogated but must rather be moderated and directed by sympathy and reason to the service of larger human ends. The common charge against the apotheosis in *Prometheus Unbound* is that it is monotonous, sentimental, and naive. The deeper charge is that it upholds an ideal of humanity emasculated of the drives essential to our constitution and proper function as social beings.

Yet *Prometheus Unbound* is above all imaginative and visionary, a work that describes not what humans are but what they might be. The major problem confronting us is that we have become so inured to struggle and competition as abiding facts of experience that we cannot visualize a culture without them. Today the advancing dimensions and the accelerating dangers of that struggle are becoming ever more apparent. At the same time we are acquiring the means through psychology, biology, and genetics to alter a human nature long thought innate and immutable. The methods for reforming human nature endorsed by the tradition of Christian humanism seem to have failed consistently in the past. Can we now, with time running out, continue to trust to them in the future? If we can embark on a radical transformation of our nature, how should we proceed and what should be our goals and expectations? *Prometheus Unbound* is of value not so much because it prefigures the means for changing humanity as because it preserves the aspiration to do so; by holding out the shape of a possible perfection, it "bear[s] the untransmitted torch of hope / Into the grave across the night of life" (III.iii.171–72). Like its alter ego, Mary Shelley's *Frankenstein, Prometheus Unbound* is certain to become increasingly relevant to the controversy over humanity's need to transform itself in the face of self-annihilation. The prophetic character of the work is assured.

Prometheus runs counter to the main current of nineteenth-century literature most of all in its refusal to grant a permanent and unchanging reality to human nature. In this respect it is opposed not merely to the style but to the basic tenets and assumptions of realism. What, for example, is more essential to the triumph of the nineteenth-century novel in England, preeminently the art of Charles Dickens, than the vigorous and healthy life it bestows on humanity's most evil instincts as a necessary prologue to the cheering victory of the good? Shelley saw how far modern society had gone in institutionalizing evil as an enduring and even vital element. In order to be considered truthful or moving, works of literature were required to revive the common drives and oppositions, the old antagonistic rhythms of familiar experience. In *Prometheus* it was Shelley's desire to envision some ultimate escape from this self-perpetuating round of expectations, to convey the liberation of a humankind free of inhibition and compulsion.

Radical as it is in implication, the retirement of Prometheus and Asia to their cave is the fulfillment of a recurrent human longing which finds expression in the work of other writers. It is the longing of Lear to center his world around Cordelia and her prison, content, after their interval of separation, like Prometheus and Asia, to "sit and talk of time and change / As the world ebbs and flows, ourselves unchanged" (III.iii.23–24). It is the desire of Yeats for "the artifice of eternity,"[3] the bird that from its golden bough sings of the present, past, and future, like Shelley's lovers who "Weave harmonies divine, yet ever new" (III.iii.38). It is the desire for Spenser's garden of Adonis where the infinite shapes of earthly existence return to their source and where new forms are nurtured for fresh dissemination. It is the center and focus of the highest intimations of imaginative power forever creating new dimensions of existence. It is the expression of man's desire for the life of pure contemplation, the condition of Plato's philosopher-king.

Shelley's cave in fact reminded Yeats of Plato's.[4] The comparison is one Douglas Bush rapidly dismisses. "The whole passage," he writes of Prometheus's description, "is a sentimental reverie; Shelley's cave is a world away from Plato's."[5] Different as the two may be, one cannot help feeling that Yeats was right in sensing a revealing analogy. The inhabitants of Plato's cave trace in the shadows on its wall the reflection of a reality that they cannot see. By contrast Prometheus and Asia retire to behold those visionary intimations which take on reality from the power of human responsiveness:

> And lovely apparitions dim at first
> Then radiant—as the mind, arising bright
> From the embrace of beauty (whence the forms
> Of which these are the phantoms) casts on them
> The gathered rays which are reality.   (III.iii.49–53)

Such intimations are the offspring of "Painting, Sculpture, and rapt Poesy," yet return, once released, to foster and extend all imaginative endeavor, indeed to propagate "arts, though unimagined, yet to be." Prometheus and Asia will trace the "shadows . . . Of all that man becomes" (III.iii.55–58) or may become. Shelley's figure of the cave and its shadows acknowledges a kinship with Plato's as well as major differences of conception. For Shelley the human imagination not merely intuits but actively creates the shape of existence.

At the command of Prometheus, the Spirit of the Hour, as her final action in the play, blows from the whorls of a carved mystic shell the music of millennial change. Endlessly expanding like one of Yeats's gyres, the prophetic strains are the expression of a limitless potentiality by which the world is instantaneously transformed. At the end of the act the spirit reappears to describe to Prometheus and Asia the effect on the world of the music which they feel but cannot see. Her long speech, delivered like that of a messenger in classical drama to report an action that has taken place offstage, has the effect of a visionary promise rather than an account of what has just occurred. All people now walk with their fellows as with equals: "None fawned, none trampled" (III.iv.133). No longer are any compelled by tyranny or custom to deny the promptings of their best nature:

> None with firm sneer trod out in his own heart
> The sparks of love and hope, till there remained
> Those bitter ashes, a soul self-consumed.   (III.iv.144–46)

"Thrones, altars, judgement-seats and prisons" lie empty and abandoned, while "Sceptres, tiaras, swords and chains, and tomes / Of reasoned wrong" (III.iv.164,166–67), the pride of kings and priests, lie scattered and exposed to common astonishment, like barbarous relics of uncouth times.

Even while he thus imagines the earthly fulfillment of the vision of perfection, Shelley acknowledges the existence of certain fundamental human limitations. Earlier in the act, on the point of entering the cave, Prometheus anticipates the pleasure of forever viewing with Asia the ebb and flow of earthly circumstance, "ourselves unchanged." "What," he immediately adds, "can hide man from Mutability?" (III.iii.24–25). The distinction implied by his question alerts us that Prometheus has by this point in the drama transcended the limits of mortality, that as a Titan he is immortal. The same recognition of human limitations reemerges, significantly, at the very end of the Spirit's account of the return of the golden age which concludes the act:

> The loathsome mask has fallen, the man remains
> Sceptreless, free, uncircumscribed—but man:
> Equal, unclassed, tribeless and nationless,
> Exempt from awe, worship, degree,—the King
> Over himself; just, gentle, wise—but man:
> Passionless? no—yet free from guilt or pain
> Which were, for his will made, or suffered them,
> Nor yet exempt, though ruling them like slaves,
> From chance and death and mutability,
> The clogs of that which else might oversoar
> The loftiest star of unascended Heaven,
> Pinnacled dim in the intense inane.   (III.iv.193–204)

Like Prometheus tormented by the furies, we cannot hope to escape the force of passion. However, we can, like the Titan, govern our emotions; nor need we feel fear or guilt for what we experience. Likewise there is no escaping the mischances of a destiny we cannot command or foresee; for death and mutability (the possibility of change for the worse) remain the inescapable givens of the human condition without which the scope of our conceivable development would indeed be boundless. Like the Stoic philosopher, we must attempt to discriminate between those things which we can and cannot control, hoping for the eventual triumph of the good while seeking through our own wisdom and determination to promote it.

The passage expresses other limitations in the form of doubts or hesitations that, if more elusive and difficult to describe, are also more ingrained. The loathsome and deceitful mask imposed on human nature has fallen away to reveal its true condition. Yet the roll of adjectives describing humanity's attributes is almost exclusively negative: "Sceptreless," "uncircumscribed," "unclassed, tribeless and nationless / Exempt from awe, worship, degree." With its repeated assertions—"the man remains / . . . but man / . . . but man"—the lines seem to struggle to assert some fundamental and enduring conception of humankind against the force of this negative description. There seems, in other words, a conflict between Shelley's idea of man as all but unlimited potentiality and the need to acknowledge a permanence or continuity of human nature.

The tension is most apparent in the famous lines that close the passage which Shelley originally conceived as the ending of his drama, the lines which describe man, except for the clogs of mortality that necessarily restrain him, as "The loftiest star of unascended Heaven / Pinnacled dim in the intense inane" (III.iv.203–4). One is struck again by the negative epithet in "unascended Heaven" and by its ambiguity. Is the adjectival past participle used here in its transitive sense—to indicate a heaven the star of man has never climbed or measured? Or is the sense intransitive—to suggest a heaven, and with it a whole panoply of stars and planets, that has never yet risen, never yet come into being? The first image of human potentiality, for all its expansiveness, is swallowed up in the immensity of the second.

The famous concluding line, "Pinnacled dim in the intense inane," in many ways the most memorable in the play, has always held a special fascination for Shelley's admirers and detractors. The powerful effects of assonance and consonance culminate in the single word "inane," a substantive which, with its suggestive negative prefix, Shelley seems to have deliberately given the climactic place at the original ending of his drama, like "vacancy" at the end of "Mont Blanc." By the word "inane" Shelley sought, of course, to signify the formless void of infinite space—a vacancy full, however, of unlimited potentiality. He was clearly using the word as a substantive and with a sense of its physical and scientific denotation. Yet he uses it elsewhere in its adjectival and more common sense as "empty," "senseless."[6] In this line the two senses of the word flow rapidly into each other. Indeed, the alternation between the positive and negative connotations creates a dizziness, a terror of the abyss which, as suggested by "Pinnacled" and "dim," characterizes the mind's encounter with the unfathomable and constitutes a major aspect of the Romantic conception of sublimity.

In the peculiar struggle it evinces between affirmation and negation, exaltation and fear, illumination and blankness, the passage that closes the third act of Shelley's *Prometheus* is one of the most remarkable evocations of the sublime in Romantic literature.[7] As in the closing stanzas of the "Ode to the West Wind," there are moments in Shelley's verse when the ecstasy of his identification with his singing master Orpheus, the type of the sublimely inspired poet, is crossed by the terror and misgiving of the overreacher. At the end of the third act of his drama, Shelley had pushed his vision of millennial bliss to the very limits of human comprehension, and the strain of the effort is reflected in his verse. That he could at the end depict his vision teetering on the very brink of meaning, or meaninglessness, is attributable not only to the heights he was attempting to scale but to his underlying honesty as poet. The very brightness of his vision creates a penumbra of surrounding shadow that constitutes a second or countermeaning, an effect of Romantic irony common to the work of all the great Romantic poets.[8]

The practice of referring to *Prometheus Unbound* as Shelley's "masterpiece" has been in some ways unfortunate. The epithet suggests a finality for the work of a poet only twenty-seven years old who produced much of his best verse in the years remaining to him and who would certainly have continued to develop as a major poet had he lived. But more important, the term suggests a consistency of form and style which we associate with works like the *Divina Commedia* and *Paradise Lost.* His decision, late in 1819, to add a fourth act to the play, a coda written in a style of heightened lyricism that notably extends the form and significance of his drama, reveals how open the conception was in his mind.[9] This openness *Prometheus* shares with much of the great work of Shelley's contemporaries, with Wordsworth's *Prelude,* Byron's *Don Juan,* and Keats's two *Hyperions.*

It is possible to conjecture Shelley's reasons for returning to *Prometheus.* He wanted most of all to provide an ending that better dramatized the millennial joy and reawakening spreading through the universe. The account delivered to Prometheus and Asia by the Spirit of the Hour at the end of the third act is somewhat awkward and oblique. Shelley's decision to depict the universal reawakening more directly required him, however, to enlarge the form as well as the dimensions of his drama. As critics have observed, the coda takes the form of a celebration whose use of song, dance, and spectacle is more reminiscent of the Renaissance masque than the effects we customarily associate with the chorus of Greek tragedy. The masque, which is presented before the cave of Prometheus and Asia and is observed and commented on by Panthea and Ione as they gradually awaken, has, as Harold Bloom observes, the effect of an epithalamium in honor of the united lovers.[10] It is appropriate that much of its imagery is overtly erotic. Shelley's celebration of the rebirth of sexuality emerges chiefly, however, through the larger change the marriage of Asia and Prometheus makes possible. At the climax of the masque the Earth and Moon, in orgiastic dance around each other, combine to bring about a new creation in space, a propagation described in an imagery rich in scientific implication which throws fresh light on the themes of potentiality and the nature and direction of human development. At the conclusion of the act an altered and now benign Demogorgon reappears, rather like Prospero at the end of the masque in Shakespeare's *The Tempest,* a play that haunted Shelley's imagination, to sum up for the participants the significance of the rites they have enacted. Demogorgon's powerful summation gives Shelley the opportunity to settle certain questions his earlier conclusion had left hanging, principally the human desire for assurance that, despite the continuance of change and the power of necessity, we can ultimately gain some permanent hold over the good.

The act that Shelley composed achieves its ends, as Donald Reiman has shown, in three clear movements.[11] We first watch the approach and greeting of the Chorus of the Spirits and the Chorus of the Hours, culminating in their union in stately dance and song. As the measures break up, Panthea and Ione behold the spectacle of the moon rolling forward in her chariot to meet the onrushing sphere that bears the little sleeping Spirit of the Earth, a scene conceived as pageant whose symbols are as elaborate and condensed as any in the drama. As the Moon and the Earth disappear together, united in the orbit of their common love, Demogorgon reascends from the abyss to deliver his concluding and decisive apostrophe.

The union of the Spirits and the Hours in cosmic dance dramatizes the conditions necessary for the emergence of mankind's best nature into the fullness of reality. Like the spirits who comfort Prometheus at the end of Act I, the Chorus of Spirits that opens Act IV represents the highest instincts and intuitions that haunt the human mind. However, they are described at the outset of the act as "unseen." The Spirits cannot achieve actualization except through union with the Hours, just as the Hours require the Spirits to realize themselves in turn. The point is driven home by the momentary confusion of Ione and Panthea as they question each other: "What charioteers are these?" "Where are their chariots?" (IV.56). Kenneth Cameron has written that "Shelley imagines the Hours as awaiting their birth through the ages."[12] However, the same is equally true of the Spirits who forever exist *in potentia* in the human mind. At the beginning of the act we watch a train of dark forms and shadows, the ghosts of past hours, on their way to "bear Time to his tomb in eternity" (IV.14). With their disappearance, the Chorus of new Hours advances. As the Spirits and the Hours converge upon each other, a single voice calls out, "Unite!" (IV.80). Immediately Panthea exclaims: "See where the Spirits of the human mind / Wrapt in sweet sounds as in bright veils, approach" (IV.81–82). She can now see the Spirits who have heretofore been invisible. Like form and embodiment or wish and fulfillment, the Spirits and the Hours both imply and need each other. Joined together in harmonious dance, they symbolize the emergence of human perfection into the plenitude of time that Shelley conceived as forever possible.

The Spirits pursue the measures of their dance with the exultance of the liberated Ariel:

> Our spoil is won,
> Our task is done,
> We are free to dive or soar or run.   (IV.135–37)

However, their joy lies not so much in mere freedom as in the more serious work of new creation they make possible:

> And our singing shall build,
> In the Void's loose field,
> A world for the Spirit of Wisdom to wield.   (IV.153–55)

Through their singing and dance the Spirits and Hours together propagate a new atmosphere (a conception important to Shelley in both its scientific and its metaphorical sense) conducive to the formation of new life. Indeed, as Cameron, following Carl Grabo, observes, the ensuing stanzas suggest "the formation of solid matter from the stuff of nebulae,"[13] the creation, inspired by Shelley's varied reading in philosophical and scientific theory, of a new planet and its emergent life:

> We whirl, singing loud, round the gathering sphere
> Till the trees and the beasts, and the clouds appear
> From its chaos made calm by love, not fear.   (IV.169–71)

Combining echoes of Genesis and Revelation with science fiction, the circling spirits summon with their rhythms the gravitational forces necessary for the constellation of a new world in space. However, the forms of life we see emerging are impelled not by fear and struggle, the driving force of former evolution, but by love.

The Spirits and the Hours break up their dance. Their combination establishes an underlying pattern for interpreting the more elaborate pageant that follows, the romance and union of the Moon and Earth. As critics like G. Wilson Knight have sensed, the latter episode introduces a new weight and density of symbolism, a metaphoric shorthand combining Shelley's interest in such varied fields as astronomy, chemistry, optics, and anthropology.[14] At the same time the image of the onrolling chariot that dominates the episode looks both backward to the mechanism of *Queen Mab* and forward to the metaphor of the victorious car in *The Triumph of*

Life, relating Shelley's vision in *Prometheus* to the beginning and the end of his poetical career.

As before, Panthea and Ione hear the approaching forms before they see them. Panthea proclaims "the deep music of the rolling world" (IV.186), while Ione detects a range of "under-notes, / Clear, silver, icy, keen" which "pierce the sense . . . / As the sharp stars pierce Winter's chrystal air" (IV.189–92). At length they descry through two openings in a wood the approaching chariots of the Moon and Earth. Ione's impression of piercing cold is elaborated in her description of the occupant of the first chariot, the "winged Infant," Shelley's figure of the Moon:

> white
> Its countenance, like the whiteness of bright snow,
> Its plumes are as feathers of sunny frost,
> Its limbs gleam white, through the wind-flowing folds
> Of its white robe, woof of ætherial pearl.
> Its hair is white,—the brightness of white light
> Scattered in strings, yet its two eyes are Heavens
> Of liquid darkness, which the Deity
> Within, seems pouring, as a storm is poured
> From jagged clouds, out of their arrowy lashes,
> Tempering the cold and radiant air around
> With fire that is not brightness.   (IV.219–30)

The dazzling brilliance radiating from the airy figure, reinforced by repeated use of the word "white," alternately attracts and repels us with an impression of the pure and frigid, the heavenly and inhuman, the captivating and a disconcerting touch of the albino. The image of the Moon and her chariot is one of Shelley's most elaborate metaphors for the power of potentiality streaming in unrefracted brilliance toward the sphere of this world. It is the same "white radiance of Eternity" (463) he was shortly to commemorate in the celebrated lines in *Adonais*, the snow-crowned power he had described in its menacing and indifferent aspects in "Mont Blanc," the influence whose sudden visitations he had invoked in his "Hymn to Intellectual Beauty." Like Asia who at the moment of her transformation screens her brilliance in smiles, "Mak[ing] the cold air fire" (II.v.51), the infant Spirit of the Moon "temper[s] the cold and radiant air around" (IV.229) to qualify its potentially destructive power. As the chariot rolls forward it awakens, like the Platonic demiurge, "sounds / Sweet as a singing rain of silver dew" (IV.234–35), the yearning and delight of the whole creation, the imagery of the opening stanzas of Wordsworth's "Intimations Ode" that Shelley was to employ more ambivalently in *The Triumph of Life.*

If the Moon in her chariot is Shelley's symbol for the universal energy informing life, his image of the whirling orb of interpenetrating spheres that bears within it the Spirit of the Earth is his symbol of a potentiality of a different but related kind—the potentiality for endless change. The sleeping child is borne forward on a sphere itself made up of "many thousand spheres," "Ten thousand orbs involving and involved" (IV.238,241). The onrushing mass reflects a multitude of colors, "Purple and azure, white and green and golden" (IV.242), the various hues of refracted light, and its surfaces are peopled with "unimaginable shapes" (IV.244). All of these symbolize the infinite possibilities of earthly evolution, past, present, and future. The orb advances with a "self-destroying swiftness" (IV.249); the work of transformation necessarily proceeds through both creation and destruction, for new cycles can emerge only as the old are effaced. The vision of ceaseless change in response to a limitless force of energy appears at the beginning of one of the greatest of Shelley's later lyrics:

> Worlds on worlds are rolling ever
>   From creation to decay,
> Like the bubbles on a river
>   Sparkling, bursting, borne away.[15]

The car that bears the infant Earth is Shelley's reworking of Queen Mab's chariot and the panorama of earthly history and future promise it makes possible. However, the space vehicle he imagines in *Prometheus* is a far more original, kinetic, and complex metaphor.

The image of the infant Earth, the child asleep at the center of the whirling spheres, remains the most striking, even unsettling, part of Shelley's figure. Yet the image is precisely apposite. The child lies sleeping at the center of the circling orb unaffected by the evolutionary changes that surround it, the emblem of a potentiality forever uncompromised and inviolate. As it sleeps its lips move in silent imitation of the sights and sounds around it, smiling contentedly but ultimately indifferent to the changing patterns of its dream of life.

Shelley's figure reminded G. Wilson Knight of Keats's youthful metaphor for the power of poetry as "might half slumb'ring on its own right arm" and again of Keats's portrait of Adonis sleeping in his bower in *Endymion.*[16] Keats's figures look outward to an awakening to a world of love and heroic achievement. Shelley's figure, by contrast, looks inward to the security and perfection of what is self-contained and unconditioned. Shelley read *Endymion* only a few weeks before composing his final act, and Panthea's elaborate description of the sleeping Spirit of the Earth recalls Keats's poem in several ways.[17] The "star upon its forehead" (IV.270) shooting golden rays like a beacon both into the universe and into "the Earth's deep heart" (IV.279) reminds one of the "orbed drop / Of light" sitting "high / Upon the forehead of humanity" and sending forth "A steady splendour" that was Keats's symbol for love (*Endymion*, I.800–811). More certain still, Shelley was remembering Keats's description of the wreckage that surrounds Endymion in his wanderings under the ocean in Book III (itself adapted from Clarence's great speech on the fears of drowning in *Richard III*, I.iv.21–32) for his vision of the secrets of the earth that the infant's rays illuminate.[18]

Yet Shelley's description reflects an evolutionary terror rooted in scientific knowledge of prehistoric archaeology. The sleeping child lies surrounded by a vast evolutionary destruction, the melancholy evidence of many "cancelled cycles" (IV.289). The "monstrous works" of "uncouth skeletons," "statues, homes, and fanes; prodigious shapes" (IV.299–300), testify to the prolonged development of cultural ignorance and superstition. "Huddled in grey annihilation, split, / Jammed in the hard black deep" (IV.301–2), they resemble the debris piled beneath the slopes of Mont Blanc, the accumulation of countless centuries. Around them lie

> The anatomies of unknown winged things,
> And fishes which were isles of living scale,
> And serpents, bony chains, twisted around
> The iron crags, or within heaps of dust
> To which the tortuous strength of their last pangs
> Had crushed the iron crags.   (IV.303–8)

The passage is remarkable not just for its obvious knowledge of the testimony of fossil remains but for the peculiar loathing of evolution it expresses. Well before the methodical investigations and conclusions of Charles Darwin, Shelley had already grasped, largely through the writings of contemporary scientists like Darwin's grandfather Erasmus, the horror of an earthly evolution that, operating through the principles of competition, rapine, and survival, had left a history that was the very antithesis of his ideal of love.

This course of evolution had gone terribly wrong, leaving earth like "an abandoned corpse" on which strange forms "multiplied like summer worms"

> till the blue globe
> Wrapt Deluge round it like a cloak, and they
> Yelled, gaspt and were abolished; or some God
> Whose throne was in a Comet, past, and cried—
> "Be not!"—and like my words they were no more.   (IV.313–18)

The lines reveal Shelley's knowledge of the geological theories of catastrophic change advanced by Sir Humphry Davy, Erasmus Darwin, Cuvier, and others, in which the earth was seen as having evolved through upheavals or floods caused by planets that periodically destroyed its life. Yet Desmond King-Hele, who along with Carl Grabo and Kenneth Cameron has done so much to help us understand the scientific orientation of Shelley's imagination, can nevertheless write of the passage that Shelley "affirms his faith in evolution by referring pointedly to city-dwellers whose fossil remains are mortal but not human. Yet he ends perversely by making Panthea mention the cataclysmic theory."[19] Shelley grasped the evolutionary pattern that the more farsighted of his scientific brethren had begun to perceive, but he put no faith in the "progress" it represented. Nor is there anything perverse in Panthea's description breaking off with the specter of a cataclysm. The point of the passage is that true worldly rehabilitation can come about only when the earth, and the principles of strife and competition that have brought it to its present pass, have been eradicated. Like John Stuart Mill, Shelley would argue that the path of true progress lies not in following nature but in correcting it. The faith that underlies Shelley's vision is an extraordinary trust in the potential for changes of the most fundamental kind in man's nature, changes that bring to mind claims made in our own day for the possibilities of human, social, and cultural engineering.

Now that Jupiter and the atmosphere of "solid cloud" and "hot thunderstones" (IV.341) surrounding him have disappeared, "drunk up / By thirsty nothing" (IV.350–51), the way is prepared for new creation. Nature abhors a vacuum, and so

> beneath, around, within, above,
> Filling thy void annihilation, Love
> Bursts in like light on caves cloven by the thunderball.
> (IV.353–55)

As the Moon and Earth approach each other to begin their dance of cosmic joy, they together create a new atmosphere, and the Earth is enfolded by a "vaporous exultation" that surrounds him like "an atmosphere of light" (IV.321,323). Through the warmth of his proximity the Earth thaws the Moon's brilliant but potentially destructive cold so that she exclaims:

> Some Spirit is darted like a beam from thee,
>   Which penetrates my frozen frame
>   And passes with the warmth of flame—
> With love and odour and deep melody
>   Through me, through me!—   (IV.327–31)

She for her part "interpenetrates [the Earth's] granite mass" (IV.370) with her own power, inspiring a quickening of new life in the chaos of his form. In imagery that is at once astronomical and erotic, Shelley prefigures the union of earth and moon, man and woman, the poet and his inspiring muse; it suggests the extent to which Shelley had idealized his relationship with Mary. Together the Earth and Moon combine to create the harmony of a new nature in which "Labour and Pain and Grief in life's green grove / Sport like tame beasts—none knew how gentle they could be!" (IV.404–5)—a condition Yeats yearned for more memorably if more wistfully when he wrote that "Labour is blossoming or dancing where / The body is not bruised to pleasure soul."[20] Shelley's lines look forward to an ideal tempering of the male and female natures, to a humankind free of the Oedipal compulsions, the feral instincts and competitive drives, the need to survive by overcoming and suppressing others. The passivity and pellucid calm at the heart of the playfulness and rejoicing that close *Prometheus* seem strange because they stand in such contrast to the ideals of our own civilization.

   As the voices of Earth and Moon fade off into the distance, Panthea calls Ione to behold the reemergence of Demogorgon, who rises as a mighty power, a cloud of darkness, from the center of the earth. His reappearance at the end of Shelley's drama is not more remarkable than the alteration in his role and character. The diction and tone of his invocation of the powers of the universe, "Ye Kings of suns and stars, Dæmons and Gods" (IV.529), recalls Prometheus's first line at the opening of the play, "Monarch of Gods and Dæmons, and all Spirits," suggesting that the wheel has come full circle. Like Prospero, he seems to summon the spirits who have been his servitors and whom he takes his leave of before dismissing: "Ye elemental Genii, who have homes / From man's high mind" (IV.539–40). Like God, he seems to survey his handiwork from the prospect of the seventh day:

    ye beasts and birds—
  Ye worms and fish—ye living leaves and buds—
  Lightning and Wind.   (IV.544–46)

If not less awesome than his former self, the Demogorgon of Shelley's last act is more forthcoming, human, and confiding.

There is an element of humility in Shelley's decision to give the final word in his drama to Demogorgon. The temptation must have been strong to bring Prometheus forward once again, perhaps as the type of the inspired poet, as final spokesman. By asserting to the last the primacy of necessity, Shelley was preserving an order essential to the intellectual decorum of his play. Although Prometheus by his endurance may keep alive the millennial spark of hope, it is only through Demogorgon and the incomprehensible working of the vast forces he controls that the promised change can come about.

Whatever the awkwardness of reintroducing Demogorgon upon the stage, it was necessary for Shelley to reinvoke his authority in order to clarify a troubling ambiguity at the heart of his drama, one apparent throughout the play which is thrown into greater prominence at the end. Shelley's play enacts as its central movement the achievement of an earthly millennium; but it does so only within a universe of change and mutability, the conditions that still surround and limit humanity amid the universal rejoicing at the end of Act III. If it does not lie within the power of Prometheus to will the good into existence, if he must depend upon the inscrutable processes that Demogorgon alone comprehends, what is there to guarantee the stability and continuance of humanity's new bliss? We have seen Demogorgon ascend in his car at the promised hour to dethrone Jupiter. May he not rise at some equally unforeseen time in the future to reinstall the tyrant? The reversibility of time and the astonishing rapidity of change that remain always potential can work on behalf of humanity's evil instincts as well as its good. And would not the return of Jupiter's empire, after all the play has envisioned, prove a disappointment too great for even Prometheus to bear?

Demogorgon's closing declamation openly raises these concerns, which Shelley, using the deity as his mouthpiece, can settle with no final assurance. The best Demogorgon can do is to deliver certain pledges:

  Gentleness, Virtue, Wisdom and Endurance,—
  These are the seals of that most firm assurance
    Which bars the pit over Destruction's strength;

> And if, with infirm hand, Eternity,
> Mother of many acts and hours, should free
>   The serpent that would clasp her with his length—
> These are the spells by which to reassume
> An empire o'er the disentangled Doom.   (IV.562–69)

The sleep of the amphisbaena, the two-headed snake that symbolizes eternity and now lies coiled in a seamless ring beneath Demogorgon's throne, may yet be broken, permitting Jupiter to reascend from the pit that now confines him. Faced with this possibility, Demogorgon can offer no easy prescription but only the qualities Prometheus has already exhibited: "Gentleness, Virtue, Wisdom and Endurance." Among these it is the last, the Titan's ability to hold out through "the last giddy hour / Of dread endurance" (IV.558–59), that seems preeminent. The example of his fortitude is the principal means Demogorgon holds out to humanity to reclaim self-rule should the kingdom of darkness ever reassume its reign:

> To suffer woes which Hope thinks infinite;
> To forgive wrongs darker than Death or Night;
>   To defy Power which seems Omnipotent;
> To love, and bear; to hope, till Hope creates
> From its own wreck the thing it contemplates;
>   Neither to change nor falter nor repent:
> This, like thy glory, Titan! is to be
> Good, great and joyous, beautiful and free;
> This is alone Life, Joy, Empire and Victory.   (IV.570–78)

The concluding stanza of Demogorgon's exordium and its imperatives go to the moral center of the Promethean situation Shelley had represented as all humankind's. To defy and to love: how can one maintain the delicate but necessary balance between such seemingly conflicting demands? Without the assurance of absolute faith, how can one continue hoping through defeat after defeat for a victory that can spring, paradoxically, only from something close to ultimate despair? How can one maintain the unsubdued assertion of the individual will and yet preserve that open responsiveness through which a greater common destiny must manifest itself? In *Prometheus Unbound* Shelley does not look to particular programs or to individual saviors but to the triumph of a universal consensus that is forever imminent in our better nature if we will allow it to emerge and overcome. Such a victory, he implies in his final line, is the only one worth having. The most remarkable aspect of *Prometheus* is Shelley's trust that that consensus can and must prevail within the world.

ethical science, that the former ought to be entirely regulated by the latter, as whatever was a right criterion of action for an individual must be so for a society which was but an assemblage of individuals, "that politics were morals more comprehensively enforced."—Southey did not think the reasoning conclusive.

"He has," Shelley went on to complain, "a very happy knack when truth goes against him of saying, 'Ah! when you are as old as I am you will think with me'—this talent he employed in the above instance" (I,223).

Tempering ethical ideals with expediency in order to achieve practical results was an issue that surfaced almost from the start of Shelley's acquaintance with William Godwin. It is clearly Godwin whom Shelley has in mind in writing again to Elizabeth Hitchener the next month:

> The persons with whom I have got acquainted, approve of my principles, & think the truths of the equality of man, the necessity of a reform and the probability of a revolution undeniable. But they differ from the mode of my enforcing these principles, & hold *expediency* to be necessary in politics in as much as it is employed in its utmost latitude by the enemies of innovation:—I hope to convince them of the contrary of this. To expect that evil will produce good, or falsehood generate truth is almost as rational as to conceive of a patriot king or a sincere Lord of the Bedchamber. (I,263)

How was it possible to act in the spirit of moderation and compromise, which Southey and Godwin were continuously urging, and preserve the integrity of one's ideals? Shelley's brief intervention in the politics of the Irish question was not conclusive, for the poet succeeded in speaking his mind forthrightly only to withdraw from the scene in deference to Godwin's increasingly agitated protests that the counsels he was urging would prove disastrous. The conflict between commitment to ethical idealism and the demands of political reality remained a potential sore spot in his conscience throughout his early years. As he wrote to Elizabeth Hitchener toward the end of 1811, "what conflict of a frank mind is more terrible than the balance between two opposing importances of morality—this is surely the only wretchedness to which a mind who only acknowledges virtue it's master can feel" (I,149).

This moral problem, the potential opposition between uncompromising idealism and practical expediency, is the very issue that, realized dramatically within a deeply moving human situation, he returned to years later in *The Cenci*. The fundamental issue upon which the drama turns is, to put it simply, was Beatrice wrong in planning the murder of her father, Count Francesco Cenci, or was she justified in following, like Antigone, the dictates of her conscience and in adopting violent means to relieve both her family and herself from an insupportable tyranny? The dilemma is one Shelley deliberately prepares for the play's readers when he declares in his "Preface":

> Undoubtedly, no person can be truly dishonoured by the act of another; and the fit return to make to the most enormous injuries is kindness and forbearance, and a resolution to convert the injurer from his dark passions by peace and love. Revenge, retaliation, atonement, are pernicious mistakes. If Beatrice had thought in this manner she would have been wiser and better; but she would never have been a tragic character.[2]

The passage underlines the inflexible moral imperative that Beatrice violates in carrying out the murder of her father.

What, however, of the practical reality of her situation, the terror disguised within the brief, unobtrusive phrase, "the most enormous injuries"? The threat of incestuous rape that her father first holds over her and then, we are led to believe, actually carries out during the course of the play is simply too terrible for her to endure. The violation, as Shelley movingly presents it, is not simply physical but psychological, one she has no means of defending herself against and which deprives her of all necessary self-possession, driving her to the point of madness. Isolated by the political corruption of the society, church, and state that surround her, Beatrice seems to have no other course than to adopt the violent means of her persecutors. Shelley deliberately centers his drama on an ethical problem, despite his disclaimer in the "Preface" that "I have endeavoured as nearly as possible to represent the characters as they probably were, and have sought to avoid the error of making them actuated by my own conceptions of right or wrong, false or true"[3]—a statement that bears most on the issue of dramatic probability. Clearly he was drawn to Beatrice Cenci not simply by the Guido Reni portrait and the legendary account of her character and fortitude but by the moral problematics of her situation. James D. Wilson is right when he argues that "The key to understanding *The Cenci* lies in the extent to which we hold Beatrice responsible for her actions,"[4] even if that question is hardly the whole of Shelley's play. The "Preface" sets forth an ideal of human forbearance; yet as the play proceeds and forces us not simply to observe but to sympathize and judge, we ask ourselves, is there no limit to what Beatrice must endure?

Although *The Cenci* brings to a head political and ethical problems of such long standing in Shelley's thought, it is remarkable that there exists today no consensus on how to interpret his drama with regard to these issues. The older view, the groundwork for which was laid in Carlos Baker's pioneering study of the poet's development,[5] is best expressed in a well-balanced and trenchant essay of Robert F. Whitman: "If Beatrice is admirable, it is in spite of, not because of, her act of rebellion. By taking what she thought to be the law of God into her own hands, she acted as a brave and desperate human being—but she was wrong."[6] Shelley's drama also lends itself to a more modern reading, however, and Beatrice emerges from Stuart Curran's full-length study of the play as an existential heroine. Faced with the necessity of acting within an illogical universe so corrupt as to be morally absurd, Beatrice has no recourse but to attempt to establish an existential order of her own, and there is neither justification nor point in condemning her in terms of simple ethical platitudes.[7] These two précis hardly do justice to the detailed and reasoned arguments they summarize; the differing viewpoints indicate, however, the extent of disagreement over the essential outlook of the play and how it invites or requires us to assess its heroine and her dilemma. The two extremes of reasoning also define a spectrum of opinion along which other judgments arrange themselves.

The questions I have touched on are material because they involve the logic of Shelley's career and the relationship *The Cenci* bears to *Prometheus Unbound*. No doubt important practical considerations, reinforced by Mary's impatience, lay behind Shelley's conversion to a radically different style of dramatic composition following his completion of the third act of *Prometheus*. But there are also overtones of psychological compensation in the remarkable transition. Having celebrated the triumph of love and the millennium in the rarefied atmosphere of *Prometheus Unbound* and its "beautiful idealisms of moral excellence,"[8] he was now impelled to depict a far darker scene, what he described in his letter dedicating *The Cenci* to Leigh Hunt as the "sad reality"[9] reflected in the despairing plight of a virtuous heroine pressed beyond the limits of human endurance.

If, by bringing him down to earth, *The Cenci* served Shelley as an emotional counterirritant, however, does it also represent a reweighting of moral emphasis? After celebrating the victory of the godlike Prometheus, was he now impelled to dramatize, through his moving study of Beatrice's ordeal, the actual likelihood of human failure, and if so, for what purpose? From everything we know of Shelley's generosity of spirit, it is hardly likely, despite the rigorous ethical precepts set forth in his "Preface," that he should want to draw down the deprecation of an audience upon a human and fallible heroine for her "error." If the play teaches, it does so, surely, in a way that transcends any such simple moral demonstration. Comparing the two plays, Earl Wasserman, Shelley's most distinguished modern critic, has argued that "it would be misleading to read them merely as exactly opposite sides of the same moral coin."[10] The warning may be salutary; however, the vagueness of the statement, highlighted by the uneasy juxtaposition of "merely" and "exactly," leaves one uncertain just how the two dramas ought to be related to each other. Coming as *The Cenci* does between the third and final acts of the longer drama, the pattern of similitude in dissimilitude that links them is striking. Despite the change to a specific historical and domestic setting, Beatrice resembles a kind of failed Prometheus. Yet, as Wasserman has gone on partly to observe, the two plays manifest totally different emotional dynamics, centered in quite different notions of catharsis.

Some works of literature lend themselves to explication through a single crux that crystallizes the vital interpretive problems; and *The Cenci* is a play of this kind. The crux I refer to is the most obvious and dramatic irony in the play: the arrival of the pope's legate, Savella, with a warrant for Cenci's arrest and summary execution only moments after Beatrice and her hirelings have carried out the Count's murder near the end of Act IV. The timing of Savella's totally unexpected and seemingly fortuitous appearance assumes, beyond any other element in the play, the aura of dramatic contrivance. The sense of irony the legate's entry generates is so powerful that it is hard not to sense that the poet saw the effect as vital to the significance of his play.[11]

But just how are we to interpret the irony? It is significant that critics of the play, differing on so much else, have found themselves in sharpest disagreement on this single issue. For some older commentators, the irony served to underline Beatrice's error in adopting violent means to do away with her father, by showing that, had she only waited, the course of justice would have been taken out of her hands.[12] For others, quite to the contrary, Savella's arrival is the culminating absurdity in a cruel and illogical world in which the only course open to Beatrice is to seek to impose a moral order of her own and in which she is punished for bringing about the very end that society itself has belatedly ordained.[13] The two analyses are closely similar in their perception of the irony but diametrically opposed in the conclusions they draw from it. Even Earl Wasserman largely begs the question when he warns that "the reader falls into a moral trap" if he interprets Savella's arrival as "an intentional cosmic irony"; for, "To think, as many readers have thought, that this is cosmic irony is to assume that the Count's crimes *should* have been entrusted to the law, an assumption that contradicts the ethics upon which the drama is built."[14] Assuming the reader avoids the moral trap Wasserman describes, how does the episode in fact affect us? If Savella's arrival is not an instance of cosmic irony, what kind of irony is it and what are its effect and purpose?

Savella's unexpected arrival crystallizes the ethical problem Shelley sought to treat in *The Cenci*. It also reveals the important psychological roots the play shares with *Prometheus Unbound*. Critics have in part observed that Promethean imagery runs throughout *The Cenci*. The struggle of wills between Jupiter and Prometheus obviously resembles that between Count Cenci and his daughter. What connects the plays at a deeper level, however, is Shelley's peculiar fascination with the Promethean situation and its major ironies. As we have seen, the essence of that relationship is summed up in the savage struggle of wills between Jupiter and Prometheus, a struggle in which, paradoxically, the Titan has his antagonist already in his power. Given the truth of the prophecies and their inevitability, the mythical equivalent of Shelley's trust in necessity and the ultimate triumph of the good, Prometheus has only to hold out in his determination in order finally to overcome. Yet as Mercury's agonizing questions make clear, although the Titan can be sure of the end of his ordeal he has no way of knowing its extent. At any point the moment of his deliverance may be at hand; yet the unexpired term of his suffering may also be long, so immense, perhaps, as to approach infinity. Without the means actually to foresee the promised hour and the manner of his deliverance, how can Prometheus summon the necessary perseverance? Faced with such incertitude, how can he, for all his invincibility, avoid falling into the pit of despair that forever awaits him? This tension is the particular terror of the Promethean situation Shelley so well understood. It accounts in no small measure for his determination to represent in *Prometheus Unbound* his vision of the final fulfillment of human aspiration.

Although the Promethean situation and its dialectics of terror are clearly revealed in the first act of *Prometheus Unbound*, understandably, they are not at the center of Shelley's vision of millennial redemption. Yet not only are they central to the drama of *The Cenci* but also Shelley gives them a new and more excruciating twist. The perilousness of Prometheus's position might seem sufficiently apparent. Yet its terror is intensified by the force of a further intimidating hypothesis. Let us suppose that, after centuries of defiance, Prometheus's endurance finally breaks so that he yields to Jupiter the fatal secret, only to discover that his promised deliverance was immediately at hand—a day, an hour, perhaps only a minute beyond the point of his capitulation. That heartbreaking, all but unthinkable possibility is the very one Shelley dramatizes at the turning point of *The Cenci* with the arrival of Savella.

The recognition of this hypothesis and its bearing on the dramatic situation in *The Cenci* sets up a powerful surge of imagination that is central to Shelley's ethical intention and effect. The reader or spectator is propelled violently back and forth between two poles of supposition, both of which are intolerable. In view of the inevitability of Prometheus's victory if only he maintains his defiance, in view of the suffering he has already endured and the dependence of all human hope on his continued resolution, the idea of his submission is virtually inconceivable. Yet when one considers his terrifying isolation and uncertainty, how can he go on? The imagination is driven back and forth between the two conflicting premises without the ability to accept either or to reconcile them.

Prometheus Unbound portrays the advent of the millennium through the triumph of a hero of godlike capacities, in an ideal vision of what is potentially achievable if only in the reaches of the future. In *The Cenci* Shelley was moved to trace, by way of contrary reaction, the undoing of a virtuous but intensely human heroine who represented the Promethean ideal. She was to fail partly on account of the overwhelming force of oppression and partly through the vulnerability of her human nature. Her drama produces that keen sense of loss we customarily associate with great tragedy, which *Prometheus* necessarily lacks. It is almost as if Shelley, having depicted the victory of Prometheus, now felt himself drawn to the mortal Io, the maiden whom the hero comforts in the latter part of Aeschylus' play but whom he is unable to save from Hera's dreadful persecution.[15] In the visionary and triumphant drama the possibility of heroic failure, if never inconceivable, is deliberately suppressed. What, however, of those human souls less fortified, less determined than Prometheus who might fail where he was destined to succeed? How, as a matter of practical ethics, were they to be judged?

In thinking about the two plays and their relationship to the myth, it is important to recognize how Shelley, although introducing the subtler psychological torments of Mercury, deliberately eschewed in *Prometheus* the primitive violence—the bird's daily dismembering attack—that is such an important part of the primeval legend. The point emerges clearly if we compare Shelley's play with the work of his contemporary, the painter Henry Fuseli, whose treatment of the bound Prometheus has that nightmare quality characteristic of the artist at his best.[16] The bird—eagle or vulture—is lurking and obscene; nor do we require the insights of depth psychology to sense, as the bird forces open the god's thigh with its talons, how Fuseli has taken the liver as an obvious euphemism in a way that goes straight to the roots of the male ego. In Shelley's *Prometheus* this aspect of the hero's ordeal is never treated. In *The Cenci* the genital threat is not merely explicit but overpowering. It is Beatrice's ability to endure everything except sexual violation that explains her collapse.

To understand how *The Cenci*, and in particular the Savella episode, is grounded in the Prometheus myth is not to resolve the controversies that surround the episode's significance or, for that matter, the interpretation of the drama. At the outset of the play, Beatrice Cenci is a maiden of exceptional fortitude and courage, defiant before the threats of her father and a tower of support to her beleaguered stepmother and younger brother. She is, in fact, a kind of feminine counterpart to Prometheus, transposed to a domestic situation. The absolute power and fiendish tyranny exercised by her father is no less terrifying than Jupiter's. Just as Jupiter is intent to break Prometheus's will, so Cenci is intent to break his daughter's; only he knows that he will succeed and exults in the weapon of his success. For Count Cenci possesses one notable advantage over Jupiter: a father's insight into the nature of his daughter. Cenci knows she cannot withstand the ordeal of being sexually forced. If Beatrice Cenci possesses a tragic flaw, it is her virginity or, more exactly, her idealization of her virginity as the center of her moral nature. It is essential to her sense of her own integrity as a human being. Shelley brings to his study of Beatrice's anguish a sympathy and psychological insight that quite transcend the celebrated treatments of rape in the fiction of the earlier century.

To say that Beatrice's tragic flaw is her idealization of her own virginity implies an element of moral condemnation. But how else are we to take the major ethical declaration of the "Preface" to the play, which Shelley himself applies specifically to his heroine, that revenge and retaliation are unjustifiable? From the outset of the drama Shelley engages our sympathies in the plight of his heroine. At the opening of the third act she staggers wildly on stage toward her stepmother, having been violated for the first time by her father:

> How comes this hair undone?
> Its wandering strings must be what blind me so,
> And yet I tied it fast.—O, horrible!
> The pavement sinks under my feet! The walls
> Spin round! . . .

> My God!
> The beautiful blue heaven is flecked with blood!
> (III.i.6–10,12–13)

By the fifth act, when the persecution by her father, condoned and extended by the authorities of state and church, has run its full course, the figure of violation recurs, but now as an image of desolation and terror enveloping the universe:

> If there should be
> No God, no Heaven, no Earth in the void world;
> The wide, grey, lampless, deep, unpeopled world!
> If all things then should be . . . my father's spirit,
> His eye, his voice, his touch surrounding me;
> The atmosphere and breath of my dead life!   (V.iv.57–62)

For all this Shelley's drama never lets us forget, as Beatrice is gradually drawn into the conspiracy to murder her father, the precepts of forbearance and nonviolence dramatized in *Prometheus* and reaffirmed in the "Preface" to *The Cenci*, a standard by which she must be ultimately judged. Planning the conspirators' first unsuccessful attempt to destroy the Count on his way to the Castle of Petrella, Beatrice describes the huge rock which she suggests can be rolled down to crush him as he passes through a ravine beneath:

> there is a mighty rock,
> Which has, from unimaginable years,
> Sustained itself with terror and with toil
> Over a gulph, and with the agony
> With which it clings seems slowly coming down;
> Even as a wretched soul hour after hour,
> Clings to the mass of life; yet clinging, leans;
> And leaning, makes more dark the dread abyss
> In which it fears to fall: beneath this crag
> Huge as despair, as if in weariness,
> The melancholy mountain yawns.   (III.i.247–57)

The stone never descends, for Count Cenci passes by the intended spot an hour too soon. The lines describe Beatrice herself as a kind of failing Prometheus, slowly giving way to the insupportable weight of her miseries as they drag her down into despair.

Borrowing a device of the Elizabethan history play, Shelley partly reverses the balance of our sympathies in the latter portion of his drama. We see the Count on his deathbed, in appearance like the gracious Duncan:

> an old and sleeping man;
> His thin grey hair, his stern and reverent brow,
> His veined hands crossed on his heaving breast,
> And the calm innocent sleep . . .   (IV.iii.9–12)

Even the hired assassins, Olimpio and Marzio, at first dare not assault him. Throughout the play, we may admire Beatrice's strength of character; but we are also appalled, near the end, as we watch her brazenly lie to her judges and mercilessly browbeat the pain-crippled Marzio into retracting his confession so that he dies upon the rack. In entertaining the malign suggestions of her treacherous lover, Orsino, in joining the ranks of the conspirators and first condoning, then urging the murder of her father, she adopts the violence and absolutism of his ways. Nor can we escape the irony that in the end she becomes her father's child in a way she was not at the outset of the play. He triumphs not by despoiling her of her virginity but by corrupting her deeper integrity, by inducing her to believe that she can escape injuries that appear to her intolerable only by assuming his power and spirit, by becoming one with the very being she detests. That at the last she is unwilling or unable to see that she has been perverted only makes her tragedy more compelling.

It remains to examine the peculiar catharsis *The Cenci* produces. Shelley's drama of divided sympathies achieves its power of ethical realization because it places the reader or spectator directly on the horns of that dilemma at the heart of the Promethean situation, the situation best crystallized in *The Cenci* by the arrival of Savella. Like Earl Wasserman, I find the central statement on the moral problem of the play in the "Preface," where Shelley writes:

> It is in the restless and anatomizing casuistry with which men seek the justification of Beatrice, yet feel that she has done what needs justification; it is in the superstitious horror with which they contemplate alike her wrongs and their revenge; that the dramatic character of what she did and suffered, consists.[17]

The statement is difficult and condensed, and the psychological process, the movement of imagination, to which it refers, demands elucidation. Let us consider the conflicting and alternative judgments we are invited to make. Beatrice's crime is murder, parricide; the most heinous of offenses; the betrayal of one's begetter to whom honor and obedience are naturally due. Yet weigh against this our revulsion at incestuous rape, a violation, moreover, that is the deliberate and culminating cruelty against an innocent child who merits love and not dishonor. Caught up in the emotional dialectics of the predicament, the imagination of the reader is propelled back and forth between two sets of ethical imperatives in the effort to establish some preponderance between them, in the attempt, that is, to justify the one enormity by the other, only to find the task impossible. The effort of mind is both "superstitious" and "pernicious" not only because, driven by some of the deepest guilts and fears of the human psyche, it is profoundly irrational in origin but also because it seeks a carefully reasoned resolution of the "either/or" kind to the human dilemma confronting it.

Paradoxically, it is out of this struggle of the imagination, misguided though it may be, that the play's catharsis—ethical and profoundly emotional—arises. Here again I turn to Wasserman, who in his analysis of the drama has shown how Shelley deliberately draws the spectator or reader into a situation that excites "pernicious casuistry." However, Shelley controls the reactions of his audience with such artifice as to convert "pernicious casuistry" into what the poet elsewhere describes as "sublime casuistry," which works toward a deliberate moral end.[18] That aim, as Wasserman goes on to declare, is self-knowledge, the highest knowledge tragedy can impart. Yet Wasserman's discussion of such realization as it arises through our understanding of Beatrice's example seems curiously judicial and impassive. Thus he argues that the play brings us to an understanding that "Inherent purity of character can coexist with moral error; and, since sublime casuistry reveals that error cannot be reconciled with the purity, that purity is unaltered by the error." What follows for Wasserman is our realization that Beatrice's "moral nature has not been corrupted by her acts; she has been 'thwarted'—turned aside—from it, but it persists." Moreover, "we misread if we believe it a sign of her corruption that after the crime she can say, 'The spirit which doth reign within these limbs / Seems strangely undisturbed'" (IV.iii.63–64).[19]

Through his grasp of Shelley's skeptical methodology, Wasserman has, I think, seen more deeply into the play than any other critic, and his discussion is one to which I am considerably indebted. Yet his scholastic determination to preserve a purity of ethical distinction has led him to neglect the emotional dynamics of the work and their crucial role in determining the drama's effect and meaning. From the time when we first see her bravely defy her father's tyranny, to the end when we watch her

excoriate her judges and prepare herself for execution in complete conviction of her own innocence, we are deeply involved with and moved by
Beatrice. The moral and emotional catharsis of the play proceeds out of
this sympathetic identification as well as from our struggle to reconcile the
inescapable recognition that she has adopted her father's violence with our
abhorrence of the forces driving her to it. Such is the power of the dilemma in which Shelley places the spectator, so traumatic our predicament, that its effect is ultimately to force us to see the necessity of moving
beyond a conventional standard of ethical judgment, based on counter-
poise and calculation, to one that is more difficult and complex but also
necessary and humane. It is to urge the transcendence of the moral imperative to love. As Shelley wrote in his review of Godwin's novel *Mandeville*,
comparing it to *Caleb Williams*, "there is no character like Falkland, whom
the author, with that sublime casui[s]try which is the parent of toleration
and forbearance, persuades us personally to love, while his actions must
forever remain the theme of our astonishment and abhorrence."[20]

In her next-to-last speech in the play Beatrice turns to her younger
brother, Bernardo, to exclaim:

> One thing more, my child,
> For thine own sake be constant to the love
> Thou bearest us; and to the faith that I,
> Though wrapped in a strange cloud of crime and shame,
> Lived ever holy and unstained.   (V.iv.145–49)

As we hear these parting words pronounced in such a solemn and au-
thoritative way, a number of conflicting thoughts run through us. Is
Beatrice mad? Is she simply self-deceived? Is she, rather, clinging to the
pretense of innocence to sustain her to the end of her ordeal? Or is she
speaking the literal truth? These questions, which are not easy to separate
one from another, demand resolution. Beatrice, we know, has erred. She
has committed an act of retaliation. She has been guilty, in the terms
Shelley himself sets out in the "Preface," of a "pernicious mistake." Yet this
line of reasoning is not by itself adequate to our understanding of her
plight. The full sense of her tragedy lies in our recognition that she has
been so wrenched by her injuries that, whether we consider her mad or
sane, she has lost the ability to judge her own situation. It is as if the
searing pain of her violation had cauterized her other faculties, leaving her
oblivious to everything but the burning sense of her injuries and the
trauma of her father's touch. This deeper wound to her psychological and
moral equilibrium is perhaps the worst that can befall a dramatic character,

a condition that the traditional ethics of tragedy are reluctant to admit. In arraigning Beatrice before her judges, in forcing us to adjudicate between her lies and their hypocrisy, Shelley places us in an intolerable situation. It is a strategy deliberately contrived to compel us to recognize the bankruptcy of conventional ethical discriminations, to force upon us the necessity of ascending to a higher level of moral awareness. It is to invite, indeed require, us to condemn Beatrice's actions unblinkingly and simultaneously to love her, an act incorporating but transcending mere forgiveness. Shelley's reasoning will strike many of his critics as an ethical relativism both sentimental and dangerous. Nevertheless it is certain that he regarded the moral recognition of his play truer to the underlying spirit of Christianity than the sacrilegious politics of false piety and self-interest he exposes in all his work. One might add that in the way it both manipulates and educates the emotions of its viewers, his drama makes its point with a characteristic ferocity of logic.

In the final scene of the play, Shelley briefly raises the hopes of his audience as Bernardo rushes off to make a last-minute appeal to the pope. There is still the chance that the pontiff may relent and dispatch some new Savella with a warrant for Beatrice's release, a possibility that puts us once again in mind of the Promethean situation. When Lucretia takes heart at the possibility of Bernardo's success, Beatrice cries out:

> O, trample out that thought! Worse than despair,
> Worse than the bitterness of death, is hope:
> It is the only ill which can find place
> Upon the giddy, sharp and narrow hour
> Tottering beneath us.   (V.iv.97–101)

No doubt Wasserman and other critics would argue that Beatrice is right in refusing to trust to the pope for either justice or mercy. Nevertheless her speech reveals her demoralization. As we have seen, in Shelley's ethics hope is the cardinal virtue (except insofar as it is subsumed within the greater power of love). Hope alone can provide the resolution necessary to await the promised hour when the tide of evil ultimately must reverse itself—the expectation that gives man the courage to outlast the term of his ordeal. Brutalized by anguish and repeated disappointment, however, Beatrice has come to see hope as not simply fruitless but as "the only ill," "worse than despair." If it serves only to draw out endlessly the period of human suffering, hope is nothing more than unpardonable self-deception. What we witness is something more terrible even than the extinction of the Promethean spark—the conversion, or perversion, of hope into its

moral opposite. It is this more dreadful kind of capitulation, or derange-
ment, that Shelley asks us both to judge and to understand in his drama.

The Cenci represents a mature reconsideration of a moral issue that
goes far back, as I have argued, in Shelley's career. The conflict between
expediency and absolute principle is one the play does not so much
definitively settle as develop through the dramatic means Shelley employs
to re-educate and heighten the moral sensibility of its audience. In this
respect the ending of the final act and in particular the way Beatrice goes to
her death emerge as crucial. One can recall Mary Shelley's judgment that
"The Fifth Act is a masterpiece. It is the finest thing [Shelley] ever wrote,
and may claim proud comparison not only with any contemporary, but
preceding, poet. The varying feelings of Beatrice are expressed with passionate, heart-reaching eloquence."[21] Above all Beatrice's final speech, the
last in the play, delivered before she steps forth to execution, best substan-
tiates Mary Shelley's judgment and marks a high point of Shelley's dramatic genius. Modern directorial practice is the art of lending old plays
new emphasis. It is disconcerting to imagine how quickly one could destroy through misemphasis the delicate balance of sympathy and ironic
awareness Beatrice creates in us in the brief speech in which she bids the
Cardinal Camillo and her mother a final farewell:

> Give yourself no unnecessary pain,
> My dear Lord Cardinal. Here, Mother, tie
> My girdle for me, and bind up this hair
> In any simple knot; aye, that does well.
> And yours I see is coming down. How often
> Have we done this for one another; now
> We shall not do it any more. My Lord,
> We are quite ready. Well, 'tis very well. (V.iv.158–65)

Our attention is caught by the imagery of knotting and untying and of
Beatrice's hair, the metaphor Shelley uses throughout with great delicacy
for his heroine's virginity, on which, as we have seen, the construction of
her character depends. The scene moves us with its domesticity and quiet
pathos: stepmother and daughter providing for each other the common
services they will never again exchange. At the same time we are struck by
the muted sarcasm of her words to Camillo, "Give yourself no unnecessary
pain, / My dear Lord Cardinal," and her tone of command toward Lucretia, "Here, Mother." The woman is summed up in all her strength of
character and all her weakness as she moves with her parent toward her
death with her insistent "Well, 'tis very well." For we know it is *not* well.

The tragedy of Beatrice Cenci is not her physical undoing but the violation of her spirit and her mind. It lies in an ultimate failure of will and endurance that is the more compelling because we are made to comprehend it so completely. If in *Prometheus Unbound* Shelley left us a model of heroic resolution to admire, he gave us in Beatrice a heroine whose failure must move us to compassion and love.

eight

ROMANTIC IRONY

The Witch of Atlas

Within Shelley's career *The Witch of Atlas* occupies the place that corresponds to *Lamia* in Keats's. Both poems hold in delicate solution shades of irony running from the playful to the bitter. Both create fables that interweave traditional mythology and original invention. Both poems develop the legends they invent to call into question and even satirize some of the author's most cherished ideals, especially as regards the nature of poetry and the poetic process—a turning back of artifice upon itself that brings to mind the criterion of Romantic irony. Both poems reveal impatience with, at times resentment of, pressures for public recognition and reward. To push such similarities further would begin to obscure major differences; but it is remarkable to find the two poets adapting similar styles and strategies at comparable points in their careers.[1]

Shelley wrote his whimsical fantasy in just three days after returning to the Baths of Pisa where he, Mary, and Mary's stepsister, Claire Clairmont, were spending the summer of 1820. The poem was the result of a brief holiday outing. Shelley accompanied Mary and Claire as far as Lucca and then went on by himself to climb Monte San Pellegrino. The expedition left him worn out but stirred in imagination. The three days of wandering across the barren landscape in the garish summer light, his only company "the quaint witch Memory,"[2] who had inspired his solitary verse letter to Maria Gisborne the preceding month, seems to have brought the whole of his poetical career—its high aims and lack of recognition—before him in imagination. The mythical progress of poetry he produced, almost in comic spite, represents yet another attempt to characterize his mistress and patron, "the witch Poesy,"[3] and to account for her capricious, sometimes less than loving behavior to her mortal votaries. The playfulness of Shelley's fanciful invention is the more brilliant for the way it partly conceals, partly suggests a host of underlying grievances and disappointments.

Mary's reaction to the poem was predictably disapproving. She saw the work as yet another instance of Bysshe's freakish tastes, "wildly fanciful, full of brilliant imagery" but "discarding human interest and passion, to revel in the fantastic ideas that his imagination suggested."[4] Just when *The Cenci* offered hope for his achieving the breakthrough to popular success, he had to turn his back on the world of common concerns to indulge himself in one more imaginative junket. Beyond such practical considerations, one cannot help sensing that Mary disliked the muted bitterness, even cynicism, that the poem for all the seeming gaiety of its idealizations at times betrays.

Shelley's response to Mary's inhospitable reaction was to incorporate it in a short, six-stanza dedication which defends against her accusations and prepares the reader for the tonal complexity of the completed narrative. For, with the possible exception of *Alastor*, *The Witch of Atlas* displays the greatest versatility of tone of any of his longer poems. He begins the dedication with a bit of playful cajolery concealing genuine reproach:

> How, my dear Mary, are you critic-bitten
> (For vipers kill, though dead) by some review,
> That you condemn these verses I have written
> Because they tell no story, false or true? (1–4)

As the case of Keats was to illustrate, the viperous criticism of the reviews could kill if taken to heart.[5] Instead of urging him to cater to the narrow-mindedness of the popular taste, Shelley wished Mary would humor his longing to escape into the kind of poetry that for the moment appealed to him, a verse of playful invention, satire, ambivalence, and irony.

> What, though no mice are caught by a young kitten,
> May it not leap and play as grown cats do,
> Till its claws come? (5–7)

The plea for time and indulgence hardly disguises the unpleasant predatory habits of the grown cat, the power concentrated in its claws. Is this really the kind of evolution Mary desires for his talent? Rather than insisting on this kind of effectiveness, let her think of his poem, he writes, shifting his metaphor, as an ephemeron, the beautiful insect of a day:

> What hand would crush the silken-winged fly,
> The youngest of inconstant April's minions,

> Because it cannot climb the purest sky
>   Where the swan sings, amid the sun's dominions?
> Not thine.   (9–13)

The concluding "Not thine," so characteristic of the poem that follows, leaves us puzzled. Is the abrupt denial intended to exonerate or to accuse by implication? Or does it amount to something like a plea? It seems impossible to say.

Shelley's tone deepens into open reproach in the stanza that follows: "To thy fair feet a winged Vision came / Whose date should have been longer than a day" (17–18). The allusion is, of course, to *The Revolt of Islam*, the labor of an earlier summer, which he had also dedicated to Mary in moving Spenserian stanzas reminiscent of Byron's *Childe Harold*. *The Revolt* had emerged to mixed critical reaction and popular misunderstanding and neglect, and Shelley feared the same fate awaited *Prometheus*. Mary was always pointing out Byron's success, and Shelley had himself immediately recognized and partly envied the brilliant innovation and popular appeal of *Don Juan*. Was it any wonder that he should now seek to capture Byron's carefree ease and nonchalance by adopting the ottava rima stanza, a measure he uses with his own grace and facility even while it continuously invites comparison with the older poet?[6]

By now he knew he could never hope for the celebrity Byron had so effortlessly achieved. His own genius was of a different kind. The sympathy and intuition he required from an audience he could expect only from cultivated readers like his friend Leigh Hunt. So he turned to Mary and the warmth of her encouragement, the glow of her "eternal smile" (15), for the atmosphere on which his verse depended. The trouble was that the vital smile was "eternal" only in imagination. Even Mary's powers of understanding and encouragement had their limits. The smile faded; "the swift Sun went his way" (22). Then the poem, the insect of a day, dropped dead. Like the sensitive plant in the poem he had composed in the spring of the same year, the flower of verse could flourish only in a garden akin to Eden and with a spirit like Eve to minister and tend it. If Shelley's dedication implies a regrettable lack of sympathy on Mary's part, it also suggests the extraordinary demands he had come to make of her. "O, let me not believe / That anything of mine is fit to live!" (23–24). Is the disclaimer an expression of despair, or simply a practical recognition of the truth the modern poet, at least his sort of poet, had to face and live by? It is possible to read the lines also as a plea to Mary not to force him to become what he couldn't.

Byron's case reinforced the sad truth that time and effort were by

themselves no guarantee of poetical success. Look at " 'the agony &
bloody sweat' of intellectual travail," as he wrote to Godwin, which he had
invested in *The Revolt* (I,578). How then could one cavil at the three days'
effort his *Witch* had taken? Perhaps there was more to be gained from the
ease and casualness of the *Letter to Maria Gisborne*, which he had only
recently written, and its free play of associations. Wordsworth by his own
admission had spent nineteen years "considering and retouching Peter
Bell" (26) in the effort to create a work worthy (in the older poet's pomp-
ous emphasis) of "filling *permanently* a station, however humble, in the
Literature of our Country."[7] The result, as Shelley viewed it, was a monstrous upas tree blocking out the light and spontaneity that poetry required. The renewed attack on Wordsworth, whose shortcomings Shelley
had so amusingly canvassed in *Peter Bell the Third*, now seems somewhat
labored and gratuitous. Moreover it leads to the recognition that although
Wordsworth had produced the abortive Peter, he had also sired offspring
as vital and enviable as "Ruth or Lucy" (34), a posterity undeniably destined to endure. What had he himself to show by comparison? The hover-
ing shades of Shelley's great poetic contemporaries, Wordsworth, Byron,
and Keats among them, in the background of his dedication reveal that
Mary's objections had crystallized latent misgivings and preoccupations
that haunt his poem as well.

    Shelley's defense against such self-questioning was to turn the tables
by making, partly playfully, partly in earnest, a hyperbolic claim for the
supremacy of his ideal of poetry. Beneath his comic trappings Wordsworth's Peter was infernally ugly. By comparison,

> If you unveil my Witch, no Priest or Primate
> Can shrive you of that sin, if sin there be
> In love, when it becomes idolatry.   (46–48)

Mary had complained of the poem's obscurity, indeed impenetrability.
But such was the characteristic of true poetry that Shelley most admired
and insisted on. "Veil after veil may be undrawn," he was to write early the
next year in his *Defence of Poetry*, "and the inmost naked beauty of the
meaning never exposed."[8] That his lady was a deliberate tease, an adept in
the arts of limited exposure that lead men on, in no way impugned the
logic of his figure. For Shelley hoped it would be impossible not to fall in
love with his Witch. Such love might approach idolatry, a sin exceeding
the power of any "Priest or Primate" to pardon. However, Shelley was no
friend of the church; nor could he countenance as moral prudence the
prudery that declines to tempt a true inamorata all the way.[9] Like Keats's

tantalizing urn, the Witch is Shelley's metaphor for art's power to arouse and attract despite the sense it leaves us of the limits of our powers and experience. In *The Witch* he was to treat yet again, if more ironically, that thirst for the divine and beautiful, which, however tormenting, is the only instinct worth obeying even if that thirst remains finally unslaked.

> Before those cruel Twins, whom at one birth
>   Incestuous Change bore to her father Time,
> Error and Truth, had hunted from the earth
>   All those bright natures which adorned its prime,
> And left us nothing to believe in . . .   (49–53)

It is remarkable to compare the opening lines of *The Witch* with those of Keats's *Lamia*, which Shelley was to read only weeks later, in October, after receiving a copy of Keats's 1820 volume:

> Upon a time, before the faery broods
> Drove Nymph and Satyr from the prosperous woods,
> Before King Oberon's bright diadem,
> Sceptre, and mantle, clasp'd with dewy gem,
> Frighted away the Dryads and the Fauns . . .[10]   (1–5)

Both poems begin by returning to a primeval world, before the growth of modern consciousness and its distinctions between objective and subjective, reality and appearance, desire and belief had made the survival of mythology impossible. Both poems commence with mythical inventions to describe the genesis of the imagination and of poetry. Lamia's transformation from serpent into fairy is achieved only through the unseemly contortions of a fiery metamorphosis which exposes the weakness and ambivalence of her nature. The birth of Shelley's Witch is, by contrast, warm and languid, virtually a spontaneous generation, which takes place when the Sun gently impregnates her mother, a nymph and one of the Atlantides, deep within the cave that symbolizes consciousness. As he proceeds to characterize his Witch, Shelley reveals her anomalies more gradually but no less decisively than Keats. For one can readily agree with critics like Wilson Knight that the Witch is Shelley's embodiment of "poetic consciousness," "an incarnation of poetry itself," and with Richard Cronin that the whole poem "can be seen as a sceptical myth designed to explore the function of poetry."[11]

As *Prometheus Unbound* illustrates, it was one of Shelley's deepest convictions that poetry, in the words of the *Defence*, "defeats the curse which binds us to be subjected to the accident of surrounding impressions," and "creates anew the universe."[12] Once established in her own right, Shelley's queen proceeds, with the bewitching beauty of her "soft smiles" (86), to reorder all creatures around her in a fresh creation. The giraffe, the elephant, the serpent, and other beasts assemble before her, just as the creatures called up by God in the first garden took their names from and paid homage to Adam and Eve: "The magic circle of her voice and eyes / All savage natures did imparadise" (103–4). Crouching beside her, the lion and the leopard lose their carnivorous appetites and lie down with the doe. She tames their savage natures by drawing them within the circle of her love, "a circle around its proper Paradise which pain and sorrow and evil dare not overleap," to recall some phrasing from the essay "On Love"[13] that looks directly back to Milton's description of the wall around the garden in *Paradise Lost*.

The miraculous apparition of the lady is, however, not more splendid than disconcerting, for all the deformities and abortions her presence brings to light. Not only nymphs and shepherdesses flock to her. The parade of creatures includes "quaint Priapus with his company" (125), "Pigmies, and Polyphemes . . . / Centaurs and Satyrs" (133–34), and even more amorphous "lumps" and monstrosities, "Dog-headed, bosom-eyed and bird-footed" (135–36), derelict and seemingly irredeemable shapes spawned by some earlier course of evolution. These creatures are drawn to her by a longing for her beauty, felt as a "want" (116) or incompleteness of their being. Undismayed by their unsightliness, the Witch presides in majesty above them: "Her love subdued their wonder and their mirth" (128). She triumphs over the uncouthness of their nature, although she cannot repress their instinctive laughter at the strange spectacle she presents. Even their father, the "Universal Pan" (113), is drawn to pay his tribute:

> He past out of his everlasting lair
>   Where the quick heart of the great world doth pant—
> And felt that wondrous lady all alone—
> And she felt him upon her emerald throne.   (117–20)

Their communion is profound and unfathomable. Nevertheless the quaint tit-for-tat reciprocity together with the unspecific emphasis on feeling leaves the suspicion that their intercourse may be something less than mystical. One is reminded of the ending of Wallace Stevens' "Cy Est Pourtraicte, Madame Ste Ursule, et Les Unze Mille Vierges":

> He heard her low accord,
> Half prayer and half ditty,
> And He felt a subtle quiver,
> That was not heavenly love,
> Or pity.[14]

The juxtaposition of the spiritual and physical creates a sense of idiosyncrasy.

Like a good Platonist, Shelley knew that although ideal beauty attracts with its splendor, it can blind with its unaccustomed radiance, that there may be the need, to cite the metaphor of the *Defence*, for some "alloy of costume . . . to temper this planetary music for mortal ears."[15] Mindful of the risk of overexposure, the Witch obligingly weaves a garment to enfold her, and the spindle and the threads of fleecy mist she appropriates for the purpose lend a homely, domesticating touch to her priestly concern. However, her condescension has its limits. When the ocean nymphs, hamadryads, oreads, and naiads, the more refined among her company, offer themselves as attendants to her person, she suddenly draws back with an air of *noli me tangere*. "This may not be" (225), she declares imperiously; and she proceeds to read them a lecture on the mutable nature they share with all earthly things, a pronouncement that, proceeding from the security of her own immortality, has the ring of class distinction. The oaks, the streams, the ocean which the nymphs inhabit may be long-lasting; but even these elements must at length vanish, "And ye with them will perish one by one" (233). The Witch's delicacy does not prevent her from phrasing the unpleasant truth bluntly. She continues, moreover, in a way that does not exactly spare the feelings of her auditors:

> "If I must sigh to think that this shall be—
> If I must weep when the surviving Sun
>   Shall smile on your decay—Oh, ask not me
> To love you till your little race is run;
>   I cannot die as ye must . . . over me
> Your leaves shall glance—the streams in which ye dwell
> Shall be my paths henceforth, and so, farewell!" (234–40)

It is enough that the Witch will stray regretfully, if not exactly impassioned, amid the littering leaves and streams, the sole memorials of her would-be attendants. To ask her to love them, to sympathize with the "little race" they have to run, is to demand too much from an immortal. There are, after all, bounds to what one can expect: "I cannot die as ye must." The simple truth might as well be faced: "and so, farewell!"

The apparent insouciance of the dismissal may seem heartless; but with mercurial swiftness the Witch's mood softens to grief:

> She spoke and wept—the dark and azure well
>   Sparkled beneath the shower of her bright tears,
> And every little circlet where they fell
>   Flung to the cavern-roof inconstant spheres
> And intertangled lines of light—a knell
>   Of sobbing voices came upon her ears
> From those departing Forms, o'er the serene
> Of the white streams and of the forest green.   (241–48)

The quiet tears would testify more eloquently to pity did they not so beautifully diversify the shifting lights and colors that ornament her cell. The knell of sobbing voices fading pathetically into the distance is hardly sufficient to recall her from a luxury of self-absorption.

The four stanzas describing the Witch's dealings with the nymphs (217–48), the most brilliant in the poem, display the dazzling subtlety of Shelley's irony working through a range of moods and implications to continually test the reactions of his readers. Harold Bloom has authoritatively identified the stanzas as "the thematic center" of the poem and one of "the heights of Shelley's poetic achievement." But even he misjudges their tone when he writes of "The Witch's gentle firmness" in "her struggle with herself," her "school[ing] herself to a stoicism bordering on a necessary cruelty," while "painfully attempting to maintain her bearing."[16] Such solemnity misses the high comedy of Shelley's portrayal. It is not that the stanzas lack pathos, any more than the Witch can be accused of calculated malice. It is just that, in her weird independence and changeability, she is unable to commit herself for very long to any human concern.

If it is difficult to condemn the Witch for her childlike whimsicality, we may find it hard to warm to her aloofness, bordering on indifference. Within her cave, part treasury, part working laboratory, she cultivates and stores her stock of visions and dreams. Her treasures include promises, intimations, and secrets—the knowledge of how "Men from the Gods might win that happy age," the golden one, "redeeming native vice" (188–89). From time to time in her labors she sends forth harmonies that descend like "Sounds of air" into the world of man,

> Such as we hear in youth, and think the feeling
>   Will never die—yet ere we are aware,
> The feeling and the sound are fled and gone,
> And the regret they leave remains alone.   (157–60)

Her visions inspire the highest human hopes and ambitions; but they are doomed to fade, leaving only the bitterness of regret. The lines for a moment come close to betraying the comic detachment of the poem with overtones of personal feeling—the poignant idealism of Shelley's youth recorded in the "Hymn to Intellectual Beauty." However, the vital balance between pathos and sardonicism is quickly reestablished.

The Witch is a diligent curator of those divinations that inspire the human spirit. Yet she cultivates her distillations with the ardor of a sybarite, collecting visions in chalices, dreams in "chrystal vials" (182), and "odours in a kind of aviary" (169). The cache resembles a cabinet of choice liqueurs, concoctions of "intensest bliss" (164), the heavenly counterpart of Pope's Cave of Spleen. Her activities are a curious mixture of the sacred and the profane, the determined and the aimless. Like a monastic, she spends her days perusing "scrolls of dread antiquity" (250), but never fails to embroider the text with some fresh fancy. She passes her sleepless nights in a trance of contemplation, "With open eyes, closed feet and folded palm" (272). The posture may suggest, as Richard Cronin among others has noted, the position of the Buddha and the state of complete inner calm and self-fulfillment that is nirvana.[17] However, her abstraction suggests less the asceticism and self-discipline of the religious devotee than the reverie of the confirmed addict. Untroubled by the seasons, she withdraws in winter to a well of crimson fire set within groves of asphodel, pine, and cedar, a resort transcending the Baths of Pisa. Here she hibernates in comfortable elegance, watching the snowflakes disappear on the surface of her pool. The priestly labors of the Witch at times suggest her dedication to what Wordsworth called the "breath and finer spirit of all knowledge,"[18] when she appears the upholder and preserver of the highest human ideals. On other occasions she seems a capricious fairy godmother, now dispensing, now withholding the magical enchantments in which she luxuriates. The two characterizations correspond to different conceptions of poetry between which Shelley found it difficult to discriminate.

The principal narrative development in the second half of Shelley's poem is a diverting exercise in self-parody. He had found the only part of Wordsworth's *Peter Bell* he could enjoy was the opening episode when the poet is carried away through the air in a magic boat which then returns him, frightened but relieved to be back on terra firma. He himself realized that it was virtually impossible to write an imaginative narrative of any length without the device of at least one boat journey, a hallmark of his poetry. In catering to the Witch's whim for travel he was really humoring his own, as well as setting himself in deliberate opposition to Wordsworth's earthbound sobriety. Not surprisingly, the mock-epic derivation of the Witch's vessel is the most elaborately worked poetical contrivance in the poem. Characteristically Shelley offers us a choice between two equally fanciful explanations for the vessel's genesis. First it is claimed that Vulcan built the boat for Venus. Despite its master craftsmanship, the goddess found the ship too fragile for her "ardours" and, so the story goes, she sold it to Apollo, who bought it for the Witch, his daughter. The indignity of secondhand possession is outweighed by the craft's distinguished history. Yet another story has it that the infant Cupid scooped out the boat from the fruit of a plant, grown from a strange seed he stole and planted in his mother's star. The exorbitance of these rival conjectures is exceeded only by the account of the strange creature the Witch creates for companionship on her journey.

For years scholars have labored to elucidate the character of the Hermaphrodite with the help of learned analogies, alchemical or Platonic, too often neglecting the essential truth that the creature is funny. The Hermaphrodite is the offspring of the Witch's supreme artistry, a composite of fire and snow, a perfect synthesis of incompatible elements. It is also sexless, or rather a perfect union of both the sexes with "no defect / Of either sex, yet all the grace of both" (330–31).[19] Nathaniel Brown, who has argued for unisexuality as a serious ideal in Shelley's thought and poetry, has written that "the unequivocally androgynous Hermaphroditus is no less lovely for its 'gentle countenance' and limbs, the 'youth' of its bosom, the 'purity' of its expression, and its 'sweet sighs.' "[20] His sober assessment testifies against itself that the Hermaphrodite is the most deliciously fatuous of all the Witch's (or Shelley's) creations. There is from the first something furious and facile about the way the Witch whips up her incredible combination, kneading "the repugnant mass / With liquid love" (322–23), a process that leaves the modern reader groping for Platonic parallels while thinking of Wallace Stevens' "kitchen cups" and "concupiscent curds."[21] The creature advances in the pride of its perfections, its "bosom swelled lightly with its full youth" (333), a phrase that inevitably catches us anticipating either more or less. It is provided with "two rapid wings" fit to bear it swiftly "to the seventh sphere" (337–38). They hang limp, however, throughout most of what follows, and we discover their real usefulness only when the Witch recalls the creature from its heavy slumbers to spread its splendid pinions and provide them with the necessary sails, an ingenious if undignified expedient. She summons it imperiously—"Hermaphroditus!"—with the grandeur of its full Latin appellation and orders it about peremptorily. "Sit here!" she directs it as they enter the boat, "And pointed to the prow, and took her seat / Beside the rudder, with opposing feet" (342–44). The precise instructions together with the click-clack of the rhyme alert us to the authority of a captain who will brook no nonsense from the crew.

It is, of course, the creature's strange passivity throughout the varied incidents of the Witch's journey that causes us the most wonder.

> And ever as she went, the Image lay
>   With folded wings and unawakened eyes;
> And o'er its gentle countenance did play
>   The busy dreams, as thick as summer flies,
> Chasing the rapid smiles that would not stay,
>   And drinking the warm tears, and the sweet sighs
> Inhaling, which, with busy murmur vain,
> They had aroused from that full heart and brain.   (361–68)

The stanza is a brilliant fusion of the beautiful and vapid. As the Witch sallies forth on her voyage, the Hermaphrodite lies oblivious to all sights and prospects, caught up in its own world of autonomous emotion, self-gratified and gently smiling. Tears follow smiles indiscriminately amid the tide of emotion suffusing "that full heart and brain." One is reminded of the little Spirit of the Earth lying asleep in his onrushing sphere in *Prometheus Unbound*, his lips "moving / Amid the changing light of their own smiles / Like one who talks of what he loves in dream" (IV.266–68). The Hermaphrodite is Shelley's invention for exploring the comic aspects of what was and remained a serious belief in the unlimited potentialities of imagination.

If the Witch is Shelley's symbol of the creative spirit of art, the Hermaphrodite is her creation and reflects her perfection. Yet it also reflects her isolation and indifference. As a complex image it reveals that Shelley, like Keats, had begun to see further into the limitations as well as the imaginative power of art. As a metaphor the Hermaphrodite bears comparison to Keats's urn in its neutrality and self-containment, forever inviolable, forever withholding conclusive response to the endless questions it arouses. The comparison is, perhaps, unduly somber, for in *The Witch of Atlas* Shelley largely reconciles himself to the fickleness and irresponsibility of his lovely patroness as well as to the impotence of her offspring. Gormless though it may be, Shelley's Hermaphrodite is at least harmless. In this sense Shelley's Witch and her creation are his playful reply to the darker view of the same paradoxes taken by Mary in *Franken-*

stein. One can no more reproach Shelley's Hermaphrodite than Words-worth's Johnny. On yet another level Shelley's poem is a metaphysical re-doing of "The Idiot Boy."

In *Alastor* and *Prometheus Unbound* Shelley had depicted boat jour-neys in quest of the sources of human consciousness and the origins of life. *The Witch of Atlas* is, by contrast, a journey poem without a goal or quest, a voyage of imagination determined entirely by the Witch's fancy, by her impulsiveness and "many quips and cranks" (453). Tended by "armies of . . . ministering Spirits" (459), she progresses through temples of cloud and solemn vistas, alternately weeping and laughing like her Hermaphro-dite but strangely uninvolved in all she perceives. Her voyage is in fact the purest expression in all English poetry of Friedrich von Schlegel's concep-tion of Romantic irony as "transcendental buffoonery," that union of the meditated and the involuntary, the transparent and the deeply hidden, the comic and the serious which reveals the artist totally engaged in his cre-ation yet at the same time detached from and transcending it, a conception of art that approximates pure play.[22] As she ascends swiftly and effortlessly in her boat, the waters burn beneath her, "Indignant and impetuous" (415), as if in protest at the speed of her inhuman passage. Descending the Nile, she pauses to survey the towers of columned cities and pyramids captured as if eternally in the calm but fragile reflection of her stream. Yet she is equally at home amid the Alexandrian luxuries of the delta where she is pleased to observe the floors of bridal chambers "Strewn with faint blooms" and "naked boys bridling tame Water snakes" (506–7)—the strenuous, exhausting phallic joys which Yeats was to view so differently in his two Byzantium poems. Her survey comprehends indifferently the sa-cred and the vulgar, the monumental and the transient, "the artifice of eternity" and "The fury and the mire of human veins."[23]

For all her independence and self-sufficiency the Witch loves to de-scend to earth and to employ her special powers to inspect human life. She is in fact an incurable voyeuse. She looks in on sleeping mortals in all their varied incongruity—on lovers linked in innocent slumber and sailors stacked in bunks like the dead "within their dreamless graves" (560). She sees with a divine clairvoyance into the secrets of each soul, the virtuous and the evil, the peasant and the priest; and she visits all impartially, "like a sexless bee / Tasting all blossoms and confined to none" (589–90). Nor is her activity confined to mere observation. She loves to "write strange dreams upon the brain" (617) of those she visits. To those she finds beauti-ful she imparts visions that make their sleep deeper and more gratifying. On those she deems "less beautiful" she inflicts perplexing fantasies that only make their "harsh and crooked purposes more vain" (618–19). Her power to invade sleeping souls she owes to a secret spell:

> she had a charm of strange device,
> Which murmured on mute lips with tender tone,
> Could make that Spirit mingle with her own.   (574–76)

The art she practices reminds one of the metempsychosis by which the fairy Mab levitates Ianthe's sleeping soul to accompany her on her visionary voyage of instruction. What in the earlier poem was a serious if questionable device of pedagogy here becomes a mere plaything of fancy. For there is no intent or method in the Witch's visitations. She is far closer to the fickle and inconstant elf of Mercutio's description than is the namesake of *Queen Mab*.

Not only does the Witch act by whimsy, but her interventions are never genuinely efficacious. She acts, for example, to protect those she approves, seeming able to cheat even death of its victim. Visiting the tomb by night, she unwinds the burial cerements as easily as "childhood's swaddling bands" (606) and celebrates the liberation of her favorite by throwing the coffin "with contempt into a ditch" (608). The comic rough handling of this bit of dispatch leaves one unprepared for the tonal change the next stanza introduces, a modulation as brilliant and astonishing as any in the poem:

> And there the body lay, age after age,
>   Mute, breathing, beating, warm and undecaying
> Like one asleep in a green hermitage
>   With gentle smiles about its eyelids playing
> And living in its dreams beyond the rage
>   Of death or life, while they were still arraying
> In liveries ever new, the rapid, blind
>   And fleeting generations of mankind.   (609–16)

One marvels at a mastery of tone that can create a sense of removal from the constant fluctuations of life at once so inviting and so eerie. The coffin remains in the ditch where the Witch has flung it, but the state of the emancipated spirit, more like an animated corpse, remains problematic. One can judge only from the heavy, constant breathing, the play of smiles upon the features, and the telltale flickering of the eyelids that accompanies the flow of dreams. If this is being finally out of nature, it resembles a living death. The Witch delivers her favorites from the dream of life only by immersing them within a reverie which, like art or the imagination, perpetuates itself eternally but without yielding any culminating recognition or transcendence. One thinks back through the smiles of the dreaming Hermaphrodite and the little Spirit of the Earth to the depiction of Ianthe just after Queen Mab has elevated her soul from her body:

> Upon the couch the body lay
> Wrapt in the depth of slumber:
> Its features were fixed and meaningless.
> Yet animal life was there,
> And every organ yet performed
> Its natural functions.   (I.139–44)

There are lurid overtones here but nothing like the breathing corpse's endless life in death. Nor can one confuse Mab's authority to enlighten with the freakish whimsies and magical half-measures of the Witch. To trace the evolution the passages suggest is to discover not the sudden emergence of a skeptical bias but the progressive definition of a complex of values present in Shelley's mind and sensibility virtually from the start. This development, which takes its form from Shelley's changing experience of life, he could articulate only through the gradual perfection of his craft.

The poem draws to its close with a triumphal outburst that constitutes its comic apocalypse. Shelley's playfulness is never more inspired than when he makes free with the Witch's powers to imagine the fulfillment of his deepest beliefs and wishes for mankind. Possessed by the Witch, the priests dream of making a recantation, of disowning their learned exegesis of hieroglyphics and confessing that the hawks, cats, and geese they make out to be gods are animals and nothing more. Not content with simply dethroning himself, the king sets up a chattering monkey in his place and then, in a hyperbolic gesture of self-mockery, directs his court to fawn and flatter in the customary way. Even the hardened soldiers at last fulfill the biblical prophecy, beating their swords into plowshares in a trance of rapt somnambulism. Lloyd Abbey rightly remarks that the stanzas envision the fulfillment of the aims of all of Shelley's serious poetry.[24] The human beings the Witch touches dream of acting out the true desires of their natures, of casting aside hypocrisy and deceit in response to their true inclinations as they would not dare in waking life. Yet it is just the tone of Shelley's comic fantasy that is so elusive. Does the fact that the Witch in a moment accomplishes with careless ease the ambitions of a lifetime strike us with amusement or despair? The renewal of honesty and goodwill she magically induces seems at once easy and artificial, so natural and yet so far from imaginable realization. The playful and saddening aspects of the scene are inseparably blended within a realization that juxtaposes idealism with self-parody, a complexity of response Romantic verse only rarely achieves and that critics have often described as Shelley's urbanity.

The tone is one, however, that Shelley does not sustain to the end. The final stanza and the abrupt, uncharacteristic conclusion it provides betray the poet's dissatisfaction with a vein of humor he no longer has the will or inclination to maintain.

> These were the pranks she played among the cities
> Of mortal men, and what she did to sprites
> And gods, entangling them in her sweet ditties
> To do her will, and shew their subtle slights,
> I will declare another time; for it is
> A tale more fit for the weird winter nights
> Than for these garish summer days, when we
> Scarcely believe much more than we can see. (665–72)

The special genius of the stanza, the way it pivots on "I will declare another time," lies in its note of menace, like the impatience of a father who decides he has sat long enough by the fire telling tales to the children. By suggesting a mood and an awareness quite beyond the prevailing tenor of the poem, the stanza unsettles in an instant the decorum the work has delicately preserved. It is as if at the last Shelley could not resist lifting up the flaps of the tent to let the common light invade the ring where his circus animals—his Witch and her Hermaphrodite, the nymphs and satyrs and all the rest—have been performing. In threatening to expose his Witch to the full glare of the modern consciousness, intimations of which leak in continuously along the seams of his poem, Shelley was threatening his enchantress, like Keats at the end of *Lamia*, with scrutiny he knew she could never endure. By doing so he was recognizing the force of Mary's criticisms as well as his own sense of the brevity and tenuousness of the spell his poetry could cast. The acerbity of his conclusion suggests that, until the arrival of a more congenial season, his style of ironic playfulness may represent the only possibility for poetic survival.

nine

LOVE'S UNIVERSE

Epipsychidion

In December 1820 Shelley was introduced by Claire and Mary to Teresa Viviani, a girl of nineteen confined by her aristocratic father and stepmother to a Pisan convent until a suitable bridegroom could be chosen for her. The plight of the "prisoner," beautiful, intelligent, and a youthful author, was bound to appeal to the knight-errantry of the poet who years earlier had rescued Harriet from the confines of her boarding school. The stage was set for one more dramatic outpouring and coalescence of sympathies. During a series of repeated visits to Teresa, Shelley found himself again strongly drawn in an emotional attraction. Like *Adonais*, the elegy to Keats which he composed later the same year, the poetical effusion he addressed to Teresa early in 1821 has much more to say about Shelley himself than about the subject or circumstances that provide the occasion for the poem.

Following Shelley's own characterization of the work as "an idealized history of my life and feelings" (*Letters*, II,434), some critics have read the poem as a chapter in the poet's spiritual autobiography. Others have insisted that it is really a treatise on poetry and the sources and processes of its creation.[1] The only reasonable view is that the poem is both, a work in which the emerging pattern of Shelley's life and the formulation of his verse are inextricably related. More specifically it is a revelation of the inveterate fatality dominating Shelley's life that is source of both his creativity and the particular character of his verse. It is a study in psychogenesis, an essay in the trials and difficulties of achieving poetic selfhood.

A deeply personal, indeed introverted work, the poem is, as critics have pointed out, in many respects a redoing of *Alastor*. Like the earlier poem, it continues the search for the poet's psychological or spiritual antitype, "this soul out of my soul" (238), the phrase in *Epipsychidion* that approximates the meaning of its title. Although it lacks the brilliant, disorienting originality of *Alastor*'s psychological insights, it possesses, for all its hectic, febrile quality, a greater self-awareness, a defensiveness revealed in its construction. If it springs directly from the intensity of Shelley's involvement with Teresa, it also moves through a series of progressive disengagements. The lines are not addressed to Teresa Viviani but to an "Unfortunate Lady, Emilia V——," or, more simply, the "Emily" of the poem. They are written, as we learn from the prefatory "Advertisement," by an unknown poet who has already died, somewhat ominously, while making preparations at Florence for the journey to "one of the wildest of the Sporades,"[2] a voyage imagined at the conclusion of the poem. The verses themselves, we are told at the very outset, are mere "votive wreaths of withered memory" (4), the tribute of a "rose" whose "petals pale / Are dead" (9–10).

The poem was published anonymously, at Shelley's request, and some time after its appearance in London he sought to have it suppressed. On few of his works has he commented in retrospect in terms so definitive and so estranging. When he sent the poem to Charles Ollier, his publisher, he wrote that it "should not be considered as my own; indeed, in a certain sense, it is a production of a portion of me already dead; and in this sense the advertisement is no fiction" (II,262–63). The following year he wrote John Gisborne: "The 'Epipsychidion' I cannot look at; the person whom it celebrates was a cloud instead of a Juno; and poor Ixion starts from the centaur that was the offspring of his own embrace." His words bring to mind his embracing his earlier soul sister, Elizabeth Hitchener, only to discover her a "brown demon."[3] "I think one is always in love with something or other," he went on to Gisborne. "The error, and I confess it is not easy for spirits cased in flesh and blood to avoid it, consists in seeking in a mortal image the likeness of what is perhaps eternal" (II,434).

The history of the poem's composition and Shelley's immediate and deepening alienation from it suggest a curiously compulsive experience. It is as if he had seen the error of his compelling emotional involvement almost from the start of his affair with Teresa and yet found himself unable to resist it. The poem appears to record a pattern of experience he was condemned by fate to reenact periodically throughout his career, a form of experience with no apparent catharsis short of death—the demise of the anonymous poet which the "Advertisement" of the poem reports. *Epipsychidion* is the record of a recurrent traumatic obsession, which reveals the workings of the poet's psyche and the demands of its creative energies. Once more we have a poem that demonstrates the inseparability of creativity and compulsion, of poetic vitality and spiritual disorder, a recognition for which the poem, like *Alastor*, ends by seeking justification and acceptance.

The first of the poem's three major formal divisions (1–189) is largely an invocation to Emily, a series of high lyrical flights in which Shelley repeatedly seeks to define both her and the nature of his attraction to her. The second part (190–387), his idealized autobiography, begins when Shelley gives over the attempt to characterize Emily directly and seeks rather to fix her within the enduring pattern of his life and feelings. The third (388–604) relates the author's imaginary voyage with Emily to the island paradise awaiting them in the Aegean. Each of the principal parts can be subdivided in various ways; more important is that the internal organization of the sections and their relationship to each other are throughout implicit rather than explicit. The logic of the sequence is tentative and exploratory rather than fixed. Indeed, one is led to wonder what the effect would be if the ordering of certain passages were altered or reversed, even to speculate if the poet—Shelley or the "Writer" cited in the "Advertisement"—was contemplating substantial changes, a speculation encouraged by the statement in the preface that "The present poem appears to have been intended by the Writer as the dedication to some longer one."[4] What we have is a work in which the trains of association connecting part with part are more than usually provisional and hypothetical but no less important, a work that makes exceptional demands on its readers.

The exordium begins on a high pitch, "as though the poem," as Harold Bloom writes, "had already been in progress for some length."[5] We proceed in a succession of brief verse paragraphs through a series of operatic leaps, each taking us higher into the empyrean: "Poor captive bird!" (5), "High, spirit-winged Heart!" (13), "Seraph of Heaven!" (21). The opening takes its cue from the poem's epigraph, a passage from Teresa's essay on love: "L'anima amante si slancia fuori del creato, e si crea nel infinito un Mondo tutto per essa, diverso assai da questo oscuro e pauroso baratro" (The loving soul launches beyond creation, and creates for itself in the infinite a world all its own, far different from this dark and terrifying gulf).[6] We err, however, if, like many critics, we attempt to conform the poem to the partly Petrarchan, partly Platonic idealism of Teresa's affirmation. The epigraph merely sets forth an initial premise against which the poem, as it continues, develops its own complex and ambivalent reaction.

There is from the first an evident strain as the poem proceeds from the image of Emily as the caged bird, shattered and stained with its own blood, to its ever more exorbitant claims for her:

> Sweet Benediction in the eternal Curse!
> Veiled Glory of this lampless Universe!
> Thou Moon beyond the clouds! Thou living Form
> Among the Dead! Thou Star above the Storm!
> Thou Wonder, and thou Beauty, and thou Terror! (25–29)

Emily evades the net of grand but empty abstractions the verse casts in its futile effort to contain her. In her sublimity she transcends the metaphoric power of the poetic imagination. Nor is it long before we are aware that we are witnessing a failure of the poetic process, a conclusion borne home by the verse itself: "Aye, even the dim words which obscure thee now / Flash, lightning-like, with unaccustomed glow" (33–34). The process of association, with its flow of epithets, is working at full intensity; but paradoxically it serves only to obscure Emily, not to reveal her. Recognizing the "mortality and wrong" (36) of his attempt, the poet can only appeal to Emily to redeem his poem with her favor—"Then smile on it" (40)—the familiar benison of the feminine smile essential to Shelley's verse.

The failure of the opening paragraphs of *Epipsychidion* raises an interesting problem in critical evaluation. To what degree are we justified in condemning the opening verses as unsatisfactory (a host of critical pejoratives offer themselves: "trite," "undisciplined," "vague," "effusive")? To what degree, on the other hand, is the failure to be seen as integral to the progress of the poem? *Epipsychidion* is highly uneven in quality. More than that, however, it is a work whose successful moments—its flights of sustained lyricism, its passages of epigrammatic wit—seem to arise directly out of failure and collapse. Like a number of Romantic works, it is a poem that can define its true direction only through a succession of false starts that involve disorder and uncertainty. Like much modern art, it is a work in which beauty and wonder are inseparable from boredom and horror. It makes special demands on our understanding and resourcefulness as readers. Whether we find the necessary patience to do justice to the work as a whole depends on whether we perceive that the poem's moments of lyrical intensity, its particular insights into the poetic psyche, could have been achieved (at least at this point in Shelley's career) in no other way.

Epipsychidion begins with the attempt to capture Emily and her significance for the poet through a series of abstract comparisons that derive their metaphoric power from the cosmos. We are not very far into the poem, however, before we begin to sense, if only indistinctly, a countermovement: "I never thought before my death to see / Youth's vision thus made perfect" (41–42). The phrase "Youth's vision" brings to mind the visionary maiden of *Alastor* and the quest for her which is really a process of inner investigation and discovery. The new countermovement is to find its full expression only with the rhapsodic flight of personal recollection of the second section. The point is, however, that the second, inner-directed movement is present from the outset and seeks to assert itself against the primary. For there are two major impulses that govern the work as a whole. One is centrifugal: the effort to externalize Emily, to see her as an influence governing nature and humankind, a power concentrated in the universe of sun, moon, and stars. The other is centripetal: the recognition that Emily and her power are constituents of the self. The first impulse attempts to project her, to discover her in the images and operations of the macrocosm. The second seeks to find her in the microcosm, the interior world of the self. The poem takes its initial momentum from the first impulse; it is, however, a momentum that cannot be maintained and that collapses. As it does so the second impulse begins to emerge and to provide a tension that polarizes the work and governs its development.

The identity of the narrator-poet now begins to grow in significance:

> Would we two had been twins of the same mother!
> Or, that the name my heart lent to another
> Could be a sister's bond for her and thee,
> Blending two beams of one eternity!   (45–48)

The problem is that of reconciling his love for Emily with his earlier emotional commitment to mother, sister, and spouse. The poet, of course, wants to see such names as interchangeable terms of a single relationship. Yet the verse goes on to acknowledge that this kind of interassimilation ("were one lawful and the other true" [49]) is neither permissible nor faithful to his experience. The verse paragraph concludes with an exclamation that conveys a shock of recognition: "How beyond refuge I am thine. Ah me! / I am not thine: I am a part of *thee*" (51–52). In his loss of self-possession, the poet feels altogether engrossed by Emily. Yet she remains a being whom he cannot identify except in terms of himself and those relationships that make up the most meaningful part of his past. Within the pattern of equivalences the verse has just offered, "I am a part of thee" is only another way of saying, "Thou art a part of me."

The recognition of the pull into the self prompts by way of reaction another outburst of centrifugal energy. Like the spiraling moth or the "dying swan who soars and sings" (54), the poet attempts one more flight into the empyrean with a series of new comparisons. "Art thou not," he asks,

> A Star
> Which moves not in the moving Heavens, alone?
> A smile amid dark frowns? a gentle tone
> Amid rude voices? a beloved light?
> A Solitude, a Refuge, a Delight?   (56,60–64)

The compiling of images recommences, the method employed in so much Romantic verse to start a flow of associations that will carry the verse forward to the coalescence of a theme or perception. Yet there is a new tone of doubt; the comparisons are phrased as questions, the interrogation mark has replaced the exclamation. Nor do the metaphors the verse heaps up lead anywhere except to a new collapse and a further realization of the poet's own limitation:

> I measure
> The world of fancies, seeking one like thee,
> And find—alas! mine own infirmity!   (69–71)

No sooner is this recognition voiced than the verse shifts its direction yet again. The beginning of the paragraph that follows, "She met me, Stranger, upon life's rough way" (72), is the closest anticipation yet of the ecstatic outburst that opens the second major section of the work: "There was a Being whom my spirit oft / Met" (190–91). It is as if, in the continuous war between the centrifugal and centripetal forces, the verse were struggling to break through a series of restraints to the recognition of its true object—the visionary maiden who haunts the recesses of the poet's interior consciousness. What kind of psychological resistance, one must wonder, accounts for a process of definition that can make its way only by overcoming repeated checks and diversions?

Already at the beginning of the new verse paragraph ("She met me, Stranger, upon life's rough way") Emily appears partly subsumed within a feminine archetype dominating the poet's psyche from his birth. The paragraph is particularly revealing because it contains the germ of primitive experience that is shortly to flower into the autobiographical recollections in the second section of the poem, rather like a leitmotif in Romantic music that appears before it is developed. Thus the verse describes the maiden and how

> from her lips, as from a hyacinth full
> Of honey-dew, a liquid murmur drops,
> Killing the sense with passion . . .   (83–85)

The lines are an unmistakable premonition of the later baleful "One" in the second section "whose voice was venomed melody" (256) and from whose "living cheeks and bosom flew / A killing air, which pierced like honey-dew" (261–62). These later lines depict a poisonous infatuation, which grows out of the earlier, more generalized attraction and the intensity that surrounds it. The central theme the paragraph expresses is the overwhelm-ing longing generated by a kind of primitive knowledge beyond the senses and almost beyond expression—"too deep / For the brief fathom-line of thought or sense" (89–90). Whereas the verse earlier sought to define the source of its attraction in terms of fixed abstractions, it now turns to the flowing, to shades "of light and motion" (94). The poet invokes the being he adores as a kind of power, an energy radiating from a single source,

> one intense
> Diffusion, one serene Omnipresence,
> Whose flowing outlines mingle in their flowing,
> Around her cheeks and utmost fingers glowing
> With the unintermitted blood, which there
> Quivers, (as in a fleece of snow-like air
> The crimson pulse of living morning quiver,)
> Continuously prolonged, and ending never,
> Till they are lost, and in that Beauty furled
> Which penetrates and clasps and fills the world.   (94–103)

The lines employ strongly erotic imagery to describe a feminine presence that is curiously vague and intangible, known or remembered by the power that radiates from her in endless reverberations. Perhaps the best gloss for the lines is the passage from Tennyson's "Tithonus" they in-spired, the description of the goddess of the dawn's diurnal revisitation to her mortal lover and of how, as her "cheek begins to redden through the gloom," he watches

> The lucid outline forming round thee; saw
> The dim curls kindle into sunny rings;
> Changed with thy mystic change, and felt my blood
> Glow with the glow that slowly crimsoned all
> Thy presence and thy portals.[7]

"Tithonus" is the most brilliant and moving of Tennyson's attempts to define the wellsprings of his own poetic temperament, and the imagery of its central section identifies it with Shelley's earlier endeavor. Like the presence Tithonus would arrest, the power is fleeting and unfixable, "Scarce visible" and sensed more by the "fragrance [that] seems to fall from her light dress, / And her loose hair" (104–6). As with the visionary maiden in *Alastor*, her beauty is experienced more as a sensation of past bliss, the recognition of a void that cannot be filled but which for that very reason inspires the keenest longing, "a wild odour [that] is felt, / Beyond the sense, like fiery dews that melt / Into the bosom of a frozen bud" (109–11). The power is frozen, dead, yet paradoxically susceptible to eternal renovation, a "motion which may change but cannot die" (114).

No sooner has the poet described the influence that haunts him as a "motion" than he seeks once again to reify it as "An image of some bright Eternity" (115), an effort that leads on to yet one more assemblage of multiplying metaphors for Emily:

> A shadow of some golden dream; a Splendour
> Leaving the third sphere pilotless; a tender
> Reflection of the eternal Moon of Love
> Under whose motions life's dull billows move;
> A Metaphor of Spring and Youth and Morning;
> A Vision like incarnate April . . .   (116–21)

The failure of the attempt is by now almost predictable, and with it the consequent disintegration into despair: "Ah, woe is me! / What have I dared? where am I lifted?" (123–24). One is struck by overtones of warning and prohibition.

In the effort to recover the forward momentum of his verse, the poet turns to reinvoke his inspiration yet again: "Spouse! Sister! Angel! Pilot of the Fate / Whose course has been so starless!" (130–31). The three quite different relationships through which he seeks to express the nature of his love are each incomplete, and illustrate once again his need to reconcile them with a more dominant feminine archetype fundamental to his experience. Hence the renewed outburst of failure and frustration:

>   O too late
> Beloved! O too soon adored, by me!
> For in the fields of immortality
> My spirit should at first have worshipped thine,
> A divine presence in a place divine;
> Or should have moved beside it on this earth,
> A shadow of that substance, from its birth;
> But not as now.   (131–38)

Had they met "in the fields of immortality," in the world of preexistence, he could have loved her entirely. But in the world of humankind, the terms "spouse," "sister," "guardian angel" point to distinct relationships that must be kept divided; and he is already married to another. Yet the fact remains that if he has loved Emily "too late," he has also loved her "too soon"—not simply too quickly but too early. For he realizes that, whether he has recognized her before or not, he has known her as a part of his first and earliest adoration, an aspect of that greater presence that still animates and drives his existence.

The tantalizing play of paradox and insinuation is suddenly broken by the portentous lines that introduce the next verse paragraph: "Thy wisdom speaks in me, and bids me dare / Beacon the rocks on which high hearts are wreckt" (147–48). The current of the poet's verse, for all its false starts and impediments, appears on the point of breaking through to some fresh clarification. What follows is a passage of verse written in a style precise, epigrammatic, fluent, which, although intimated earlier, is distinct from anything preceding it—a condensation in both the stylistic and the psychological sense:

> I never was attached to that great sect,
> Whose doctrine is, that each one should select
> Out of the crowd a mistress or a friend,
> And all the rest, though fair and wise, commend
> To cold oblivion, though it is in the code
> Of modern morals, and the beaten road
> Which those poor slaves with weary footsteps tread,
> Who travel to their home among the dead
> By the broad highway of the world, and so
> With one chained friend, perhaps a jealous foe,
> The dreariest and the longest journey go.   (149–59)

The lines are remembered by many readers, and known by heart by some, who have forgotten everything else in *Epipsychidion*, even the situation that occasioned them. The passage has always been described as Shelley's most forthright attack, at least in verse, upon the institution of marriage, his most fervent assertion of free love. However, the lines spring from a deeper, secret understanding. They convey a message that many find suspect, meretricious, even offensive, but one that Shelley represents in its most compelling light. It is a message writ large throughout Byron's poetry, which that poet was never able or willing to distill with such succinctness. It is the truth that no single woman can ever prove adequate to satisfy man's appetite for love or beauty (although it is wrong to define the principle along sexist lines). The limitlessness of human desire, the declaration of each individual's eternal birthright, the charter of his uniqueness and his independence constitutes equally his glory and his curse. For the very insatiability of longing that preserves the individuality of each being at the same time ensures its isolation, the realization that it will never meet its ideal mate or double of the Platonic fable, Yeats's "yolk and white of the one shell."[8] The journey remains the dreariest and the longest whether one undertakes it accompanied or alone.

Why are the two verse paragraphs that follow and conclude the first section of the poem, "sermons," as Bloom characterizes them,[9] less memorable and satisfying? They have been often taken as one of Shelley's major paeans to the universality of love and the imagination, seen as correlative powers, a Dantean hymn to the ennobling effect of human aspiration for what is divine.[10] Yet the two paragraphs seem forced and stilted after the declaration that precedes them. They struggle to dispel the darker implications of the central insight through a series of metaphysical paradoxes ("to divide is not to take away," "Each part exceeds the whole" [161,181]) that in their condensation and rapidity seem mere scholastic platitudes. Once again one detects a strong centrifugal impulse, as the verse struggles to objectify and mediate its understanding if not within the imagery of nature and the macrocosm then through the eternal philosophical principles behind them. The verse becomes more involuted, more hyperbolic in its transcendental claims, then suddenly gives way to the autobiographical rhapsody that commences the second section of the poem.

It is unfortunate that Shelley's own phrase, "an idealized history of my life and feelings,"[11] has been adopted as a description of the middle section of his poem. The word "idealized" in particular suggests a history ordered and set down as a pattern or a model. What we have in the narrator's account is rather the most revealing section of what Richard Holmes has called "the most nakedly autobiographical poem [Shelley] ever wrote,"[12] the record of a series of recurrent personal crises. The pattern of the history is "idealized" primarily because it is struggling to condense and define itself and to emerge into conscious recognition. Inevitably the events it recounts invite, indeed demand, elucidation in light of what we know of Shelley's own life and psychological history. To be sure, he writes in his "Advertisement" that "The present Poem, like the *Vita Nuova* of Dante, is sufficiently intelligible to a certain class of readers without a matter-of-fact history of the circumstances to which it relates."

Yet he goes on to add: "Not but that, *gran vergogna sarebbe a colui, che rimasse cosa sotto veste di figura, o di colore rettorico: e domandato non sapesse denudare le sue parole da cotal veste, in guisa che avessero verace intendimento*" (Great would be his shame who should rhyme anything under the garb of metaphor or rhetorical figure; and, being requested, could not strip his words of this dress so that they might have a true meaning).[13] The two statements, contradictory in their effect if not in their assertions, testify to the ambivalence that marks the work throughout, to a desire both to reveal and to conceal. Taken together the two statements constitute an invitation to read the narrator's account of his life history as a condensation of Shelley's own, a condensation, however, that reflects Shelley's effort to crystallize and comprehend it.

It has not been sufficiently observed that the autobiographical aura pervades the second section, albeit more suggestively than explicitly, from its very beginning:

> There was a Being whom my spirit oft
> Met on its visioned wanderings, far aloft,
> In the clear golden prime of my youth's dawn,
> Upon the fairy isles of sunny lawn,
> Amid the enchanted mountains, and the caves
> Of divine sleep, and on the air-like waves
> Of wonder-level dream, whose tremulous floor
> Paved her light steps;—on an imagined shore,
> Under the grey beak of some promontory
> She met me, robed in such exceeding glory,
> That I beheld her not. In solitudes
> Her voice came to me through the whispering woods,
> And from the fountains, and the odours deep
> Of flowers, which, like lips murmuring in their sleep
> Of the sweet kisses which had lulled them there,
> Breathed but of *her* to the enamoured air.   (190–205)

The lyrical exordium is in sharp contrast to the metaphysical conceits preceding it. With its harmonic flow and power the verse transports us to a range of sensibility we recognize at once as uniquely Shelley's. In a way that is by now familiar, the lines revive the fragmentary impressions of the child's expanding consciousness, a world pervaded by the imagery of sleep and dreams in which lips murmur and kisses lull, a "youth's dawn" presided over by the dominant feminine presence, the supreme expression of maternal love. The passage culminates in tribute to this earliest remembered influence, a being who

> Makes this cold common hell, our life, a doom
> As glorious as a fiery martyrdom;
> Her Spirit was the harmony of truth. (214–16)

The dramatic assertion seeks to snatch victory from defeat. For the fundamental truth the passage, like Wordsworth's "Intimations Ode," acknowledges is that the world of childhood rapture has forever faded. The feminine presence at its center has vanished, leaving only the memory of her being, a recollection more like a lack or thirst that never can be satisfied and that drives the quester ever onward.

Like the Poet in *Alastor*, the autobiographical narrator in *Epipsychidion* seeks to reunite himself with the spirit who has withdrawn from him, abandoning him to the needs and longings she has aroused:

> And as a man with mighty loss dismayed,
> I would have followed, though the grave between
> Yawned like a gulph. (229–31)

The rift between them, however, is too great to overcome, and with the failure comes the sense of separation and change intimated in "And as a man." The phrase marks the first and only appearance of the principal male noun within the poem. It is as if the experience of loss the passage records were definitive, the initiation into adulthood, the mark of one's humanity, perhaps even the crucial determinant of the male ego or identity.

The reassuring voice that whispers, "O thou of hearts the weakest, / The phantom is beside thee whom thou seekest" (232–33) provides the motive for the quest related in the remainder of the section. However, the brief exchange that ensues, "Then I—'where?'—the world's echo answered 'where!' " (234), unmistakably recalls the story of Echo and Narcissus: "dixerat: 'ecquis adest?' et 'adest' responderat Echo" ("He asked, 'Is anyone here?' and 'Here!' cried Echo back.")[14] The voice seems a mere repetition of the quester's own. Moreover, though he now begins his search to discover "Whither 'twas fled, this soul out of my soul" (238), the presence he seeks seems irrecoverably lost:

> neither prayer nor verse could dissipate
> The night which closed on her; nor uncreate
> That world within this Chaos, mine and me,
> Of which she was the veiled Divinity,
> The world I say of thoughts that worshipped her. (241–45)

The lines expose a paradox central to the poem. The "veiled Divinity" may have vanished, but she remains crucial to the identity of her lover. Thus he insists on distinguishing between two parts of himself, a dark and engulfing "Chaos" that is "mine," and a central core of being, an immutable "me," formed and indelibly marked by her spirit.[15] The division reflects an idealization that involves splitting of the ego into separate parts, one pure and harmonious, reflecting only her, the other evil and demonic and subject to the malign influences of the world.[16] The idealization is essentially the same as that in "On Love," Shelley's earlier, fragmentary essay, which provides a valuable gloss for *Epipsychidion*. "We dimly see within our intellectual nature," Shelley had written, "a miniature as it were of our entire self, yet deprived of all that we condemn or despise, the ideal prototype of every thing excellent or lovely that we are capable of conceiving as belonging to the nature of man." This interior ideal, this "soul within our soul," now provides the model to which "we eagerly refer all sensations, thirsting that they should resemble or correspond with it," while life becomes the quest for the "discovery of its antitype."[17] The description epitomizes the process of idealization by which the narrator is driven, following his loss, to wander through "the wintry forest of our life" seeking amid its various apparitions "one form resembling hers" (249,254).

Understanding this idealization is crucial to interpreting the autobiographical reminiscences that follow, passages that from at least the time of Newman Ivey White have been recognized as the most astonishing and revealing of Shelley's self-disclosures in verse. As Richard Holmes has written, "The shadows of Elizabeth Shelley, Harriet Grove, Harriet Westbrook, Elizabeth Hitchener, Cornelia Boinville, Sophia Stacey and perhaps others all fit along the margins of the verse."[18] Yet the problem, intimated from the start in the poem's "Advertisement," has been how to interpret the apparent allusions to the most intimate and important relationships in Shelley's life. Even before the major autobiographical revelation—the thinly veiled allegory of his changing ties with Mary, Claire, and others—we have the problem of interpreting the narrator's initiatory liaison with "One, whose voice was venomed melody" (256), a malignant and withering attraction:

> The breath of her false mouth was like faint flowers,
> Her touch was as electric poison,—flame
> Out of her looks into my vitals came,
> And from her living cheeks and bosom flew
> A killing air, which pierced like honey-dew
> Into the core of my green heart. (258–63)

Following Thornton Hunt's report of an indiscretion Shelley committed at Oxford, a number of scholars have accepted the notion that the passage refers to the poet's having contracted venereal disease from a prostitute while at university.[19] Whether the lines refer directly to an encounter during which Shelley became infected will never, in all probability, be proved. Yet the narrower reading obscures the deeper truth the passage conveys. For the imagery of mouth and touch, of melody and perfume, connects the mysterious beguiler with the larger prototype of the dream maiden who emerges at the outset of the second section. The enchantress of the later lines diverges from this primary model as her dark and evil antithesis. If the splitting of the ego leads to the projection of its idealized half in the form of the visionary dream maiden, it leads also to the personification of its other half as her wicked and deceiving opposite.[20]

Shelley throughout his life consistently tended to imagine women in terms of these extremes. He went on, moreover, to visualize his life and his career within governing relationships he constructed in imagination, which led to his conceiving those close to him in terms of the moral abstractions—either good or evil—he projected onto them. It is in this more exact sense that *Epipsychidion* is indeed, as he called it, "an idealized history of my life and feelings." The deeper truth the poem reveals is the difficulty of maintaining these abstract divisions, the fact that the changing pressures of life inevitably wrenched and ultimately collapsed the system of imaginative relations seemingly so essential to the preservation of his identity. As one system split up, another had to be created to replace it. As a personal history *Epipsychidion* reveals the psychological cost of creating these idealized relationships, the difficulty of maintaining them, and the extraordinary pain of their disintegration.

The introductory episode involving the dark lady leads directly to the autobiographical passage. The narrator recounts how he long wandered in search of some faithful embodiment of his ideal, until at last

> One stood on my path who seemed
> As like the glorious shape which I had dreamed,
> As is the Moon, whose changes ever run
> Into themselves, to the eternal Sun;
> The cold chaste Moon, the Queen of Heaven's bright isles,
> Who makes all beautiful on which she smiles,
> That wandering shrine of soft yet icy flame
> Which ever is transformed, yet still the same,
> And warms not but illumines. (277–85)

Long ago, Newman Ivey White, drawing together the conjectures of earlier commentators, conclusively showed that the passage must be taken as Shelley's most revealing if problematic analysis of his relationship with Mary. Kenneth Cameron, who went on to correct and elaborate details of White's discussion, especially in the "planet-tempest passage," showed that Mary herself recognized and accepted her identification with the moon and was, moreover, hurt by it, how deeply one can only guess.[21] *Epipsychidion* is the one long poem of her husband's on which she vouchsafed no comment in her edition of 1839, and there is little difficulty in guessing why. Although she makes all she smiles on beautiful, the "cold chaste Moon" is a wan and fading power, casting a "soft yet icy flame" that "warms not but illumines." The passage seems to suggest that for all the beauty of her presence, for all the calm and intellectual power she exercised over Shelley's life, Mary failed to provide the human warmth and sympathy the poet required.

These implications reemerge as the narrator goes on to depict his strange passivity beneath the moon's commanding influence:

> And I was laid asleep, spirit and limb,
> And all my being became bright or dim
> As the Moon's image in a summer sea,
> According as she smiled or frowned on me;
> And there I lay, within a chaste cold bed:
> Alas, I then was nor alive nor dead.   (295–300)

The lines return us to the mood of *Alastor* and its account of the Poet's dependency. Indeed, the passage directly recalls some of Shelley's phrasing and imagery in a letter to Mary in autumn, 1814, a letter that serves as an important gloss on the earlier poem: "Your thoughts alone can waken mine to energy. My mind without yours is dead & cold as the dark midnight river when the moon is down. It seems as if you alone could shield me from impurity & vice. If I were absent from you long I should shudder with horror at myself" (I,414). In the letter Shelley's idealization of Mary is less qualified and more rapturous, his apparent subjection more willing. Yet both his letter and the passage from *Epipsychidion* reflect the same ambivalence. If one part of him delights in glorifying Mary as the presiding influence of his life, another part struggles against the enervation that idealization demands.

The impression that, on the point of celebrating Emilia as the newly discovered Sun of his existence, Shelley was drawn back in recollection to his earliest years with Mary is confirmed in the way the trancelike sleep beneath the moon is broken by the apparition of

> twin babes, a sister and a brother,
> The wandering hopes of one abandoned mother,
> And through the cavern without wings they flew,
> And cried "Away, he is not of our crew."
> I wept, and though it be a dream, I weep.   (303–7)

As Cameron has argued, it is impossible not to connect the two babes, "a sister and a brother," with Shelley's children by Harriet, Ianthe and Charles.[22] "Abandoned mother," moreover, puts Harriet's case more simply and directly than Shelley anywhere else confessed. The overtones of guilt are even more evident in the exclamation of rejection and reproach the children utter in their flight: "Away, he is not of our crew." The words suggest the realization of Shelley's deepest fears: that they would be not simply taken from him but turned in sympathy against him. The final line and its implicit rebuttal of some of these accusations as illusory and baseless—"I wept, and though it be a dream, I weep"—reveals how deeply traumatic the experience had been and continued to be.

What follows is the celebrated "planet-tempest" passage, at once the most difficult and most potentially revealing part of Shelley's own idealized autobiography:

> What storms then shook the ocean of my sleep,
> Blotting that Moon, whose pale and waning lips
> Then shrank as in the sickness of eclipse;—
> And how my soul was as a lampless sea,
> And who was then its Tempest; and when She,
> The Planet of that hour, was quenched, what frost
> Crept o'er those waters, 'till from coast to coast
> The moving billows of my being fell
> Into a death of ice, immoveable;—
> And then—what earthquakes made it gape and split,
> The white Moon smiling all the while on it,
> These words conceal:—If not, each word would be
> The key of staunchless tears. Weep not for me!   (308–20)

It is clear that under the figure of "The Planet of that hour" Shelley is writing of the intensely painful circumstances of Harriet's suicide in November 1816. The passage reflects the manner of her death by drowning and catches the wintry quality of the Serpentine which Shelley afterward visited, a scene he recalled in one of the rare places in his poetry that allude to the tragedy:

> The cold earth slept below,
>   Above the cold sky shone;
> And all around, with a chilling sound,
>   From caves of ice and fields of snow,
>   The breath of night like death did flow
>   Beneath the sinking moon.[23]

Under the shock of this event and its emotional "storms" the moon is enveloped by sickness and obscurity, while the tempest rages above the prostrate soul which lies like a helpless sea beneath it. Here once again Cameron helps elucidate the biographical nature of the crisis with his convincing argument that the tempest should be identified with Eliza Westbrook, Harriet's sister, whom Shelley first accepted as his wife's companion and trusted advisor, then came to loathe as his worst enemy.[24] In Shelley's eyes, Eliza increasingly became Harriet's dark counterpart or double, a dichotomy that permitted him to blame her for the destruction of his marriage and the loss of his children while preserving Harriet's innocence to the very end.

As important as the autobiographical keys for reading and interpreting Shelley's spiritual allegory is the deeper psychological reality that underlies the scene. The moon is thrown into eclipse by the cosmic upheaval, leaving the soul "a lampless sea." The event may indeed reveal some kind of frigidity, some failure of sympathy on Mary's part. Yet as the moon continues to smile down patiently, she seems, with "pale and waning lips," to survey with horror a convulsion she has not herself brought about but is rather caught up in, obscured by, and helpless to resist. The fiction that the soul of the narrator is merely passive, that he takes his character and motivation from the planetary forces that surround him, conceals the realization that he provides the center of their orbit and that they take their value and identity from him. Undoubtedly the most striking images describe the freezing of the soul-waters as the tempest passes over them, then the way they "gape and split" under the pressures contorting the ice. What we witness is the counterpart of that original splitting of the ego in the act of idealization, that is to say the waning and collapse of idealizations under pressures too great to withstand. The shock of Harriet's suicide and the tide of guilt and accusation it occasioned exceeded Shelley's efforts to justify or rationalize. Indeed, they came to cast a dark and blighting shadow over Mary, the bright Moon in that ideal firmament he projected about him. Yet the passage ends with the partly defiant "Weep not for me," as if, even in the face of the disasters he has just depicted, the narrator must end by reasserting that "me," that idealized part of himself to which he must remain faithful.

Why was Shelley drawn to recollect some of his most painful experiences with Harriet and Mary on the very point of celebrating his new attraction for Emily? No sooner has the autobiographical passage and its veiled summation of past failure and disappointment run its course than the narrator suddenly hails the new and glorious apparition that breaks upon him in his despondency:

> At length, into the obscure Forest came
> The Vision I had sought through grief and shame.
> . . . . .
> Soft as an Incarnation of the Sun,
> When light is changed to love, this glorious One
> Floated into the cavern where I lay.
> . . . . .
> I knew it was the Vision veiled from me
> So many years—that it was Emily. (321–22,335–37,343–44)

Yet the adoption of Emily as the Sun is hardly simple, for it requires yet one more reconstruction of the narrator's subjective cosmos and its network of personal relationships. Thus Mary will remain to play an important, if perhaps subordinate, role, so that there will now be "Twin Spheres of light who rule this passive Earth, / This world of love, this *me*" (345–46). Once again there is the fiction of the narrator's passivity. With superb male egoism he surrenders himself up to the domination of their influence within a planetary system he himself has created, which is in fact the projection of "this *me*," the ideal and idealizing part of the self. Even Claire, whose intimate involvement with Shelley was so distressing and unsettling to her stepsister, Mary, is to be reintegrated within the harmony of the new planetary configuration.

> Thou too, O Comet beautiful and fierce,
> Who drew the heart of this frail Universe
> Towards thine own; till, wreckt in that convulsion,
> Alternating attraction and repulsion,
> Thine went astray and that was rent in twain;
> Oh, float into our azure heaven again! (368–73)

It is no matter that Claire brings to light the peculiar instability of Shelley's past attachments, that "Alternating attraction and repulsion" in which adulation could pass so rapidly into rejection. It is no matter that she brings with her the recollection of yet another past "convulsion" that has left the universe containing her and the idealizing ego "rent in twain," broken down into its contradictory constituents. Despite such vestiges of past destruction, Shelley, or his narrative alter ego, can turn to Emily to beg her to lend herself to one more attempt at idealization, to pass over "whatsoe'er of dull mortality / Is mine" (389–90) in favor of his true, abiding image of himself:

> To the intense, the deep, the imperishable,
> *Not mine but me,* henceforth be thou united
> Even as a bride, delighting and delighted.   (391–93; my emphasis)

Indeed he asks all the women in his life to cooperate in bringing about this reconstellation of his imaginative desires and energies.

In its curious mixture of revelation and disguise, of apology and confession, *Epipsychidion* adumbrates the enduring fatalism of Shelley's career as poet. It brings almost to conscious recognition the pattern of repeated effort and failure that underlies both the poetry and the life. It reflects the poet's struggle to project and objectify within the macrocosm of the outer world those values dearest to the self in symbols and personifications that, under the pressure of reality, were forever collapsing back into the microcosm of the ego from which they originated. The poem demonstrates the difficulty, if not the impossibility, of reconciling the microcosm and the macrocosm, art and life. Yet the poem at the same time represents this desire as the ineradicable impulse of the true poetic soul; and it concludes by seeking understanding, tolerance, and even praise for the recurrent failure it brings to light.

The third major movement of the poem commences with the imaginary depiction of the lovers' union and flight: "The day is come, and thou wilt fly with me" (388). The pull of the verse is inexorable, reinforced by the emblems of a commanding necessity. "The hour is come:—the destined Star has risen" (394). The walls confining Emily are high but not sufficient to restrain true love. "A ship is floating in the harbour now" (408), and all the winds and portents are propitious. It is striking, as White has pointed out, that no sooner has Shelley imagined the reunification of his psychological and spiritual existence beneath the mutual sway of Emily, Mary, and Claire, a goal intimated from the poem's opening lines, than every trace of this design should vanish in the all-engrossing desire for union with Emily alone.[25] It is as if the power of the new attraction, like that of the star for the moth, overwhelmed every other remembrance or consideration. Mary drops from the poem until the concluding lines of the envoi, while every hope for the fulfillment of happiness is concentrated in

Emily. For the third movement of the poem takes the form of an elopement, the withdrawal of the lovers to a lone Aegean island, "Beautiful as a wreck of Paradise" (423), which still reflects the harmony of a lost golden age and where the two are to consummate their union.

Like Asia's journey in *Prometheus Unbound*, the voyage is a regression backward to the sources of life, toward the recovery of a lost wholeness of primitive experience. Few poets have evoked the regressive impulse so powerfully as Shelley, as echoes in the poetry of a later age, from Tennyson's "Lotos-Eaters" to the concluding stanzas of Arnold's "Scholar-Gipsy," testify. The island among the Aegean is inhabited by a few survivors of an earlier pastoral time, "Simple and spirited; innocent and bold" (429). The air is laden with the scent of flowers; strains of music "fall upon the eye-lids like faint sleep" (449). The tidal undulation rhythmically blends the various sense impressions synesthetically into one apprehension of an underlying source where

> every motion, odour, beam, and tone,
> With that deep music is in unison:
> Which is a soul within the soul—they seem
> Like echoes of an antenatal dream.   (453–56)

Veil after veil of imagery falls away as the verse draws ever closer to the center of all sensory experience, the animating soul, the counterpart of the narrator's own,

> a Soul no less [which]
> Burns in the heart of this delicious isle,
> An atom of th' Eternal.   (477–79)

If Emily is the projection of the narrator's "me," that ideal part of himself, it is clear that the Edenic setting both harmonizes with and reflects the perfection of their love. As Wasserman has written, "the union of the lovers with [the island] is of the same order as their union with each other. For the island is but the 'internal' conceived of as 'external,' just as Emily is the finite self projected as perfect and infinite."[26] There is no longer any division between macrocosm and microcosm; the two have been conflated.

The lovers will inhabit "a lone dwelling," the architectural "marvel of the wilderness" (483–84), which he has stocked with books and music for their pleasure. Yet their imaginary existence together recognizes no division between culture and nature.[27] Built no one knows "by whom or how"

(484), the structure ready for their habitation seems to have taken its form within the heart of the earth, "then grown / Out of the mountains, from the living stone" (495–96). Its decoration, "all the antique and learned imagery" (498) that once adorned it, has long since been replaced by ivy and wild vines. The substitution of art by nature is significant: a later form of development is replaced by one more primitive. So parasite flowers with their "dewy gems" (502) take the place of lamps to illuminate the halls. The dilapidations the building has suffered through the years have only rendered its galleries more airy and open to the lights of night or day, which provide a natural and ever-changing pattern of mosaic decoration. So perfectly is the building integrated with its setting that there seems no distinction between interior and exterior, the domestic and the out-of-doors. The view from the high terraces is of an all-subsuming harmony and dreamlike interassimilation, in which

> Earth and Ocean seem
> To sleep in one another's arms, and dream
> Of waves, flowers, clouds, woods, rocks, and all that we
> Read in their smiles, and call reality.   (509–12)

Here the two lovers will dwell, like the ancient king and builder with his sister-spouse before them, where minutes are measured by the pant of sleeping deer and years by the silent accumulation of leaves, until their existence together merges inseparably with all that surrounds them:

> Let us become the over-hanging day,
> The living soul of this Elysian isle,
> Conscious, inseparable, one.   (538–40)

They will become both the circumference and the vital center of the heavenly canopy enfolding them, united with each other and with all else (for "conscious" here means chiefly "thinking and feeling as one").

The scene represents the most extended and intense effort of imagination in Shelley's poetry to characterize that unity with the ideal of his own soul for which he longed. Yet the attempt is hardly unique. One is reminded of the harmony of the kingdom where Laon and Cythna are drawn into their incestuous relationship at the opening of the second canto of *The Revolt of Islam*. As in the earlier poem, the first destabilizing movement originates with the sexual impulse. Overtones of the erotic are present everywhere within the landscape, in the "lightest winds [which] touch their paramour," the island, or the shore which "Trembles and sparkles as with ecstacy" beneath "the quick, faint kisses of the sea" (545,547–48). Like Laon and Cythna before them, the two lovers are led to the embrasure of a cavern, throughout Shelley's verse the customary setting for consummation. Quiet words proceed to looks and looks to kisses while the rapture of their embrace leads on irresistibly to culminate in sexual orgasm:

> Our breath shall intermix, our bosoms bound,
> And our veins beat together; and our lips
> With other eloquence than words, eclipse
> The soul that burns between them, and the wells
> Which boil under our being's inmost cells,
> The fountains of our deepest life, shall be
> Confused in passion's golden purity.   (565–71)

The desire for complete union can consummate itself in no other way than through sexual fulfillment. Yet the rapture ends in the distressing recognition of division: "We shall become the same, we shall be one / Spirit within two frames, oh! wherefore two?" (573–74). The ecstasy of their imaginary union concludes in the recognition of a fundamental division. It is as if the struggle to achieve identity (in the sense of "sameness," "oneness") led only to a fuller realization of identity as "personal or individual existence." The ambivalence of the concept suggests the impossibility of its achievement:

> One passion in twin-hearts, which grows and grew,
> 'Till like two meteors of expanding flame,
> Those spheres instinct with it become the same,
> Touch, mingle, are transfigured; ever still
> Burning, yet ever inconsumable.   (575–79)

The planetary imagery here specifically recalls the scene at the culmination of the first canto of *The Revolt of Islam* in which two lights roll forward on the floor of the Temple of the Spirit, ascending "Like meteors" and "commingling into one, / One clear and mighty planet" (625,627–28) to reveal the majestic, bisexual figure who takes its seat beneath it.[28] The figure emerges from the sphere, however, only to preside over the appearance of Laon and Cythna and the account of their separation, adventures, and reunion after death.

The larger prospect of repeated divisions and higher reintegrations progressing steadily toward an ever-nearer ideal of human perfection advanced in *The Revolt* is implicitly rejected in *Epipsychidion* in the quest for total union. All else gives way to the burning desire to merge totally with the ideal:

> One hope within two wills, one will beneath
> Two overshadowing minds, one life, one death,
> One Heaven, one Hell, one immortality,
> And one annihilation. Woe is me!   (584–87)

The more relentlessly "one" struggles to assert itself over "two," the more apparent it makes the underlying division.[29] The effort to compound two bodies, minds, and wills as one ends not in unification but annihilation. The current of the verse sinks back into the recognition of rhetorical failure and the limitations of its medium:

> The winged words on which my soul would pierce
> Into the height of love's rare Universe,
> Are chains of lead around its flight of fire.—
> I pant, I sink, I tremble, I expire!   (588–91)

The fact is that language, even the symbolic language of verse, depends ultimately on nature, and can only approach those idealizations conceived within the self. At the same time the perpetuation of the sexual metaphor in the final line, the last in the poem proper, suggests that ecstasy can be achieved only at the cost of ultimate dissemination and collapse. As Wasserman has written, "the poem closes with the same desperate and ecstatic confusion" we have noted from the beginning.[30] The rhetorical breakdown is symptomatic of the poem's alternating construction and deconstruction.

How is one to account for the analysis of recurrent failure in a love poem dedicated to Teresa Viviani, a failure that in various ways casts such a long shadow over Shelley's relationship with Mary? For if his attraction for Teresa, however intense and ecstatic, was virtually dead from the start of composition—actually more a catalyst for a deeper range of personal concerns—Mary was still a vital part of his existence. *Epipsychidion* is a hymn to love, an autobiography, a manifesto, a confession, an apology, a kind of prophecy, and, last, a prayer or entreaty. Above all it is the anatomy of a compulsion central to the poet's life and art. Unless we see the poem as all of these, we miss some element essential to its composition. The best clue we have for interrelating such different functions lies in the thirteen lines of irregularly rhymed verse Shelley appended by way of an envoi.

The envoi has often been passed over without comment. When considered at all, its burden has usually been summarized in one aphorism: love's "reward is in the world divine / Which, if not here, it builds beyond the grave" (597–98). Ideal love can find its perfect consummation only in the world to come, not in this.[31] Yet one wonders if such a summation is adequate to the psychological depth and complexity of the completed work. Not surprisingly, Shelley begins his envoi by returning once more to the theme of his governing compulsion, bidding his verses kneel in farewell at their mistress's feet to reaffirm both her rule and their triumph over the poet: "We are the masters of thy slave" (593). Yet the ending of the envoi is less predictable, as Shelley goes on to ask the verses to intercede for him with "Marina, Vanna, Primus" and to appeal to them to "love each other" and to "leave the troop which errs, and which reproves, / And come and be my guest,—for I am Love's" (603–4). What is this Dantesque company of partly allegorized initiates? Why are they entreated to love each other, and what and why are they asked to cease reproving?

At the very end of his poem, Shelley turns to Mary (Marina) and to Jane and Edward Williams, shortly to become two of his closest friends. The Williamses, living together as husband and wife though actually unmarried, were to join the Shelleys in occupying Villa Magni, the forlorn little house on the Italian coast at Lerici in the summer of 1822, when Shelley's life came to an end. Jane (Gio*vanna*) was to become the last of Shelley's passionate attachments, to whom he wrote his greatest love lyrics. Edward (Primus) was the inseparable companion of his last days, who drowned with him when their boat foundered during a squall in the gulf of La Spezia in July. It is curious to find a poem that lays bare the troubled history of Shelley's past idealizations ending with an appeal to Mary to take her place with the Williamses in what was ultimately to become one more constellation of idealized relationships. It is disconcerting to find prefigured a situation in which Shelley was to become deeply involved with Jane while at the same time pleading loyalty both to Edward and to his wife.[32]

In writing *Epipsychidion* Shelley laid to rest a brief but extraordinary episode of his life. Yet the work represents a very imperfect catharsis. At a deeper level the poem is the revelation of an enduring compulsion too strong to be checked or moderated, a desire that overrides all testimony and reasoning against it. In the words of the envoi, "Love's very pain is sweet" (596). It suited Shelley, in writing his apology, to adopt the high style of Dante in *La Vita Nuova*. Yet the enduring life the poem reveals is neither new nor, in Dante's sense, transformed. If the work is a manifesto, it is less metaphysical, less a Platonic testament of beauty than the admission of personal and psychological necessity. By invoking with remarkable clairvoyance the sympathy of Jane and Edward Williams, the figures who, along with Mary, were destined to play the principal roles in the next and last act in the idealized drama of his life, he was really entreating under-standing and forgiveness. At the end of his remarkable self-revelation, he was soliciting the pardon of those few who could truly understand him; he was asking for the acceptance of a part of himself that could never change.

ten

TRAGIC IRONY

The Triumph of Life

Shelley's last great poem, *The Triumph of Life*, was left uncompleted when he drowned in the bay of Spezia on 8 July 1822. Earlier in the year, at the end of April, the Shelleys had moved with Edward and Jane Williams into Villa Magni, a small, isolated house situated directly on the sea amid the rugged beauty of the Italian coast near San Terenzo. Claire joined them there early in June. Mary hated the lonely, forlorn setting from the start. Shelley was improved in health and spirits and perhaps as happy as at any time in his life, delighting in a situation approximating the "wreck of Paradise" he had imagined at the end of *Epipsychidion*. By day he enjoyed the companionship of Williams on boating expeditions. In the evening he cast his spell over Jane, who sang the love lyrics he composed for her, accompanying herself on the guitar. Despite this outward calm, however, Shelley was troubled in imagination. Not long before the fatal voyage to Livorno to greet Leigh Hunt, newly arrived in Italy from England, Mary was awakened in the night by Shelley's screams. He had had a vision of Edward and Jane covered with blood and shouting, "Get up, Shelley, the sea is flooding the house & it is all coming down." He then had another vision of his own figure in the act of strangling Mary, so that he rushed into her bedroom to reassure himself; her jumping out of bed awakened him. On another occasion, he reported that while walking on the terrace at Villa Magni he had met his own figure, who inquired of him, "How long do you mean to be content?" Even Jane acquired the infection. She recounted that, while standing by a window, she had seen Shelley follow himself across the terrace, when in fact he was far off at the time.[1]

This doubling had a long history in Shelley's life. Whatever their reality in fact or in Shelley's imagination, the assailant who knocked him senseless by his cottage door at Keswick, the famous Tanyrallt intruder who fired at him, the English officer who knocked him down and stunned him while collecting his mail in Italy are too much a part of the Shelley legend to be dismissed as meaningless fantasy.[2] Nor can they be attributed simply to Shelley's obvious persecution complex. Occurring at times of emotional crisis or nervous tension, such manifestations are reflections of internal conflict, the rebellion of one part of his psyche against another. They dramatize the increasing strain of the division between his bright, idealizing impulses and his recognition of the darker reality of human instability, impermanence, and death.

Against this background of idyllic beauty and contentment and underlying perturbation Shelley composed one of the greatest Romantic fragments. The work has long been taken to mark a new stylistic departure. T. S. Eliot, who thought it Shelley's greatest poem, found in it, significantly, "traces of a struggle toward unification of sensibility," "a precision of image . . . and an economy that is new."[3] Shelley's handling of the terza rima measure shows a mixture of strength and delicacy, of sensuous intensity and ironic withdrawal, a combination that brings to his verse a new, intriguing subtlety. This tone, at once so striking and elusive, greets one from the outset of the induction, which describes the morning sunrise and places the narrator within the newly revealed landscape, the background for his coming vision. The thirteen stanzas that make up this prologue constitute one of the most remarkable passages in all of Shelley's verse, the evidence of a new stylistic level of achievement. It should be added that the stanzas contain the germ of significance for the entire fragment, so that the visions that follow and their allegorical enactments only elaborate a meaning that is implicit from the start.

The opening is remarkable in its vigor:

> Swift as a spirit hastening to his task
>   Of glory and of good, the Sun sprang forth
> Rejoicing in his splendour . . .   (1-3)

The rush of alliterative *s* sounds hurries us forward even while the emphatically balanced *g*'s of "glory and of good" and the counterpoint of verbal adjectives, "hastening," "rejoicing," provide a center of stability. The opening powerfully recalls the most majestic of all the Psalms declaring the glory of God's handiwork:

> In them hath he set a tabernacle for the sun, Which is as a bridegroom coming out of his chamber, and rejoiceth as a strong man to run a race.   (*Psalms* 19:4-5)

The triumphant upsurge of exultation at the birth of the new day is carried forward in such strong verbs as "fell," "flamed," "arose," until it is checked for the first time by a curiously muted note:

> and at the birth
>
> Of light, the Ocean's orison arose
>   To which the birds tempered their matin lay.   (6–8)

The odd word "temper" (a verb so important in the visionary narrative that follows), used here in the sense of "qualify" or "mitigate," provides the first suggestion that the joy of the reawakened world that seems so full and spontaneous is actually conditioned by circumstances we can as yet only dimly imagine.

The note of ambivalence, so subtly introduced, recurs as a kind of solemn undersong to the joyful chorus of creation:

> All flowers in field or forest which unclose
>
>   Their trembling eyelids to the kiss of day,
> Swinging their censers in the element,
>   With orient incense lit by the new ray
>
> Burned slow and inconsumably, and sent
>   Their odorous sighs up to the smiling air.   (9–14)

The delightful anthropomorphism of the first conceit, in which flowers are likened to infants awakened to the light by the kisses of the maternal day, is checked by the heavier liturgical overtones already introduced by "orison" and "matin." From natural propagation the flowers suddenly change to ritual objects in a ceremony in which all are compelled to participate, censers set alight by the sun and burning slowly toward extinction. The figure reminds one, ominously, of the metaphor of burning that runs throughout *Alastor* and the implacable logic of its energy-time equation. Nor is it easy to decide whether the sighs sent up like prayers are to be taken as a Te Deum or an expression of universal tedium.[4]

The opening of Shelley's induction to *The Triumph of Life* can be considered an extended play on the word "burden," taking the word first in the sense of a lifting up of the voice, a chorus or refrain, and then in the more common sense of load, labor, or oppression. The life and death impulses are exquisitely balanced in a divided consciousness that pervades and dominates the entire poem. The darker implications emerge like shadows so gradually from the chorus of praise that arises with the first break of light over the world that they are at first all but imperceptible. Yet it is not long before they are borne home:

> And in succession due, did Continent,
>
>> Isle, Ocean, and all things that in them wear
> The form and character of mortal mould
>> Rise as the Sun their father rose, to bear
>
> Their portion of the toil which he of old
>> Took as his own and then imposed on them. (15–20)

The gravity of rhythm and diction and the convoluted yet rigorously logical syntax together convey an inexorability that contrasts sharply with the primal joy and spontaneity of the opening verses. The sun is no longer a young man, a son, but rather a "father" who cannot save his children but can only reimpose the burden of toil he has inherited on them in a series of unending transferrals. The splendor and expectation of the daybreak lead to a reaffirmation of the habitual and recurrent.

Against this background of divided consciousness, arising at first purely through the natural creation, we become aware of the presence of the narrator and his strange apartness. While the world about him has slept, he has been kept wakeful by mysterious "thoughts which must remain untold" (21) beneath the multitude of stars the sun has now obscured. While the night flees before him, he lies extended on the ground with his back to the onrushing day, as if preparing for sleep when all around him has just awakened to the light. The isolation of his position is emphasized by his proximity to the hoary trunk of an old chestnut, in whose decaying roots he is to recognize, in an instant of vestigial reconstruction, the features of the dead philosopher Rousseau, shortly to become his interlocutor and guide. We seem poised on the threshold of one more poem written in the familiar tradition of dream-vision. Yet the narrator assures us his state of mind is more like a trance than slumber because it proceeds from a sense of déjà vu, the conviction that he has already sat on the same slope of lawn and known the dawn with its awakening birds, fountains, and ocean and felt the same cold dew, like a baptism, on his brow and hair.

The poetic figure that conveys this sense of remembrance, at once so intense and so obscure, is perhaps the most difficult extended metaphor in the entire poem:

> a strange trance over my fancy grew
> Which was not slumber, for the shade it spread
>
> Was so transparent that the scene came through
>   As clear as when a veil of light is drawn
> O'er evening hills they glimmer.   (29–33)

The passage is more intelligible if we repunctuate its last two lines: "As clear as, when a veil of light is drawn / O'er evening hills, they glimmer." *The Triumph of Life* is dominated by the imagery of shades and shadows darkening the objects of perception. Here, however, the shade that falls over the narrator's vision highlights rather than obscures the scene, in the same way that the dying light of sunset can sometimes briefly illuminate a fading landscape to recall the radiance of dawn. The flight of time and with it the perpetual erosion of vision, together with the persistence of something deeply buried and enduring in imagination, are contradictory impressions that Shelley's induction subtly combines. In their alternation the two convictions determine the figuration and significance of the vision that follows.

Following the prologue, the narrative is divided into three principal sections. First we have the narrator's waking vision of the triumphal pageant of the car of life and its multitude of victims (41–175). At his dismayed exclamation, "And what is this?" (177), Rousseau abruptly makes himself known from the root of the old chestnut and proceeds in the second part (176–300) to comment on the desolating spectacle and on some of its chief historical participants. The third section (300–543), a kind of retrospect, consists of Rousseau's description of the earliest of his recollections, his romance with the mysterious "shape all light" (352)—an apparition overwhelmed by the deafening music of the same savage pageant the narrator has just depicted and into which, Rousseau relates, he himself has already been drawn. His autobiographical reflection takes us to the point where the fragment breaks off, with the narrator's final—and tantalizingly unanswered—question, "Then, what is Life?" (544).[5]

Two metaphors dominate and unify the allegory of these narratives. The first is the conquering chariot, which appears initially in the narrator's vision and then in Rousseau's, and the dusky "Shape" (87) crouching within, above the host of prisoners drawn in the car's train. The second metaphor is the "shape all light" (352) that remains at the center of Rousseau's memories of his origins. Now these two figures, while not identical, are nevertheless corollary. They are aspects of that doubling that had become a growing phenomenon of Shelley's awareness. They portray a single continuous progression, but from different perspectives, the one from its inception, the other from its end. In *The Triumph* Shelley was seeking to articulate his answer to two questions that had long preoccupied his imagination. What is the origin of that power that animates all existence, the energy that propels all life and that we recognize most immediately as joy and desire? Second, where does it conduct man, and what is its ultimate resolution or end? The two principal metaphors and the logic of their interrelationship within the design of Shelley's allegory provide the clues for understanding his answers to these great questions which had come increasingly to weigh upon his spirit.

Recent criticism of *The Triumph* has partly sensed the intimate connection between the two principal figures, both female, of Shelley's allegory.[6] The "shape all light" that appears to Rousseau in his dream of reawakening burns with an intense incandescence, but it is a brilliance that is already fading even as she appears before him:

> "the fierce splendour
> Fell from her as she moved under the mass
> Of the deep cavern." (359–61)

At the time the spectacle of the onrushing chariot of life is about to burst upon Rousseau's vision, the figure of the "shape all light" is already dissolving:

> "And the fair shape waned in the coming light
> As veil by veil the silent splendour drops
> From Lucifer, amid the chrysolite
>
> Of sunrise." (412–15)

She fades away to a kind of shimmering, a faint beam that "Glimmers, forever sought, forever lost" (431), a presence vaguely sensed beside him on his path. Now the "Shape" the narrator perceives in his vision of the triumphal car of life is the end product of this process of dissolution. She sits

> as one whom years deform
> Beneath a dusky hood and double cape
> Crouching within the shadow of a tomb,
> And o'er what seemed the head a cloud like crape

> Was bent, a dun and faint etherial gloom
> Tempering the light. (88–93)

While the car itself irradiates a cold, icy glare, she sits within, bent and deformed by age, the center of a light that is so muffled and obscured by the heavy coverings that enshroud her as to be more like gloom or shadow than genuine illumination. If the "shape all light" of Rousseau's earlier vision is associated with birth, spring, renewal, and the radiance of a "light diviner than the common Sun" (338), the shape that dominates his vision of the conquering car is linked to age, disfiguration, obscurity, decomposition, and the ultimate extinction of the grave. The latter shape is simply the spent and diminished replica of the other.

The progression from one figure to the other provides the fragment with its central structure and significance. Several related metaphors control the development of the poem. One is of burning and irradiation and, as an inevitable result, waning and dissolution. The other is encrusting, blurring, and adulteration—a process of distortion that refracts light ultimately to its opposite, deceiving shadow. Intimately related, the two metaphors share a long history in Shelley's work and thought. In *The Defence of Poetry*, for example, he had likened great poetry to "a burning atom of inextinguishable thought," a brightness, however, whose source of inspiration "is already on the decline" from its inception. He had written, too, of the power of poetry to "strip the veil of familiarity from the world," even while speculating whether some veil of language or meter were necessary to temper such splendor for human senses.[7] In *The Triumph* the imagery of waning and veiling, formerly subordinate to the great affirmative metaphors for poetry and its operation, now emerge as primary and subversive. From its beginning life involves us inexorably in progressive diminutions and distortions. Angela Leighton has perceptively distinguished between life and living, between life as origin and life as process: "Life is something which is lost even while it is lived. Punningly, origin and process converge in the same word . . . the one is always a loss of the other."[8] To recall the great figure Shelley had invented in *Adonais* to describe everything Keats had escaped, it is "the contagion of the world's slow stain" (356) that now emerges as triumphant and obliterating. As the logic of the "Intimations Ode" after all suggests, human experience is defined not so much by the wonder of birth and illumination as by the inescapable darkening of impulse and perception.

One can argue, of course, that Shelley's perception of the splendor of the ideal remains in *The Triumph* as intense as ever. It is just that the

splendor is so transient and impermanent. Rousseau describes to the narrator how he once awakened in the April dawn beneath a cavern in a
mountain, alongside a gentle rivulet that flowed from it. As Donald
Reiman has suggested, the archetypal features of the landscape unmistakably depict the birth of human consciousness and the ties that connect it to
the world beyond, "the realm without a name" (396), the sources of its
being which it can intuit but never comprehend.[9] So sweet and lulling is
the stream that the recollection of its melody annihilates "All pleasure and
all pain, all hate and love" (319), the habitual contraries of man's experience, together with the pangs of desire itself. It is significant that Rousseau, in describing so great a state of tranquillity, should declare that

> "A sleeping mother then would dream not of
>
>   The only child who died upon her breast
> At eventide." (321–23)

For the contentment he describes is like the sleep of the newborn infant by
the side of its mother, a repose "The thought of which no other sleep will
quell / Nor other music blot from memory" (329–30). In a poem so much
concerned with obliterations of memory, the lines seem to define a sub-
stratum of recollection that defies annihilation.

From the first the scene is characterized by strong effects of synesthesia, of many sounds and motions gradually "woven into one / Oblivious melody, confusing sense" (340–41). The experience of sensuous con-
vergence and unification together with the curious sense of confusion and
loss are significant. As David Quint has argued, the lines prefigure the
development of the child from a preconscious state toward adult consciousness, a reading that accords with the events that follow as Rousseau
describes them.[10] Thus the "shape all light," the symbolic figure that most
nearly comprehends the whole complex process Rousseau recounts, now
emerges from the reflection of the sun as it blazes in its first brilliance on
the surface of a forest well. From the outset the shape is, as Reiman has
observed, a reflected figure, an image of a power too overwhelming or
intense to be observed directly. She is the figuration of what cannot be
fully figured to the senses or the intelligence, a metaphor that only approximates the reality it represents. She "fling[s] / Dew on the earth, as if she
were the Dawn" (352–53), a figure whose simile implies the onset of loss
and deterioration and suggests deception. Already she is accompanied by
Iris with "her many coloured scarf" (357), the rainbow, which, for all that

Wordsworth's heart might leap to behold it, was for Shelley the symbol of the diffusion of light into its constituent colors and the loss of original purity. The "fierce splendour" (359) that surrounds the Shape as she moves is, as Tilottama Rajan observes, "curiously similar" to the bright, withering light of the triumphal car of the narrator's earlier vision.[11]

It would be wrong to overemphasize the subtly darker overtones that qualify the grace and beauty of the Shape's appearance. She seems to arise from the synesthetic coalescence of the play of winds and waves and shadows like one of Botticelli's allegorical figures, a deity to preside over and symbolize their harmony. So delicately does she move upon the surface of the stream that her feet and trailing hair scarcely unsettle the reflection, the surface of illusion. She ascends from the idyllic setting, a figure answering to the mind's need to personify a loveliness and splendor it can conceive in no other way. She is the archetype of Shelley's dream women, the shape within the "mirror whose surface reflects only the forms of purity and brightness: a soul within our soul,"[12] the type, as Leslie Brisman writes, of "all the psychidions of his poems and others'."[13] She is also the inspiration of the poet's verse, his muse. As she progresses, her feet move to the measure of one "sweet tune" (382), a figure that, as Paul de Man has observed, invites us to think of "feet" in the sense of meter, rhythm, scansion, and all the other organizing forms of verse.[14] At the same time, however, she is too bright and dazzling to look at, and her very feet, as Rousseau watches them,

>   "blot
> The thoughts of him who gazed on them, and soon
>
> All that was seemed as if it had been not,
>   As if the gazer's mind was strewn beneath
> Her feet like embers, and she, thought by thought,
>
>   Trampled its fires into the dust of death."   (383–88)

In his great metaphor in *The Defence of Poetry* Shelley had earlier compared the mind in creation to "a fading coal which some invisible influence, like an inconstant wind, awakens to transitory brightness,"[15] a gleam already fading even while the artist struggles to capture and objectify it in one of the arts. In *The Triumph* the whole task of representation comes to seem hopeless. The "shape all light" actively tramples out the very thoughts she inspires. She transfigures with delight and at the same time vitiates all attempts to fix or to conceptualize her presence. Like a deeply buried dream, so lifelike and engrossing, she remains, though fading, a haunting influence throughout the remainder of the dreamer's life, one that resists every effort to draw it upward into consciousness.

It is no wonder Rousseau is moved to ask the Shape the great but simple and inevitable questions, irresistible to humankind: "Shew whence I came, and where I am, and why" (398). Nevertheless, the questions are self-betraying because they reveal the growth of self-awareness, the self-preoccupation that, as *Alastor* had shown, is ultimately destructive. Moreover, the interrogations are ones for which, as Demogorgon had declared, no answers can be given. Indeed, the way Rousseau poses his queries, "as one between desire and shame / Suspended" (394–95), lines that reveal to what effect Shelley could assimilate the subtlety of Dante's style, suggests the impropriety of his asking. In response the Shape holds out to him her cup of bright Nepenthe: " 'Arise and quench thy thirst' " (400).

There has been an extraordinary difference of critical opinion about Rousseau's drinking of the draught. Some critics condemn him for temerity in aspiring to the sources of divine illumination. For others, like Harold Bloom, the Shape is the parody of such an ideal and actually a deceiving "type of Rahab, the New Testament Great Whore embodied in the natural world."[16] Yet there is no point in condemning her as malicious or seductive for undertaking to satisfy Rousseau's desire, any more than there is in condemning him when, like Keats's dreamer who drinks the transforming elixir in the garden near the outset of *The Fall of Hyperion*, he seeks to assuage his thirst. Both actions are part of a larger fatality that defines the individual's initiation into the common world of human experience. Hence the subtle play of implication in the simile that describes Rousseau at the crucial moment when he rises to drink:

> And as a shut lily, stricken by the wand
>   Of dewy morning's vital alchemy,
>
> I rose.   (401–3)

The image of the stricken lily creates at first the impression of some deleterious enchantment. As the simile unfolds, however, like the flower it describes, we see that the magic practiced is only the natural alchemy of the spring and of the morning as they cause the flower to open to the sun. As in the opening tercets of the induction, the natural and the artificial, the healthy and the baleful, the spontaneous and the ominous are inextricably combined.

The draught Rousseau drinks is no deceiving potion but simply a distillation too potent for his human senses. Paradoxically, its power destroys the knowledge it conveys, transforming his brain to "sand" (405) and accelerating the dissolution of the scene before him. As the first vision fades, the second, the procession of the triumphal car, breaks upon his senses. Yet the "shape all light," although waning to a glimmer, does not disappear entirely to his consciousness. She remains with him, "The ghost of a forgotten form of sleep" (428), a being sensed more through absence than actual presence, a dreamlike shape "forever sought, forever lost" (431) beside him on his way.

The Triumph of Life: the irony of Shelley's title is striking. Behind the title stands, of course, the convention of the Roman triumph, the ceremonial reentry into Rome by the conquering emperor in his car, surrounded by captives and the spoils of victory, a ritual commemorated throughout the poetry and painting of the Renaissance. In Shelley's *Triumph*, Life the conqueror prevails over himself. His victory is the triumph of actualization over potential, of life as process over life as inception. His conquest represents the defeat of hopeful instinct, the corruption of virtuous impulse, the decline and degeneration of life's vital energies to a shadowy procession of forms that mock and disfigure the light from which they once proceeded. The vision is more a life in death, a *danse macabre,* than a pageant of the living. Because it directly follows the fading of the "shape all light" in Rousseau's narration, the new vision of the onrushing car and its procession appears as the direct result of the earlier episode. It follows from the constellation of the "shape all light" out of the harmonious rush of interwoven waves and music in Rousseau's imagination, from his longing to approach and question her, and from his thirst for the draught of knowledge she holds out in answer to his queries. The progression represents the growth of self-consciousness out of self-obliviousness, of identity and ego out of immersion in the undifferentiated flow of universal existence, of desire and intellectual ambition out of contentment and repose. The stunning speed with which the second vision bursts upon the first dramatizes through violent temporal compression Shelley's sense of the inevitability of the cycle into which humans are by nature born and reborn.

As in Wordsworth's "Intimations Ode," the logic of Rousseau's first episode, his rapture with the enchanting shape, is elucidated through images of light that supervene upon and occlude one another. The same kind of metaphoric progression occurs in Rousseau's and the narrator's descriptions of the triumphal car and its procession. As the car breaks upon Rousseau's sight, Iris, spreading her triumphal arch of the rainbow directly overhead, " 'forbade / Shadow to fall from leaf or stone' " (444–45), as at high noon or the midpoint of life. When the car climbs the slope before it, however, the grove where Rousseau remains

> "Grew dense with shadows to its inmost covers,
>   The earth was grey with phantoms . . .

> thus were

> Phantoms diffused around, and some did fling
>   Shadows of shadows, yet unlike themselves,
> Behind them."   (481–82,486–89)

Amid the gathering dusk, vague forms like elves and apes disport themselves with capes and tiaras and other emblems of worldly power in a monstrous parody of human existence. Rousseau follows with his eyes the disappearance of "the car's creative ray"(533), a phrase that is resoundingly ironic. Like the sun at the poem's outset, the light of the car strips the veil of darkness from the eyes of those it awakens only to leave them weltering in deforming shadows when it vanishes.

The same logic of metaphor pervades the development of the narrator's earlier vision of the car and its triumphal progress. The "maniac dance" (110) that greets the car's arrival changes to a desperate race to keep up with its departing light. The dancing celebrants cast lengthening shadows that are terrifying portents. As the car advances, the old are ruthlessly abandoned:

> Behind,
> Old men, and women foully disarrayed
>   Shake their grey hair in the insulting wind,

> Limp in the dance and strain with limbs decayed
>   To reach the car of light which leaves them still
> Farther behind and deeper in the shade.   (164–69)

More fortunate, perhaps, are the young who, caught up in the frantic ecstasy and "Convulsed" (144) with pleasure, consume each other in the destructive intensity of sexual delight. As in *Alastor*, the choice is between burning swiftly and brightly, or smoldering dully to the socket. All alike must burn.

The metaphor of burning, which is inseparable from that of light and shadow, is equally central to the poem. In an important pronouncement Rousseau declares to the narrator:

> "if the spark with which Heaven lit my spirit
>   Earth had with purer nutriment supplied
>
> Corruption would not now thus much inherit
>   Of what was once Rousseau—nor this disguise
> Stained that within which still disdains to wear it." (201–5)

All men are set alight with the fire of desire or ambition, the flame of which Rousseau boasts, or confesses, he himself has transmitted to others. However, some alloy within the stuff of human nature prevents the flame from burning purely, so that it gutters and darkens from impurities.

The metaphor of burning and exhaustion is specially important because it determines our attitude toward the broad historical perspective the poem projects through the procession of the car and its prisoners. Rousseau identifies some of the principal captives to the narrator. Critics have often interpreted the vision of the rout of prisoners as reproachful: "Chained hoary anarchs, demagogue and sage" (237)—Voltaire, Frederick the Great, Immanuel Kant, Catherine of Russia, Emperor Leopold II, Aristotle, Alexander, and the rest. However, the kind of condemnation the poem invites is far from simple, for the group includes

> "The Wise
>
> The great, the unforgotten: they who wore
>   Mitres and helms and crowns, or wreathes of light,
> Signs of thought's empire over thought." (208–11)

These historical figures are embodiments of vital energies that have been perverted or diverted from their proper course. Even the noblest of them, Plato, was led astray at the last by his infatuation for his favorite, the youth Aster. Nor would the narrator's glimpse of the fallen Napoleon hold him spellbound in awe and pathos did he not sense so keenly the lost possibilities of greatness, a wealth of talent and ambition misdirected and betrayed. Even spiritual visionaries like "Gregory and John and men divine" have arisen only to end as "shadows between Man and god" (288–89), obscuring the true light they would clarify and define. Similarly, the great poets of antiquity, those "who inly quelled / The passions which they sung," transmit a "living melody" that "Tempers its own contagion to the vein / Of those who are infected with it" (274–78). The flow of passionate feeling which the poets of old controlled within the ruling order of their lives seduces and corrupts the modern auditor incapable of similar self-mastery and discipline. The prospect Rousseau reveals to his pupil is a long history of human aspiration and endeavor that, time after time, has been tempered and stained by some taint of human nature, vitiated by "the mutiny within" (213), by a fatal susceptibility or intractability. The prospect of the universality of perverted aims is so desolating that it causes the narrator to wonder why

>   power and will
> In opposition rule our mortal day—
>
>   And why God made irreconcilable
>   Good and the means of good.   (228–31)

With those thoughts, as Reiman has observed, he comes around toward the dark view propounded by the last Fury in the first act of *Prometheus*, who torments the hero with the vision of a world of "all best things . . . confused to ill" (I.628).[17] Nor is the pessimism of the scene alleviated, as has been argued,[18] by those missing from the procession, "they of Athens and Jerusalem" (134)—Socrates, Christ, and their followers. These few who "could not tame / Their spirits to the Conqueror," who flee back "like eagles to their native noon" (128–29,131), represent no practicable course for dealing with life's evils but only dramatize through their revulsion the hopelessness they perceive. For the great generality of humankind there is no escaping the destructive vortex created by the juggernaut of life in its triumphal passage.

The larger fatalism of the poem brings us ultimately to the paradox that the narrator's guide is incapable of saving himself; he has himself been swept up into the disfiguring procession. Why, one must ask, did Shelley choose Rousseau as his narrator's mentor and why, among the historical figures in the poem, does he command such prominence? The question assumes added importance in view of Bloom's recent rereading of *The Triumph* within the context of his theory of poetic influence and posteriority, a reading in which he argues that Rousseau is a surrogate for Shelley's older Romantic contemporaries, Coleridge and specially Wordsworth. "Rousseau," Bloom declares in a judgment that seems remarkably wrongheaded, "might just as well be named Wordsworth or Coleridge in the poem, except that Shelley was too tactful and urbane to thus utilize those who were still, technically speaking, alive."[19]

There is little doubt that *The Triumph*, like so much of Shelley's other work, looks back to Wordsworth and in particular to the "Intimations Ode" as a major source of inspiration. At the same time it would be wrong to imagine that his choice of Rousseau was fortuitous or that the latter is merely the mouthpiece for an older and defeated generation of English poets. Vanquished though he may be, it is precisely Rousseau's invincibility of spirit that gives him his commanding position in Shelley's drama and justifies Shelley's choice of the great dreamer, lover, writer, and prophet. For Shelley's reading of Rousseau, above all *Julie, ou La Nouvelle Héloïse*, had taught him what we have come increasingly to recognize today—Rousseau's preeminence as the supreme exponent of European Romanticism. Rousseau above all emerges as the high priest of desire and aspiration, the life force that, for better or for worse, animates Shelley's *Triumph* and accounts for its peculiar fatalism. "All baser things pant with life's sacred thirst," as the poet had written in *Adonais* (169), a desire from which humans cannot hope to escape. This truth was writ large throughout Rousseau's work and in his life. It was a truth Shelley had keenly felt while avidly touring Meillerie and many of the scenes associated with *Julie* in company with Byron in the summer of 1816, scenes that Shelley was reliving in imagination while at work upon *The Triumph*.[20] The trip had inspired Byron's memorable portrait of Rousseau as "wretched," "blasted," yet still the supreme proponent

> of ideal Beauty, which became
>   In him existence, and o'erflowing teems
> Along his burning page, distempered though it seems.[21]

"Rousseau," Shelley declared at the end of the trip, "is indeed in my mind the greatest man the world has produced since Milton."[22]

The key to Rousseau's character and role in Shelley's poem is the anomaly of his position, as one unable to resist the lure of the degrading spectacle yet who remains up to the last unrepentant, even defiant. He declares that he is "one of those who have created, even / If it be but a world of agony" (294–95). In view of the depth of suffering from which it springs, the utterance strikes one as a strange sort of boast. Yet such unyieldingness most characterizes Rousseau throughout the poem. Pointing out all those whom life has conquered, he distinguishes himself from the rest with a pride that borders on arrogance:

> "I was overcome
> By my own heart alone, which neither age
>
>   Nor tears nor infamy nor now the tomb
> Could temper to its object."   (240–43)

The assertion has been taken to mean several things.[23] It seems most clearly, however, to advance the claim that whereas others channeled their best energies into particular goals or objects that ultimately failed them,

Rousseau alone remained loyal to the heart itself, to its irrepressible springs of longing—that is, to the principle of the insatiability of human desire.

Hence although Rousseau admits that perhaps he "had well forborne" (189) to join the dance, he never actually urges the narrator to do so. Indeed, the most moving and rhetorically compelling part of his narration comes when he describes the manner in which he at last has been drawn into life's tumult:

> "I among the multitude
> Was swept; me sweetest flowers delayed not long,
>   Me not the shadow nor the solitude,
>
> Me not the falling stream's Lethean song,
>   Me, not the phantom of that early form
> Which moved upon its motion,—but among
>
>   The thickest billows of the living storm
> I plunged, and bared my bosom to the clime
>   Of that cold light, whose airs too soon deform.—"
>
> (460–68)

"I plunged": the prolonged succession of inverted constructions is broken by the active verb which rings out with a desperate but triumphant authority that is, ironically, the poem's challenge to the vision of the triumph of life the conqueror. Better to create, even if creation is doomed to betray and mock its author. Better to remain faithful to the heart and its impulses, even if they draw one toward perdition. For the course of human destiny is in any case inevitable. One thinks of the words in Shelley's minute hand that Reiman has tentatively recovered from the last leaf of the manuscript of *The Triumph*: "Alas I kiss you Julie."[24] If the textual reconstruction is correct, the words refer to the moment in the *Nouvelle Héloïse* when Saint-Preux receives the fatal kiss from Julie in the grove at Clarens, the incident that is in many ways the determining moment in Saint-Preux's life and in the structure of Rousseau's novel. As Reiman has gone on to argue, the episode corresponds to the moment in *The Triumph* when Rousseau drinks from the glittering elixir held out to him by the "shape all light."[25] That moment is the prologue to his perception of the onrushing car of life and his immersion in its violent and exhausting procession. However, Shelley's Rousseau remains, despite the evidence of his violation, to vaunt rather than deplore the truth of his experience. What he blazons forth is the inalienable testimony of his own humanity. Like one of Yeats's old scarecrows, he emerges weirdly from the tree's shrunken root to defy life even from the depths of his desolation with an energy of self-assertion that has little in common with Wordsworth. He remains one of the most remarkable images in Romantic poetry.

As Lloyd Abbey among others has argued, *The Triumph of Life* plumbs the depth of Shelley's mature skepticism.[26] This quality is nowhere better illustrated than in the condensed and hauntingly memorable judgment Rousseau delivers to his pupil, of life as a "false and fragile glass":

> "Figures ever new
> Rise on the bubble, paint them how you may;
>   We have but thrown, as those before us threw,
>
> Our shadows on it as it past away." (247–51)

We can give significance to life only by casting on it the shadow of our own configuration. The shapes we perceive are the reflection of our own and, as the sphere whirls forward, are endlessly obliterated and replaced by a multitude of others. Like the greater image of the chariot of life, the metaphor seems a sad parody of Shelley's earlier symbol for life as infinite potentiality—the revolving sphere that conveys the sleeping Spirit of the Earth in the last act of *Prometheus* (IV.236ff). In a different way the metaphor of the glass also recalls Plato's allegory of the cave, a figure forever intriguing to Shelley, which he redacted in different forms throughout his career.

It is not surprising that many critics have viewed the poem as a palinode to the poet's earlier work and its Promethean power of affirmation, the expression of the final triumph of the death impulses over those of life. Trailing off into sketches of sailboats on its final leaf, the manuscript of the work has even been taken as an elaborate suicide note, the rationalization for the death the poet foresaw with such extraordinary clairvoyance in the last stanza of *Adonais*—the death, it has been argued, he actively cooperated with the elements to achieve when the *Don Juan* sank on the afternoon of July 8.[27] Certainly it is difficult to imagine how he would have continued the poem or proceeded to answer the question the narrator poses with his last words: "Then, what is Life?" (544). Rousseau's answer, the concluding words in the draft, breaks off with "Happy those for whom the fold / Of" . . . (547–48). For Reiman the words suggest that Shelley was moving toward the image of the sheepfold and Hesperus, the evening or folding star associated with the nightly gathering of the flock, as affirmative symbols of human salvation.[28] One can only say that, within its context, the passage rather seems, as Miriam Allott has brilliantly suggested, a first step toward a restatement of the lines Yeats rendered from the Greek in "From Oedipus at Colonus" as:

> Never to have lived is best, ancient writers say;
> Never to have drawn the breath of life, never
> To have looked into the eye of day . . .²⁹

Before committing oneself to viewing the fragment as the expression of a final and despairing pessimism, one would do well to recollect how protractedly optimism and hopelessness, affirmation and negation struggle throughout Shelley's verse. As with Blake, the one state evokes the other. More than that, each intensifies, indeed validates the other. The one is virtually inconceivable without its opposite. Even in *The Triumph*, where, one might argue, the skeptical background is darkest, Rousseau's example of defiance in the face of the fate that overwhelms him takes on such power precisely because the forces that have borne him forward seem so irresistible. In poem after poem, Shelley returns to some version of the inveterate conflict between the entrenched powers of good and evil, each equally unconquerable. The true resourcefulness of his poetry lies in its adaptation of occasion, its formal and stylistic innovation, to provide a multitude of changing insights, from the comic to the tragic, on the essential human situation.

In *The Triumph* Shelley depicts the fading of the vision of the "shape all light" into the devastating glare of common day, a daylight shading into growing darkness. Life and its processes involve us in a world of shadows that progressively refract and obscure the true light of our origins. Yet the impression of our first romance, our first encounter with that spirit of transcendent brightness, is ineradicable. Even while the Shape fades for Rousseau, he senses it forevermore beside him, a "presence" that

> "Although unseen is felt by one who hopes
>
>   That his day's path may end as he began it
> In that star's smile." (417–19)

Throughout his career Shelley struggled against the forces of cynicism and oppression, forces he associated with the brutality of a false ideal of masculinity. Throughout his career he was animated and sustained by something even more powerful because more primitive: the kindling smile of love whose power irradiates his earliest experience. He expressed his sense of that power in the penultimate stanza of *Adonais*:

> That Light whose smile kindles the Universe,
> That Beauty in which all things work and move,
> That Benediction which the eclipsing Curse
> Of birth can quench not, that sustaining Love
> Which through the web of being blindly wove
> By man and beast and earth and air and sea,
> Burns bright or dim.   (478–84)

Shelley imbibed the power of that smile from the earliest days of his infancy and childhood. It was invisibly and intricately woven into the very essence of his being. The light of the smile irradiates the whole of his poetry and burns more brightly for the forces of darkness opposing it. It is impossible that anything could have extinguished it short of death.

NOTES · INDEX

ABBREVIATIONS

Letters	*The Letters of Percy Bysshe Shelley,* ed. Frederick L. Jones, 2 vols. (Oxford: Clarendon Press, 1964)
MLQ	*Modern Language Quarterly*
Reiman and Powers	*Shelley's Poetry and Prose,* ed. Donald H. Reiman and Sharon B. Powers (New York: Norton, 1977)
RES	*Review of English Studies*
WC	*The Wordsworth Circle*

NOTES

1. *Queen Mab*

1. Carlos Baker, *Shelley's Major Poetry: The Fabric of a Vision* (Princeton: Princeton University Press, 1948), p. 29.
2. The intellectual sources of the poem have been discussed at length by Kenneth N. Cameron in *The Young Shelley: Genesis of a Radical* (New York: Macmillan, 1950), pp. 239–74, and by Desmond King-Hele in *Shelley: His Thought and Work,* 3rd ed. (London: Macmillan, 1984), pp. 27–47.
3. Baker, pp. 23–28, traces the sources of the poem's allegorical machinery.
4. *Letters,* II, 304. References by volume and page number to this edition are hereafter included in the text.
5. *Queen Mab,* dedication, "To Harriet *****," 1–10. Unless otherwise noted, all quotations from Shelley's poetry are from Reiman and Powers. References are hereafter included in the text. Unless otherwise noted, italics are Shelley's.
6. W. H. Hildebrand is virtually alone among critics in discussing the importance of the poem's frame. He writes that Henry's "real function in the poem is somewhat obscure and, artistically, he seems superfluous. Because Shelley makes no attempt to characterize him, he hovers in the corners of the poem like ectoplasm or a stillborn idea, passive yet curiously disturbing." He goes on to note that "the relationship between Shelley and Harriet, as described in the [dedicatory] poem, exactly parallels that of Henry and Ianthe" and comments pointedly that "if Ianthe is the source of 'Light, life and rapture' for Henry, then the vision is bestowed on Ianthe as much for Henry's sake as for her own." "Shelley's Early Vision Poems," *Studies in Romanticism,* 8 (1969), 203–4.
7. *The Revolt of Islam,* 3792. For the text of this poem I have used that of Thomas Hutchinson's *Shelley: Poetical Works,* 2nd ed., corrected by G. M. Matthews (London: Oxford University Press, 1971).
8. Reiman and Powers, p. 473.
9. Newman Ivey White, *Shelley* (New York: Knopf, 1940), I, 76.
10. Thomas Jefferson Hogg, *The Life of Percy Bysshe Shelley,* ed. Edward Dowden (London: Routledge, 1906), p. 168.
11. For this practice of Shelley, see White, I, 89, and his comment that although Shelley "sincerely desired to get at the truth," the "truth is that his motives were curiously mixed."

12. *Shelley and His Circle: 1773–1822,* ed. Kenneth Neill Cameron and Donald H. Reiman (Cambridge, Mass.: Harvard University Press, 1961–), II, 739–40.

13. Roger Ingpen, *Shelley in England* (London: Kegan Paul, Trench, Trubner, 1917), p. 237.

14. See Ingpen, pp. 333–34 and A. M. D. Hughes, *The Nascent Mind of Shelley* (Oxford: Clarendon Press, 1947), 109–10.

15. White, I, 131.

16. See *Shelley and His Circle,* II, 623, and Ingpen, pp. 340–41.

17. There is also a second, jocular verse letter to Graham that alludes to the affair, published by Neville Rogers in "An Unpublished Shelley Letter," *Keats-Shelley Memorial Bulletin,* 24 (1973), 20–24.

18. Ingpen, p. 347.

19. Hutchinson, p. 837.

20. Richard Holmes, *Shelley: The Pursuit* (London: Weidenfeld and Nicolson, 1974), p. 202.

21. Hutchinson, p. 820.

2. *Alastor*

1. The relationship between the two is discussed by Jay Macpherson in *The Spirit of Solitude: Conventions and Continuities in Late Romance* (New Haven and London: Yale University Press, 1982), p. 151, a work that suggests the centrality of *Alastor* to a major current of the romance tradition in Western literature.

2. Richard Holmes, *Shelley: The Pursuit* (London: Weidenfeld and Nicolson, 1974), p. 300.

3. See Mary Shelley's note on *Alastor* in Thomas Hutchinson, ed., *Shelley: Poetical Works,* 2nd ed., corrected by G. M. Matthews (London: Oxford University Press, 1971), p. 30, and Holmes, pp. 286, 290.

4. Holmes, p. 287.

5. Hutchinson, p. 30.

6. Ibid.

7. "Memoirs of Percy Bysshe Shelley," in *Thomas Love Peacock: Memoirs of Shelley and Other Essays and Reviews,* ed. Howard Mills (London: Rupert Hart-Davis, 1970), pp. 54, 68.

8. Kenneth Neill Cameron, *Shelley: The Golden Years* (Cambridge, Mass.: Harvard University Press, 1974), pp. 16–17.

9. Reiman and Powers, pp. 473–74.

10. Ibid., p. 69.

11. Shelley wrote later the same year to Elizabeth Hitchener on the subject of Hogg's "apostacy": "How have I loved him *you* can *feel*—but he is no longer the being whom perhaps twas the [?warmth] of my imagination that pictured. I love no longer what is not that which I loved" (*Letters,* I, 213).

12. Reiman and Powers, p. 69. The charge of inconsistency and confusion was made early by Raymond D. Havens in "Shelley's *Alastor*," *PMLA,* 45 (1930),

1098–1115, and by Frederick L. Jones in "The Inconsistency of Shelley's *Alastor*," *ELH*, 13 (1946), 291–98, and has often been repeated.

13. Carlos Baker, *Shelley's Major Poetry: The Fabric of a Vision* (Princeton: Princeton University Press, 1948), p. 43.

14. Reiman and Powers, pp. 69–70.

15. Donald H. Reiman, *Percy Bysshe Shelley* (New York: Twayne, 1969), pp. 37–38.

16. See Harold Bloom, *The Visionary Company* (Garden City, N.Y.: Doubleday, 1961), p. 280. Bloom's claim that "the poet" who pronounces the invocation "speak[s] as the element of fire" seems questionable. Fire is mentioned earlier in the poem (64, 89) but as extinguished or hidden and buried.

17. Reiman and Powers, p. 474.

18. The lines are discussed by Glenn O'Malley, who calls them "perhaps the most striking passage of the poem," as an instance of Shelley's fascination with the figure of the "air-prism" in *Shelley and Synesthesia* (Evanston, Ill.: Northwestern University Press, 1964), pp. 50–52.

19. The many echoes of Wordsworth, especially of the "Intimations Ode," have sometimes tempted critics into readings narrowly focused on Shelley's ambivalent attitude toward his older contemporary that ignore the poem's deeper range of implication. The old argument of Paul Mueschke and Earl L. Griggs for "Wordsworth as the Prototype of the Poet in Shelley's *Alastor*," *PMLA*, 49 (1934), 229–45, has been revived in more sophisticated form by Yvonne M. Carothers in "*Alastor*: Shelley Corrects Wordsworth," *MLQ*, 42 (1981), 21–47. Among recent studies that of William Keach, "Obstinate Questionings: The Immortality Ode and *Alastor*," *WC*, 12 (1981), 36–44, is especially balanced and discerning.

20. Baker argues that the "curse-motif" is suggested only in the poem's title and the second paragraph of the "Preface," not in the poem itself. He goes on to surmise that Shelley adopted the title and added the sentence in the "Preface" that "The Poet's self-centred seclusion was avenged by the furies of an irresistible passion pursuing him to speedy ruin" only after completing the poem and in deference to Peacock, who in his memoirs asserted that Shelley "was at a loss for a title, and I proposed that which he adopted: *Alastor; or, the Spirit of Solitude*. The Greek word *alastor* is an evil genius . . . The poem treated the spirit of solitude as a spirit of evil" (Mills, p. 60). Baker is right to question aspects of Peacock's interpretation. Nevertheless, he is wrong to deny the presence of the "alastor" motif within the poem itself and to assert that in adopting Peacock's suggestion Shelley wrenched the logic of his theme, which Baker contends (pp. 41–42) is "the law of love" as opposed to the "natural law" or necessity celebrated in *Queen Mab*. See Carothers' conclusions, pp. 46–47. The fact is that, following the Poet's indifference to the Arab Maiden, the spirit of human love dispatches her second "gift" to him less from deliberate malice than from a principle of compensation akin to emotional or psychological necessity. Similarly, the Poet should not be blamed (as he is by many critics) for neglecting the Arab Maiden, whom he not so much spurns as simply never sees and whose primary role is to dramatize his otherworldly longing and uniqueness. See Note 23. In "Shelley's 'Alastor' Again," *PMLA*,

46 (1931), 947–50, Marion Clyde Wier points out that the Greek word can denote either the avenging demon or its victim.

21. Earl Wasserman, who has best discussed this characteristic of the poem, attributes it to Shelley's philosophical skepticism. He writes that "much of the art of the poem lies in the appearance of similar image patterns that reflect ironically on each other. Skeptically uncertain of both the value of human life and the probability of afterlife, Shelley can only test tentatively by watching the esthetic consequence of placing the same image or ironically similar images in opposing contexts." *Shelley: A Critical Reading* (Baltimore and London: Johns Hopkins University Press, 1971), p. 34.

22. See particularly "The Wild Swans at Coole," *The Variorum Edition of the Poems of W. B. Yeats,* ed. Peter Allt and Russell K. Alspach (New York: Macmillan, 1957), p. 332.

23. That Shelley wrote *Alastor* "to point out [the Poet's] neglect of human love through his fondness for solitude [and] his dream of an ideal mate" is an assumption going back at least as far as Raymond D. Havens' influential "Shelley's *Alastor,*" *PMLA,* 45 (1930), 1108, and the notion continues to recur. Marcel Kessel writes that "the incident of the Arab maiden is evidently intended to show the Poet's spurning of love. He not only fails to cultivate human sympathy and friendship, but he also ignores the love of others for him." "The Poet in Shelley's *Alastor*: A Criticism and a Reply," *PMLA,* 51 (1936), 303. Bryan Cooper asserts that "The Poet's sin has been to turn his back—not simply on human society as many critics have asserted—but on the entire natural world." "Shelley's *Alastor*: The Quest for a Vision," *Keats-Shelley Journal,* 19 (1970), 67–68. James C. Evans declares that "The Poet's rejection of the love offered him during his odyssey is his great fault." "Masks of the Poet: A Study of Self-Confrontation in Shelley's Poetry," *Keats-Shelley Journal,* 24 (1975), 73. The best answer to such contentions is provided by Norman Thurston, who argues simply but astutely that "the Arab maiden never exists as a real possibility for the Poet." "Author, Narrator, and Hero in Shelley's *Alastor,*" *Studies in Romanticism,* 14 (1975), 121.

24. "The Choice," Allt and Alspach, p. 495.

25. My late colleague, E. Talbot Donaldson, informed me that he was the first to call this fact to the attention of Frederick Pottle. Donald Reiman has emphasized the detail in *Percy Bysshe Shelley,* pp. 39, 39n. Evan K. Gibson, who has gone further than any other critic in attempting to read the details of the Poet's journey symbolically, interprets the voyage upstream as a quest for "the mysterious source of life." "*Alastor*: A Reinterpretation," *PMLA,* 62 (1947), 1042. The essay is reprinted in Reiman and Powers, pp. 545–69.

26. The recurrence of the imagery of eyes, culminating at the moment of the Poet's death, has been often pointed out by commentators. See for example Peter Butter, *Shelley's Idols of the Cave* (New York: Haskell House, 1954), pp. 53–54.

27. In his reading of *Alastor,* the most influential interpretation of the poem to date, Earl Wasserman argues for a radical and deliberate division in the poem's focus between a Wordsworthian narrator committed to a faith in natural piety, a commentator roughly equivalent to the Wanderer in *The Excursion,*

and the Poet dedicated to his quest for fulfillment of his visionary ideal. In Wasserman's analysis the two perspectives, the natural and Wordsworthian and the otherworldly and ideal, continually play off against each other to expose the shortcomings of each position in the manner of Shelley's skeptical dialogue, *A Refutation of Deism*, a process that removes Shelley himself from the poem as a kind of ironical observer. In recent years Wasserman's analysis has come to seem increasingly fallacious. The sharp dichotomy in character he draws does not sustain close scrutiny. How is one to explain the narrator's dedication, from the start of the poem, to the un-Wordsworthian arts of graveyard conjuration (23–29) and alchemy (29–37)? Keach has written that "the narrator's echoes of the Immortality Ode show his Wordsworthianism to be much less secure and consolidated from the outset than Wasserman allows." "Obstinate Questionings," p. 36. More recently Tilottama Rajan has written perceptively of "a curious dissociation of sensibility which causes the poem to move in two contradictory directions," a "troubled ambivalence . . . symptomatic of the dialogue of Shelley's mind with itself," a "dialogue [that] seems to stop well short of the sort of self-awareness that Wasserman envisages." "*Alastor*," she declares, "is not an ironic poem in which Shelley has two points of view disciplining each other . . . The narrator and the Poet, far from representing contrary positions, are essentially similar beings, like Wordsworth and his younger sibling in 'Tintern Abbey.' " *Dark Interpreter: The Discourse of Romanticism* (Ithaca and London: Cornell University Press, 1980), pp. 75–76. Still more recently, William Keach writes in his book-length study, "What Shelley presents in *Alastor* is one poetic consciousness (the narrator) gradually coming to terms with and recognizing the depth of his attachment to another poetic consciousness (the wandering poet)." *Shelley's Style* (New York and London: Methuen, 1984), p. 87.

28. Thurston, p. 128.
29. Albert S. Gérard has written: "It should be obvious that Shelley hardly means to condemn his hero. The poem is rather a lament on the fate to which he is doomed because of the very sublimity of his mind . . . His guilt is not a sin. It is a tragic hubris, similar to that of the heroes of Greek drama." *English Romantic Poetry: Ethos, Structure, and Symbol in Coleridge, Wordsworth, Shelley, and Keats* (Berkeley and Los Angeles: University of California Press, 1968), p. 158.
30. Gérard writes of *Alastor* as "a cathartic poem, in which Shelley embodies the dramatic wrestling of his saner self against the temptation of extreme idealism" (p. 137). For Gérard, however, the catharsis is philosophical rather than psychological, stemming from "the ontological problem from which [*Alastor*] arises," and "the poem is to be considered primarily an implicit repudiation of [Shelley's] extreme idealism" (pp. 162, 160), a reading that leads on to Wasserman.

3. *The Revolt of Islam*

1. See Donald Reiman's essay, "The Composition and Publication of *The Revolt of Islam*," in *Shelley and His Circle: 1773–1822*, ed. Kenneth Neill Cameron and

Donald H. Reiman (Cambridge, Mass.: Harvard University Press, 1961–), V, 145–46.

2. For the text of *The Revolt,* printed only in part in Reiman and Powers, I have followed Thomas Hutchinson, *Shelley: Poetical Works,* 2nd ed., corrected and revised by G. M. Matthews (London: Oxford University Press, 1971). For the circumstances under which the poem was written, see Mary Shelley's note in Hutchinson, pp. 156–58, and Reiman, "Composition and Publication," pp. 146–48.

3. As Harold Orel has written, "entire volumes dedicated to the analysis of Shelley's poems may do no more than allude to the fact of its existence." "Shelley's *The Revolt of Islam*: The Last Great Poem of the English Enlightenment?" *Studies in Voltaire and the Eighteenth Century,* 89 (1972), 1187. In Brian Wilkie's phrase, it is "the orphan of Shelley criticism." *Romantic Poets and Epic Tradition* (Madison: University of Wisconsin Press, 1965), p. 112. Wilkie's chapter on *The Revolt* is an interesting study of the poem's epic qualities.

4. "Preface" to *The Revolt of Islam,* Hutchinson, p. 32.

5. Carlos Baker, *Shelley's Major Poetry: The Fabric of a Vision* (Princeton: Princeton University Press, 1948), p. 64. See also Wilkie, p. 113.

6. Reiman's conclusion, based on a study of the relevant manuscript material, that Shelley composed the second half of Canto I only upon completing Canto XII, suggests how closely the beginning and concluding episodes were connected in the poet's mind. "Composition and Publication," pp. 148–51. Richard H. Haswell has argued that *The Revolt* is a poem "far better designed and unified than commonly believed" in "Shelley's *The Revolt of Islam*: 'The Connexion of Its Parts,' " *Keats-Shelley Journal,* 25 (1976), 81.

7. *Letters,* I, 563.

8. Desmond King-Hele has alluded briefly to the poem's plot as "dictated by subconscious fantasy" in *Shelley: His Thought and Work,* 3rd ed. (London: Macmillan, 1984), p. 82.

9. A useful summary of interpretive views of the eagle and serpent imagery is given in James Lynn Ruff's *Shelley's "The Revolt of Islam"* (Salzburg, Austria: University of Salzburg, 1972), pp. 17–26.

10. Noted by Walter E. Peck, in *Shelley: His Life and Work* (London: Ernest Benn, 1927), I, 430. For relevant discussion, see Douglas Bush, *Mythology and the Romantic Tradition in English Poetry* (Cambridge, Mass.: Harvard University Press, 1927), p. 159 and n. 62. Bush identifies passages in Homer and Virgil that are closer in expression, yet Ovid's story of the creation of Hermaphroditus suggests a revealing context for Shelley's image. We know of his acquaintance with and interest in Aristophanes' account of the division of the original androgynous sex into male and female from the poet's early reading in and later translation of Plato's *Symposium.* See James A. Notopoulos, *The Platonism of Shelley* (Durham, N.C.: Duke University Press, 1949), pp. 30, 35, 46, 214, 429–31.

11. *Ovid's Metamorphoses,* trans. Brookes More, rev. ed. (Francestown, N.H.: Marshall Jones, 1978), I, 134.

12. *Examiner,* 527 (1818), p. 75 (my emphasis).

13. Following Hunt, Carl Grabo suggested such an interpretation in *The Magic*

Plant: The Growth of Shelley's Thought (Chapel Hill: University of North Carolina Press, 1936), p. 210. Grabo's suggestion was vigorously attacked by Frederick L. Jones in "Canto I of *The Revolt of Islam*," *Keats-Shelley Journal*, 9 (1960), 31–33, who found such a reading "without any basis in the text." His own explanation to account for the Lady's disappearance, "that in this realm of spirits she, as a living mortal, had no place" (p. 32), and his conclusion that "Shelley himself was a bit confused and inconsistent" (p. 33) are less convincing. Hunt's intimacy with Shelley gives his interpretation special weight. See also Ruff's conclusion that "Hunt's suggestion . . . seems reasonable" (p. 37).

14. *Shelley: The Critical Heritage,* ed. James E. Barcus (London: Routledge & Kegan Paul, 1975), pp. 124–25.

15. See Canto V, 1741–64.

16. There have been several attempts to provide allegorical designations for the principal characters. I agree with E. B. Murray, " 'Elective Affinity' in *The Revolt of Islam*," *Journal of English and Germanic Philology*, 67 (1968), 580–81, that the evidence for such a practice is "at best tendentious." Thus I find his own conjecture that Laon represents fraternity; Cythna, equality; and their later child, liberty, unsatisfying because from the start Laon himself seems closest to liberty, an ideal struggling to realize itself. See Baker, p. 82; Ruff, p. 91, n. 20; and Haswell, pp. 88–89.

17. *Letters,* I, 564.

18. See Nathaniel Brown, *Sexuality and Feminism in Shelley* (Cambridge, Mass.: Harvard University Press, 1979), pp. 71–72, on this characteristic setting for sexual culmination.

19. Within the complicated chronology of the poem, Cythna's ordeals are related in Canto VII as part of a lengthy flashback she narrates following the celebration of their "bridal-night" (2681) in Canto VI.

20. Ruff (pp. 69–88), Haswell, and Alicia Martinez in *The Hero and Heroine of Shelley's "The Revolt of Islam"* (Salzburg, Austria: University of Salzburg, 1976), pp. 67–71, 99–104, all consider the poem revealingly in terms of such a general paradigm but with emphases different from my own.

21. "Sailing to Byzantium," *The Variorum Edition of the Poems of W. B. Yeats,* ed. Peter Allt and Russell K. Alspach (New York: Macmillan, 1957), p. 408.

22. Murray (p. 573) was the first to point out this correspondence.

23. Haswell (pp. 84–85) has pointed out a number of correspondences between the two poems.

24. Freud, in a discussion of identification, describes this cannibalism as symbolic of consuming desire for a loved object and for its assimilation. *Group Psychology and the Analysis of the Ego,* in *The Standard Edition of the Complete Psychological Works of Sigmund Freud,* trans. and ed. James Strachey (London: Hogarth Press, 1955), XVIII, 105. Ruff (pp. 74, 89n), in making a similar point, cites James George Frazer's *The Golden Bough.* Freud's discussions of the function of identification have a special bearing on the course of Shelley's development.

25. Thomas Jefferson Hogg, *The Life of Percy Bysshe Shelley* (London: Edward Moxon, 1858), I, 35–36. Dr. Lind, formerly physician to the Royal Household, was retired at Eton, teaching part-time at the College.

26. Hogg's additions to Mary Shelley's statements in his *Life* are especially sug-

gestive. "I have heard Shelley speak of his fever and this scene at Field Place more than once, in nearly the same terms as Mrs. Shelley adopts. It appeared to myself, and to others also, that his recollections were those of a person not quite recovered from a fever, which had attacked his brain, and still disturbed by the horrors of the disease" (I,33). Grabo (pp. 214–15) notes the connection between Laon's nightmare and Shelley's illness. See also Edward Carpenter and George Barnefield, *The Psychology of the Poet Shelley* (London: George Allen & Unwin, 1925), pp. 101–3.

27. White considers 1806 the most probable date, the only time Shelley was sent home from Eton for an illness, and adds that the episode "indicates the time at which [Shelley] began to consider his father an enemy." *Shelley* (New York: Knopf, 1940), I, 47–48, 573, n. 58.

28. In *Shelley: The Pursuit* (London: Weidenfeld and Nicolson, 1974), Richard Holmes refers to Lind as "an emotional father-figure" to the poet (p. 26) and adds: "If Dr. Lind had gradually inherited over the years the position of spiritual father and guide, Timothy, by contrast, was to be transformed into the type of false father, betrayer and tyrant" (p. 28).

29. Donald Reiman, *Percy Bysshe Shelley* (New York: Twayne, 1969), pp. 57–58. See also Haswell, p. 82ff.

30. I reject Haswell's contention that Cythna is punished for repulsing the tyrant, that is, for her "refusal to accept sexual pleasure" (pp. 85–86). The poem is pervaded by the ideal of free love; but the notion that a woman must submit to the advances of one she does not love is strikingly un-Shelleyan. If Cythna is, properly speaking, punished, it is for the despondency into which her ordeal plunges her, a despondency symbolized by the introversion of her cave and which has its counterpart in the real dejection Mary suffered.

31. Kenneth Neill Cameron, *Shelley: The Golden Years* (Cambridge, Mass.: Harvard University Press, 1974), p. 328.

32. *The Letters of Mary Wollstonecraft Shelley,* ed. Betty T. Bennett (Baltimore and London: Johns Hopkins University Press, 1980–), I, 10–11.

33. *The Journals of Mary Shelley, 1814–1844,* ed. Paula R. Feldman and Diana Scott-Kilvert (Oxford: Clarendon Press, 1987), I, 68–71.

34. Hutchinson, p. 33.

35. Noting the pun on "Shelley," Neville Rogers has observed that "The Nautilus was a name [Shelley] used for himself." *The Complete Poetical Works of Percy Bysshe Shelley* (Oxford: Clarendon Press, 1975), II, 390.

36. "An Essay on Man," III.177–78, in *Pope: Poetical Works,* ed. Herbert Davis (London: Oxford University Press, 1966), pp. 263–64.

37. Samuel Johnson, *The History of Rasselas, Prince of Abissinia,* in *Johnson: Prose and Poetry,* selected by Mona Wilson (London: Rupert Hart-Davis, 1969), pp. 454, 482.

38. Arthur Rimbaud, "Le bateau ivre," *Oeuvres complètes,* ed. Antoine Adam (Paris: Gallimard, 1972), p. 69.

39. White, I, 391.

40. Murray, p. 578.

41. "Preface" to *The Cenci,* Hutchinson, p. 276.

42. In "The Detestable Distinctions of Sex," the last chapter of his *Sexuality and*

Feminism in Shelley, Nathaniel Brown deals with *Laon and Cythna* (pp. 215–18) to support his claim for Shelley's advocacy of "the total annihilation of the traditional gender stereotypes and sex roles" (p. 224), a contention that would place the poet in the forefront of "The New Androgyny." One may grant that Shelley's ideal of love contemplates an ultimate fusion—physical, emotional, and intellectual—between the sexes. Yet Brown's argument for "mono- or unisexuality" (p. 224) ignores or oversimplifies the crucial evolution Laon and Cythna undergo in *The Revolt* as well as aspects of Shelley's own development. One can contrast with Brown the argument of Alicia Martinez (esp. pp. 100–101), which finds the culmination of *The Revolt* in the resolution of distinct but complementary male and female attributes.

4. *Prometheus Unbound,* Act I

1. Reiman and Powers, p. 135.
2. *A Defence of Poetry,* Reiman and Powers, p. 508.
3. *Shelley: Poetical Works,* ed. Thomas Hutchinson, 2nd ed., corrected by G. M. Matthews (London: Oxford University Press, 1971), p. 271.
4. Earl R. Wasserman, *Shelley: A Critical Reading* (Baltimore and London: Johns Hopkins University Press, 1971), pp. 109–11. See also Melvin M. Rader, "Shelley's Theory of Evil," in *Shelley: A Collection of Critical Essays,* ed. George M. Ridenour (Englewood Cliffs, N.J.: Prentice-Hall, 1965), pp. 103–10; and Timothy Webb, "The Unascended Heaven: Negatives in 'Prometheus Unbound,'" in *Shelley Revalued: Essays from the Gregynog Conference,* ed. Kelvin Everest (Leicester: Leicester University Press, 1983), pp. 37–62.
5. Kenneth Neill Cameron, *Shelley: The Golden Years* (Cambridge, Mass.: Harvard University Press, 1974), p. 540.
6. Timothy Webb, *Shelley: A Voice Not Understood* (Manchester: Manchester University Press, 1977), p. 143. Compare the judgment of D. J. Hughes that "Shelley *is* concerned with reform in the poem, but the reform is more metaphysical than political and more ontological than social" (Hughes' italics). "Potentiality in *Prometheus Unbound,*" in Reiman and Powers, p. 617.
7. *The London Magazine and Monthly Critical and Dramatic Review,* September and October 1820, reprinted in James E. Barcus, *Shelley: The Critical Heritage* (London and Boston: Routledge & Kegan Paul, 1975), p. 245.
8. *The Prelude or Growth of a Poet's Mind,* ed. Ernest de Selincourt, 2nd ed. rev. by Helen Darbishire (Oxford: Clarendon Press, 1959), XI.134, 139–44 (1850 version). Shelley would himself have known these verses from "French Revolution as It Appeared to Its Enthusiasts at Its Commencement," printed on October 26, 1809, in *The Friend* and reprinted in the 1815 edition of Wordsworth's collected works.
9. I allude to the influential argument advanced in M. H. Abrams, *Natural Supernaturalism* (New York and London: Norton, 1971).
10. Reiman and Powers, p. 508.
11. Wordsworth, *The Prelude,* VI.607–8 (1850). The sentiment behind the verses is thoroughly Johnsonian.
12. Reiman and Powers, p. 133.

13. Distinguishing between Shelley's treatment of the myth and Aeschylus', William H. Hildebrand has denied that Shelley's Prometheus possesses any secret. "As Shelley's Prometheus knows nothing of the fatal marriage that waits in ambush for Jupiter," he writes, "the desire to learn the secret (which is in fact no secret) has nothing to do with Jupiter's reasons for intensifying Prometheus' torments." *Shelley's Polar Paradise: A Reading of "Prometheus Unbound"* (Salzburg, Austria: University of Salzburg, 1974), p. 34. Nevertheless, Prometheus's possession of the secret seems implied throughout in Jupiter's attempt, through Mercury and the Furies, to break his resistance, and is especially suggested in the hero's reply to Mercury's question, "Thou knowest not the period of Jove's power?"—"I know but this, that it must come" (I.412–13). As we see later, Jupiter's overthrow in Act III, Scene i comes about in a fashion that suggests the fulfillment of the prophecy. It seems clear that for the broader, ideal design of his dramatic allegory Shelley sought to transmute the secret of his legend into prophecy.

14. See for example Carlos Baker, *Shelley's Major Poetry: The Fabric of a Vision* (Princeton: Princeton University Press, 1948), p. 97; and Milton Wilson, *Shelley's Later Poetry* (New York: Columbia University Press, 1959), p. 57.

15. John Sewell Flagg, *"Prometheus Unbound" and "Hellas": An Approach to Shelley's Lyrical Dramas* (Salzburg: University of Salzburg, 1972), p. 71.

16. See Philip Drew's "Shelley: A Note on *Prometheus Unbound*," in his *The Meaning of Freedom* (Aberdeen: Aberdeen University Press, 1982), especially his argument that "it is no unfounded paradox to say that, far from Prometheus' regeneration enabling Demogorgon to cast Jupiter from his throne, it is the inevitability of Demogorgon's overthrow of Jupiter which has enabled Prometheus to continue his resistance, and that his certain vision of the fatal hour alone enables him to pity Jupiter (I.53)" (p. 178). I have discussed Shelley's continuing adherence to the doctrine of necessity and its relation to the problem of motivation in the play in greater detail in "Necessity and the Role of the Hero in Shelley's *Prometheus Unbound*," *PMLA*, 96 (1981), 242–54.

17. Reiman and Powers, pp. 503–4. The passage is similarly cited by Ross Woodman in "The Androgyne in *Prometheus Unbound*," *Studies in Romanticism*, 20 (1981), 231, an article that touches on the limitations of will in the action of the drama.

18. Reiman and Powers, p. 133.

19. See *Letters*, II, 177.

20. The analogy, which Baker made years ago in undergraduate lectures, underlies much of his discussion of *Prometheus* in *Shelley's Major Poetry*, pp. 89–118, 251–52.

21. Philip Drew, "Shelley's Use of 'Recall,'" *Times Literary Supplement*, December 16, 1955, p. 761.

22. G. M. Matthews, reply to "Shelley's Use of 'Recall,'" *Times Literary Supplement*, January 20, 1956, p. 37. Matthews' letter was one of several controversial responses to Drew's.

23. Leon Waldoff, "The Father-Son Conflict in *Prometheus Unbound*: The Psychology of a Vision," *Psychoanalytic Review*, 62 (1975), 92.

24. P. M. S. Dawson, *The Unacknowledged Legislator: Shelley and Politics* (Oxford: Clarendon Press, 1980), p. 11.

25. Reiman and Powers, p. 240.

26. Karl Kerenyi, *Prometheus: Archetypal Image of Human Existence* (London: Thames and Hudson, 1963), p. 117.

27. Compare Yeats's lines, "The best lack all conviction, while the worst / Are full of passionate intensity," in "The Second Coming," *The Variorum Edition of the Poems of W. B. Yeats,* ed. Peter Allt and Russell K. Alspach (New York: Macmillan, 1957), p. 402.

28. *The Letters of John Keats, 1814–1821,* ed. Hyder Edward Rollins (Cambridge, Mass.: Harvard University Press, 1958), I, 184.

5. *Prometheus Unbound,* Act II

1. *The Letters of John Keats, 1814–1821,* ed. Hyder Edward Rollins (Cambridge, Mass.: Harvard University Press, 1958), I, 243.

2. William H. Hildebrand endorses this idea when he writes that "the existence of Spring depends on [Asia's] greeting, which in turn presupposes her being open or present to it, and on her naming it." "Naming-Day in Asia's Vale," *Keats-Shelley Journal,* 32 (1983), 196. Hildebrand's elaboration of the scene in terms of "a hermeneutics (reading and telling) within a comprehensive process of symbolization" (p. 201) is suggestive but prolix.

3. Shelley, "To the Moon," 1, *Shelley: Poetical Works,* ed. Thomas Hutchinson, 2nd ed., corrected by G. M. Matthews (London: Oxford University Press, 1971), p. 621.

4. Stuart Curran, *Shelley's Annus Mirabilis* (San Marino, Calif.: Huntington Library, 1975), pp. 99–100.

5. Shelley's depiction of Asia has reminded many commentators of Sandro Botticelli's *Birth of Venus.* See Lawrence John Zillman, *Shelley's "Prometheus Unbound": A Variorum Edition* (Seattle: University of Washington Press, 1959), pp. 486–87; and Kenneth Neill Cameron, *Shelley: The Golden Years* (Cambridge, Mass.: Harvard University Press, 1974), p. 509. In "Shelley's Asia and Botticelli's Venus: An Infectious Shelley Myth," *Keats-Shelley Memorial Bulletin,* 28 (1977), 32–35, Frederic S. Colwell, however, argues against the likelihood of Shelley's actually having seen Botticelli's Venus by the time he composed the second act.

6. Desmond King-Hele, *Shelley: His Thought and Work,* 3rd ed. (London: Macmillan, 1984), p. 177.

7. Something like this progression is suggested by A. H. Koszul in his "Les océanides et le thème de l'amour dans le *Prométhée délivré* de Shelley," *Revue Anglo-Américaine,* 2 (1925), 385–93.

8. Jacques Lacan, "The Mirror Stage as Formative of the Function of the I," in *Écrits,* trans. Alan Sheridan (London: Tavistock, 1977), pp. 1–7.

9. See for example Sir Karl Popper's discussion of the theories of Ludwig Boltzmann in his *Unended Quest* (London: Fontana/Collins, 1976), p. 169.

10. See Earl R. Wasserman, *Shelley: A Critical Reading* (Baltimore and London:

Johns Hopkins University Press, 1971), pp. 338–345, esp. p. 344, where he writes of "Demogorgon's realm of absolute potentiality."

11. Donald H. Reiman, *Percy Bysshe Shelley* (New York: Twayne, 1969), p. 77.
12. See Wasserman, p. 345.
13. See the note to these lines in Ellsworth Barnard, *Shelley: Selected Poems, Essays, and Letters* (New York: Odyssey Press, 1944), p. 138.
14. G. J. Whitrow, *The Natural Philosophy of Time*, 2nd ed. (Oxford: Clarendon Press, 1980), p. 8. Whitrow is summarizing the views of G. N. Lewis.
15. The phrase is that of A. S. Eddington.
16. See Reiman and Powers, p. 175n.
17. Cameron, p. 524.
18. Ibid., pp. 523–24.
19. F. R. Leavis, *Revaluation: Tradition and Development in English Poetry* (London: Chatto & Windus, 1936), pp. 206, 214. Leavis writes of Shelley's verse generally, but his remarks apply preeminently to the two lyrics. For a comparable judgment, see Cleanth Brooks, *Modern Poetry and the Tradition* (London: Poetry London, 1948), 230–31.
20. Shelley's major philosophical source is the myth in Plato's *Statesman*. See E. M. W. Tillyard, "Shelley's *Prometheus Unbound* and Plato's *Statesman*," *Times Literary Supplement*, 31 (September 29, 1932), 691; and Irene H. Chayes, "Plato's *Statesman* Myth in Shelley and Blake," *Comparative Literature*, 13 (1961), 358–69.
21. Leavis, p. 222.
22. See Wordsworth's comments in *The Poetical Works of William Wordsworth*, ed. Ernest de Selincourt and Helen Darbishire (Oxford: Clarendon Press, 1947), IV, 463.
23. Coleridge, *Biographia Literaria*, ed. J. Shawcross (Oxford: Clarendon Press, 1907), II, 109, 111–12.
24. See Wordsworth, *Poetical Works*, IV, 464.
25. Writing of *Prometheus Unbound*, with particular reference to the second act, C. S. Lewis declares in his notable defense of Shelley: "But for my own part I believe that no poet has felt more keenly, or presented more weightily the necessity for a complete unmaking and remaking of man, to be endured at the dark bases of his being. I do not know the book (in profane literature) to which I should turn for a like expression of what von Hügel would have called the 'costingness' of regeneration." "Shelley, Dryden, and Mr Eliot," in *Rehabilitations and Other Essays* (London: Oxford University Press, 1939), p. 33.

6. *Prometheus Unbound*, Acts III and IV

1. Edward E. Bostetter, *The Romantic Ventriloquists: Wordsworth, Coleridge, Keats, Shelley, Byron* (Seattle: University of Washington Press, 1963), pp. 193–95.
2. Earl R. Wasserman, *Shelley: A Critical Reading* (Baltimore and London: Johns Hopkins University Press, 1971), pp. 346–47.
3. "Sailing to Byzantium," *The Variorum Edition of the Poems of W. B. Yeats*, ed. Peter Allt and Russell K. Alspach (New York: Macmillan, 1957), p. 408.

4. W. B. Yeats, "The Philosophy of Shelley's Poetry," in *Essays* (New York: Macmillan, 1924), p. 99.

5. Douglas Bush, *Mythology and the Romantic Tradition in English Poetry* (Cambridge, Mass.: Harvard University Press, 1937), p. 150.

6. Compare *The Cenci*, III.i.277: "some inane and vacant smile."

7. In *Shelley and the Sublime: An Interpretation of the Major Poems* (Cambridge: Cambridge University Press, 1984), Angela Leighton provides a valuable discussion of Shelley's relationship to the tradition of the sublime. She does not, however, discuss this particular part of Shelley's drama.

8. Harold Bloom has observed how " 'the intense inane' might bear an unflattering double meaning" and has written of the lines that conclude the act that "The greatness of this passage is in its passionate undersong, which presents a contrary to every one of its overt affirmations." *Shelley's Mythmaking* (New Haven: Yale University Press, 1959), p. 138. This way of reading Shelley, as well as the other major Romantics, is shared by Tilottama Rajan in her justly influential *Dark Interpreter: The Discourse of Romanticism* (Ithaca and London: Cornell University Press, 1980).

9. Donald H. Reiman has contended that, at the time he composed Act IV, Shelley also made substantial changes in the earlier acts. *Shelley and His Circle,* ed. Kenneth Neill Cameron and Donald H. Reiman (Cambridge, Mass.: Harvard University Press, 1961–), VI, 1071.

10. Bloom, pp. 138–39.

11. Donald H. Reiman, *Percy Bysshe Shelley* (New York: Twayne, 1969), pp. 85–87.

12. Kenneth Neill Cameron, *Shelley: The Golden Years* (Cambridge, Mass.: Harvard University Press, 1974), p. 543.

13. Cameron, p. 546.

14. Knight writes of a style in which "the rush of excited thought and the repose of myth and symbol, enjoy perfect union." *The Starlit Dome: Studies in the Poetry of Vision* (London: Oxford University Press, 1941), p. 223.

15. *Hellas,* 197–200, Reiman and Powers, p. 416. As commentators have pointed out, Shelley's chariot of the Earth, while distinct in its details, echoes Milton's description of the "Chariot of Paternal Deitie" in *Paradise Lost,* VI.749ff., and earlier depictions in Ezekiel and Dante. See in particular Bloom, pp. 143–45.

16. Knight, p. 222.

17. See Lawrence John Zillman, *Shelley's "Prometheus Unbound": A Variorum Edition* (Seattle: University of Washington Press, 1959), p. 595.

18. This parallel has been noted by Desmond King-Hele, in *Shelley: His Thought and Work,* 3rd ed. (London: Macmillan, 1984), p. 191 and n. 19.

19. King-Hele, p. 191.

20. W. B. Yeats, "Among School Children," 57–58, Allt and Alspach, p. 445.

7. *The Cenci*

1. *Shelley: Poetical Works,* ed. Thomas Hutchinson, 2nd ed., corrected by G. M. Matthews (London: Oxford University Press, 1971), pp. 334ff.

2. Reiman and Powers, p. 240.

3. Ibid.

4. James D. Wilson, "Beatrice Cenci and Shelley's Vision of Moral Responsibility," *Ariel*, 9 (1978), 80.

5. Carlos Baker, *Shelley's Major Poetry: The Fabric of a Vision* (Princeton: Princeton University Press, 1948), pp. 138–53.

6. Robert F. Whitman, "Beatrice's 'Pernicious Mistake' in *The Cenci*," *PMLA*, 74 (1959), 253.

7. See Stuart Curran, "The Tragic Resolution," in his *Shelley's "Cenci": Scorpions Ringed with Fire* (Princeton: Princeton University Press, 1970), pp. 129–54.

8. "Preface" to *Prometheus Unbound*, Reiman and Powers, p. 135.

9. Reiman and Powers, p. 237.

10. Earl Wasserman, *Shelley: A Critical Reading* (Baltimore and London: Johns Hopkins University Press, 1971), p. 101.

11. The arrival of the papal legate is probably Shelley's most important addition to his source. See Paul Smith, "Restless Casuistry: Shelley's Composition of *The Cenci*," *Keats-Shelley Journal*, 13 (1964), 84, and Donald H. Reiman, *Percy Bysshe Shelley* (New York: Twayne, 1969), p. 91.

12. For the clearest statement of this viewpoint, see Whitman, p. 253.

13. See Curran, pp. 141–42.

14. Wasserman, p. 93.

15. Stuart Curran has perceptively pointed out a number of resemblances between Shelley's Beatrice and Aeschylus' Io in *Shelley's Annus Mirabilis: The Maturing of an Epic Vision* (San Marino, Calif.: Huntington Library, 1975), pp. 130–33.

16. The pen-and-ink drawing in the British Museum, reproduced as this book's frontispiece, is closely related to another drawing in Kunsthaus Zurich as well as to an oil painting. See Paola Viotto, *L'opera completa di Füssli* (Milan: Rizzoli, 1977), p. 88.

17. Reiman and Powers, p. 240.

18. See Wasserman, pp. 118–20.

19. Wasserman, pp. 119, 125.

20. *Shelley's Prose; or, The Trumpet of a Prophecy*, ed. David Lee Clark (Albuquerque: University of New Mexico Press, 1954), p. 309. The passage is cited by Wasserman, p. 119.

21. "Note on *The Cenci*, by Mrs. Shelley," Hutchinson, p. 337.

8. *The Witch of Atlas*

1. Richard Cronin has called attention to the general stylistic and thematic similarity of the two works in *Shelley's Poetic Thoughts* (New York: St. Martin's, 1981), pp. 58–61.

2. *Letter to Maria Gisborne*, 132.

3. "Mont Blanc," 44.

4. "Note on *The Witch of Atlas*, by Mary Shelley," *Shelley: Poetical Works*, ed. Thomas Hutchinson, corrected by G. M. Matthews (London: Oxford University Press, 1971), p. 388.

5. Shelley believed that Keats's fatal illness was brought on by the hostile reviews of his *Endymion*. In *Adonais*, his elegy to Keats, Shelley refers to the reviewer

in the *Quarterly* as a "viperous murderer," a "nameless worm" quick "To spill the venom when thy fangs o'erflow" (317, 319, 330). Shelley had earlier heard from John Gisborne and others the report of how Keats had burst a blood vessel in the "paroxysms of his disappointment" (*Letters,* II, 289) on reading the reviews of his poem. Keats was especially in Shelley's mind at the time he composed *The Witch* for the reason that he had received only a few days earlier Keats's letter declining an invitation to visit the Shelleys in Italy, a letter Keats begins by foretelling his own death. In *"Adonais:* Shelley's Consumption of Keats," *Studies in Romanticism,* 23 (1984), 296–301, James A. W. Heffernan has argued that Shelley deliberately fabricated from unsubstantiated rumors the version of the death his elegy made famous.

6. Newman Ivey White has pointed out that only a few weeks before *The Witch of Atlas* was written Bysshe and Mary had together been reading the *Ricciardetto* of Niccolò Forteguerri, the imitator of Luigi Pulci, whose *Morgante Maggiore* was, as Donald Reiman and Sharon Powers say, "the ultimate source" of Byron's ottava rima satiric style. See White's *Shelley* (New York: Knopf, 1940), II, 219–21, and Reiman and Powers, p. 347.

7. Dedicatory letter to Robert Southey, *The Poetical Works of William Wordsworth,* ed. Ernest de Selincourt, 2nd ed. (Oxford: Clarendon Press, 1952), II, 331.

8. Reiman and Powers, p. 500.

9. Compare a stanza from *Peter Bell the Third*:

> But from the first 'twas Peter's drift
> To be a kind of moral eunuch
> He touched the hem of Nature's shift,
> Felt faint—and never dared uplift
> The closest, all-concealing tunic. (313–17)

10. *The Poems of John Keats,* ed. Jack Stillinger (Cambridge, Mass.: Harvard University Press, 1978), p. 452.

11. G. Wilson Knight, *The Starlit Dome: Studies in the Poetry of Vision* (London: Oxford University Press, 1941), pp. 226–27; Cronin, p. 74. In "Metaphor and Metamorphosis in Shelley's 'The Witch of Atlas,' " *Studies in Romanticism,* 19 (1980), 327–53, Jerrold E. Hogle has interpreted the Witch more specifically as symbolic of the infinite transformations of poetic texts and language.

12. Reiman and Powers, p. 505.

13. Reiman and Powers, p. 474.

14. *The Collected Poems of Wallace Stevens* (New York: Knopf, 1955), p. 22.

15. Reiman and Powers, p. 487.

16. Harold Bloom, *Shelley's Mythmaking* (New Haven: Yale University Press, 1959), pp. 188, 190–91.

17. Cronin, p. 68.

18. "Preface to *Lyrical Ballads,*" in *The Prose Works of William Wordsworth,* ed. W. J. B. Owen and Jane Worthington Smyser (Oxford: Clarendon Press, 1974), p. 141.

19. David Rubin has written perceptively of the Witch's ability to unite irreconcil-

able elements and of the "limitations in the nature of her creation" as an expression of Shelley's "sense of the potentialities and limitations of poetry" in "A Study of Antinomies in Shelley's *The Witch of Atlas*," *Studies in Romanticism*, 8 (1969), 227. In "Shelley's Ironic Vision: *The Witch of Atlas*," *Keats-Shelley Journal*, 29 (1980), 67–82, Andelys Wood goes further in discussing the anachronism not just of the Hermaphrodite but of all the Witch's activities in an essay that sensitively defines the poem's comic quality.

20. Nathaniel Brown, *Sexuality and Feminism in Shelley* (Cambridge, Mass., and London: Harvard University Press, 1979), p. 23.

21. "The Emperor of Ice-Cream," *Collected Poems of Wallace Stevens*, p. 64.

22. In her *English Romantic Irony* (Cambridge, Mass., and London: Harvard University Press, 1980), Anne K. Mellor takes Schlegel's theories as the principal model for her own formulation. See esp. pp. 7–29, and pp. 17–19 for "transcendental buffoonery." She does not, however, discuss Shelley. Wood refers to Shelley as a "romantic ironist" in her essay on *The Witch of Atlas* (p. 82).

23. "Sailing to Byzantium" and "Byzantium," *The Variorum Edition of the Poems of W. B. Yeats*, ed. Peter Allt and Russell K. Alspach (New York: Macmillan, 1957), pp. 408, 497.

24. Lloyd Abbey, *Destroyer and Preserver: Shelley's Poetic Skepticism* (Lincoln, Neb., and London: University of Nebraska Press, 1980), pp. 102–4. In his brief discussion of *The Witch of Atlas*, Abbey treats the poem as a skeptical and ironic commentary on the ideals of *Prometheus Unbound*.

9. *Epipsychidion*

1. Newman Ivey White and Kenneth Neill Cameron have been at the head of those for whom the primary interest and meaning of the work are the light it sheds on Shelley's life and its quality of autobiographical revelation. See White's *Shelley* (New York: Knopf, 1940), II, 259–69, and Cameron's "The Planet-Tempest Passage in *Epipsychidion*," *PMLA*, 63 (1948), 950–72, reprinted in slightly revised form in Reiman and Powers, pp. 637–58, and incorporated in Cameron's *Shelley: The Golden Years* (Cambridge, Mass.: Harvard University Press, 1974), pp. 275–88. On the other hand, Earl R. Wasserman, in *Shelley: A Critical Reading* (Johns Hopkins University Press, 1971), pp. 417–61, takes the poem as an extended philosophical and aesthetic meditation whose ideas exist in an intellectual realm totally removed from Shelley's life. Harold Bloom, who resembles Wasserman in eschewing biographical elucidation, writes that the poem "is a poem about poetry, and consciously so." *Shelley's Mythmaking* (New Haven: Yale University Press, 1959), p. 210. Likewise, Daniel J. Hughes declares that "the poem is ultimately about poetry itself and the process by which it is created." "Coherence and Collapse in Shelley, with Particular Reference to *Epipsychidion*," *ELH*, 28 (1961), 265. Among readings that try to strike some balance, the brief account by Donald H. Reiman in *Percy Bysshe Shelley* (New York: Twayne, 1969), pp. 125–33, is especially notable.

2. Reiman and Powers, p. 373.

3. The comparison is made by White, II, 325.

4. Reiman and Powers, p. 373. See also the statement in one of the canceled prefaces to the work that the poem "was evidently intended to be prefixed to a longer poem or series of poems—but among [the author's] papers there are no traces of such a collection." *Shelley: Poetical Works,* ed. Thomas Hutchinson, 2nd ed., corrected by G. M. Matthews (London: Oxford University Press, 1971), p. 426.

5. Bloom, p. 209.

6. Reiman and Powers' translation, p. 373.

7. "Tithonus," *The Poems of Tennyson,* ed. Christopher Ricks (London: Longmans, 1969), pp. 1116–17.

8. "Among School Children," *The Variorum Edition of the Poems of W. B. Yeats,* ed. Peter Allt and Russell K. Alspach (New York: Macmillan, 1957), p. 443.

9. Bloom, p. 216.

10. See Earl Schulze, "The Dantean Quest of *Epipsychidion,*" *Studies in Romanticism,* 21 (1982), 191–216.

11. Shelley so characterized the work in his letter of 18 June 1822 to John Gisborne (*Letters,* II, 434).

12. Richard Holmes, *Shelley: The Pursuit* (London: Weidenfeld and Nicolson, 1974), p. 635.

13. Reiman and Powers' translation, p. 373.

14. Ovid, *Metamorphoses,* III.380.

15. Carlos Baker calls attention to the distinction, which he analyzes in a somewhat different way, in his note glossing the passage in *Shelley's Major Poetry: The Fabric of a Vision* (Princeton: Princeton University Press, 1948), p. 229, n. 28. See also Donald H. Reiman, *Percy Bysshe Shelley,* p. 129.

16. The splitting of the ego is a phenomenon discussed throughout Freud's work. See for example the discussion in "The Neuro-Psychoses of Defence" and the later paper, "Splitting of the Ego in the Process of Defence," in *The Standard Edition of the Complete Psychological Works of Sigmund Freud,* trans. James Strachey (London: Hogarth Press, 1964), III, 45–47; XXIII, 275–78. Among later analysts Melanie Klein has discussed "the weakening and impoverishment of the ego resulting from excessive splitting and projective identification" in idealization and their relation to certain forms of schizophrenia, in a way that throws special light on Shelley, in "Notes on Some Schizoid Mechanisms," in *Developments in Psycho-Analysis,* ed. Joan Riviere (London: Hogarth Press, 1952), esp. pp. 301–4, 306, 308–9, 315–16, 319–20. See also her essay "On Identification," in *New Directions in Psycho-Analysis,* ed. Melanie Klein, Paula Heiman, et al. (London: Tavistock, 1955), esp. pp. 310–12. Throughout her *Contributions to Psycho-Analysis 1921–1945* (London: Hogarth Press, 1968), she discusses "how a failure to maintain the identification with both internalized and real loved objects may result in psychotic disorders" (p. 309). See esp. pp. 290, 308–9, 317, 320, 321–22, 331, 337–38.

17. Reiman and Powers, pp. 473–74.

18. Holmes, p. 632.

19. Cameron, for example, has written that "The obvious meaning of this passage is that Shelley, early in life, encountered a prostitute and contracted a venereal disease" (*Shelley: The Golden Years,* p. 280; see also pp. 56–57). See further Cameron's fuller analysis of Hunt's account in *The Young Shelley: Genesis of a Radical* (New York: Macmillan, 1950), pp. 145–46, where he concludes that Hunt's "deduction from the *Epipsychidion* passage is clearly justified." In *Sexuality and Feminism in Shelley* (Cambridge, Mass., and London: Harvard University Press, 1979), Nathaniel Brown considers the evidence on both sides and writes that Hunt's "explanation has much to recommend it . . . Without external corroboration, however, the lines stop far short of being conclusive. It is equally possible that the imagery conveys a strictly emotional experience" (pp. 209–10). In *Percy Bysshe Shelley,* pp. 129–30, Reiman argues for a more general interpretation of the passage. Very recently Nora Crook and Derek Guiton have reargued for the probability that Shelley was infected by venereal disease, in their elaborately researched *Shelley's Venomed Melody* (Cambridge: Cambridge University Press, 1986). Like others before them they take the passage as a piece of leading evidence (see pp. 147–55) in support of a contention they admit from the outset of their study they cannot prove.

20. It is notable that Crook and Guiton in good part perceive the underlying archetypal relationship even while pressing the case for their clinical diagnosis. Thus they write: "However this does not mean that the One is a particular prostitute. Thornton Hunt did not say that she was. She could be a personified abstraction" (p. 150); and again, "Shelley presents Emily as Love, the elixir of True Life, who will redeem him from the consequences of encountering the poisonous One. She is described in terms that contrast almost point for point with the latter's baleful physical features. The honey-dew example has already been given; in addition, Emily's voice, cheeks, perfume and eyes are presented in the same way" (p. 154).

21. See White, II, 262–68; Cameron, "The Planet-Tempest Passage in *Epipsychidion,*" in Reiman and Powers, pp. 637ff.

22. Cameron, "The Planet-Tempest Passage in *Epipsychidion,*" in Reiman and Powers, p. 651. See also Cameron's *Shelley: The Golden Years,* pp. 284–85.

23. "Lines," 1–6, Hutchinson, p. 527.

24. Cameron, "The Planet-Tempest Passage in *Epipsychidion,*" in Reiman and Powers, pp. 651–53. See also *Shelley: The Golden Years,* pp. 285–86.

25. White, II, 268.

26. Earl R. Wasserman, *Shelley: A Critical Reading* (Baltimore and London: Johns Hopkins University Press, 1971), p. 450. In *Shelley and Synesthesia* (Evanston, Ill.: Northwestern University Press, 1964), pp. 106–7, Glenn O'Malley discusses the way effects of synesthesia create the impression that "the lovers merge with the island's soul."

27. J. Hillis Miller elaborates this point in his brief but suggestive consideration of *Epipsychidion* in "The Critic as Host," in Harold Bloom et al., *Deconstruction and Criticism* (New York: Seabury Press, 1979), pp. 238–47.

28. O'Malley, p. 111, calls attention to the resemblance between these two scenes.

29. The irony has been noted by Miller: "The more the poet says they will be one

the more he makes them two by reaffirming the ways they are separated" (p. 245).

30. Wasserman, p. 460. In his essay Daniel Hughes also studies the pattern of repeated collapse, tracing it in other poems and relating it to the *Defence* and to Shelley's conception of the poetical process. More recently Jean Hall takes a surprisingly optimistic view of this same pattern in reading *Epipsychidion,* in pointed contrast to Wasserman, "as a radical and spectacularly successful enactment of the poet's power to create the worlds he wishes for." "He stops," she writes of the poet at the conclusion of the poem, "not because he has failed but because he has completely succeeded. The ideal of the poem has been so far attained that there is no more room for movement, and in the final rapture of universal fusion his world passes beyond existence . . . The Shelleyan poem simply dies of its own happiness." *The Transforming Image: A Study of Shelley's Major Poetry* (Urbana: University of Illinois Press, 1980), pp. 104, 146 n.19.

31. Such, for example, is Wasserman's conclusion: "the poet is aspiring to an identity of the finite and the infinite that is not possible in life," an "identity possible only in afterlife" (p. 460).

32. The nature of Shelley's relationship with Jane remains something of an issue. G. M. Matthews argues that Shelley conducted a highly passionate love affair with her during the weeks immediately preceding his death. "Shelley and Jane Williams," *RES,* 12 (1961), 40–48; and "On Shelley's 'The Triumph of Life,' " *Studia Neophilologica,* 34 (1962), 104–34. Cameron also concludes that "by June [1822], Shelley's feeling for Jane had become deeply passionate" (*Shelley: The Golden Years,* p. 302; see also p. 310). Donald Reiman, after a thorough review of the evidence, asserts that there are no grounds for proving that their intercourse was anything but chaste. "Shelley's 'The Triumph of Life': The Biographical Problem," *PMLA* 78 (1963), 536–50. Whether or not the relationship was physical, the lyrics Shelley composed for her are sufficient evidence of the intensity of his emotional involvement.

10. *The Triumph of Life*

1. These accounts are given by Mary in her letter of 15 August 1822 to Maria Gisborne. See *The Letters of Mary Wollstonecraft Shelley,* ed. Betty T. Bennett (Baltimore: Johns Hopkins University Press, 1980–), I, 244–45. As has been occasionally pointed out, the second relation bears a striking resemblance to the monster's strangling of Elizabeth in vol. 3, chap. 6 of Mary's *Frankenstein.*

2. See *Letters,* I, 238, and Newman Ivey White, *Shelley* (New York: Knopf, 1940), I, 193, 622 nn.109–10; *Letters,* I, 355–56 and n.2, White, I, 280–85, Richard Holmes, *Shelley: The Pursuit* (London: Weidenfeld and Nicolson, 1974), 190–97; and White, II, 178, 589 n.6.

3. See T. S. Eliot, *The Use of Poetry and the Use of Criticism* (London: Faber and Faber, 1933), p. 90, and Eliot's essay, "The Metaphysical Poets," in *Selected Essays* (New York: Harcourt Brace, 1950), p. 248. The stylistic characteristics of the poem have been discussed by Donald H. Reiman in *Shelley's "The*

Triumph of Life": *A Critical Study* (Urbana, Ill.: University of Illinois Press, 1965), pp. 87–109.

4. The ambivalence of the opening lines has been sensitively commented on in different ways by Merle R. Rubin in "Shelley's Skepticism: A Detachment beyond Despair," *PQ,* 59 (1980), 361; by Richard Cronin in *Shelley's Poetic Thoughts* (London: Macmillan, 1981), pp. 208–9; and by Angela Leighton in *Shelley and the Sublime* (Cambridge: Cambridge University Press, 1984), pp. 154–55.

5. I have adopted the divisions set out by Carlos Baker in *Shelley's Major Poetry: The Fabric of a Vision* (Princeton: Princeton University Press, 1948), p. 259.

6. Tilottama Rajan, for example, has written that "the language used to describe the Car is already present in the language used to describe the Shape all light, [and] the reverse is also true." *Dark Interpreter: The Discourse of Romanticism* (Ithaca, N.Y., and London: Cornell University Press, 1980), pp. 68–69.

7. Reiman and Powers, pp. 500, 504, 505, 487.

8. Leighton, pp. 152–53.

9. See Reiman's discussion of the symbolism of the scene in *Shelley's "The Triumph of Life,"* pp. 60–61. Reiman stresses the obliterating power of the stream and its music, which destroy all knowledge of the soul's antenatal existence, contrary, as he says, to the logic of the "Intimations Ode." It is possible however to see the "shape all light," like the "clouds of glory" that accompany Wordsworth's child at birth, as vestiges that surround the newly born soul which never entirely disappear. One can agree with Reiman that Shelley believed in the impossibility of man's retaining any absolute knowledge of his life before birth and yet feel that the "shape all light" is Shelley's metaphor for those intimations Wordsworth had so powerfully described.

10. David Quint, "Representation and Ideology in 'The Triumph of Life,' " *Studies in English Literature,* 18 (1978), 648.

11. Rajan, pp. 63–64.

12. "On Love," Reiman and Powers, p. 474.

13. Leslie Brisman, *Romantic Origins* (Ithaca, N.Y., and London: Cornell University Press, 1978), p. 178.

14. Paul de Man, "Shelley Disfigured," in Harold Bloom et al., *Deconstruction and Criticism* (New York: Seabury Press, 1979), p. 60.

15. Reiman and Powers, p. 504.

16. Harold Bloom, *Shelley's Mythmaking* (New Haven: Yale University Press, 1959), p. 271. The broad spectrum of critical viewpoints is described and documented at the outset of Linda E. Marshall's "The 'Shape All Light' in Shelley's *The Triumph of Life,*" *English Studies in Canada,* 5 (1979), 49–56.

17. See Reiman, *Shelley's "The Triumph of Life,"* pp. 45–46. Reiman denies, however, that this darker view prevails in *The Triumph.*

18. See Fred L. Milne, "The Eclipsed Imagination in Shelley's 'The Triumph of Life,' " *Studies in English Literature,* 21 (1981), 692–93.

19. Harold Bloom, *Poetry and Repression: Revisionism from Blake to Stevens* (New Haven and London: Yale University Press, 1976), p. 104. Bloom's contention seems to me typical of several instances in which the theoretical commitment of his later criticism has led to forced or doubtful readings.

20. The opening of *The Triumph* with its description of "The smokeless altars of the mountain snows" (5) and the "old chestnut" (25) shortly to become Rousseau are reminiscent of Shelley's memorable description of the area around Meillerie in his letter of 12 July 1816 to Peacock: "St. Gingoux is even more beautiful than Meillerie; the mountains are higher, and their loftiest points of elevation descend more abruptly to the lake. On high, the aerial summits still cherish great depths of snow in their ravines, and in the paths of their unseen torrents. One of the highest of these is called Roche de St. Julien, beneath whose pinnacles the forests become deeper and more extensive; the chestnut gives a peculiarity to the scene, which is most beautiful, and will make a picture in my memory, distinct from all other mountain scenes which I have ever before visited . . .

    "We went between the mountains and the lake, under groves of mighty chestnut trees, beside perpetual streams, which are nourished by the snows above, and form stalactites on the rocks, over which they fall. We saw an immense chestnut tree, which had been overthrown by the hurricane of the morning . . .

    "We returned to St. Gingoux before sunset, and I passed the evening in reading Julie" (*Letters*, I, 484).
21. *Childe Harold's Pilgrimage*, III.77.5, 78.3, 7–9, *Byron's Poetry*, ed. Frank D. McConnell (New York: Norton, 1978), pp. 67–68.
22. *Letters*, I, 494. Edward Duffy has traced Shelley's deepening appreciation of Rousseau in *Rousseau in England: The Context for Shelley's Critique of the Enlightenment* (Berkeley and London: University of California Press, 1979), pp. 86–105. He concludes, however, that in *The Triumph* Shelley's vision of Rousseau is essentially that of "a visionary *manqué*, a poet done in by his own egotism" (p. 95).
23. Emphasizing "the arrogant and boastful tone" of this and the preceding speech, Duffy takes them as instances of Rousseau's "bragging" and "self-dramatization," the mark of one who "has failed even as [he] keeps insisting on just where he has stood fast" (pp. 116–18). Such a negative interpretation misrepresents the force of Rousseau's role and character in the poem.
24. See Donald H. Reiman, "Shelley's 'The Triumph of Life': The Biographical Problem," *PMLA*, 78 (1963), pp. 545ff., and Reiman, *Shelley's "The Triumph of Life*," p. 211.
25. Reiman, *Shelley's "The Triumph of Life*," pp. 74–75.
26. See Lloyd Abbey's discussion of *The Triumph* in *Destroyer and Preserver: Shelley's Poetic Skepticism* (Lincoln, Neb., and London: University of Nebraska Press, 1979), pp. 119–43.
27. See the last chapter of James Rieger, *The Mutiny Within: The Heresies of Percy Bysshe Shelley* (New York: George Braziller, 1967), which, partly through a study of accounts of the foundering of the *Don Juan*, argues that the poet's death was primarily an act of suicide.
28. Reiman, *Shelley's "The Triumph of Life*," pp. 82–83.
29. Miriam Allott, "The Reworking of a Literary Genre: Shelley's 'The Triumph of Life,' " in *Essays on Shelley*, ed. Miriam Allott (Liverpool: Liverpool University Press, 1982), p. 240.

INDEX

Abbey, Lloyd, 156, 199, 220n24, 225n26
Abrams, M. H., 70, 213n9
Aeschylus: *Io*, 134, 218n15; *Prometheus Bound*, 72, 73, 74, 83, 109, 214n13
Ahasuerus. *See* Wandering Jew
Alexander the Great, 195
Allott, Miriam, 200, 225n29
Archimedes, 3
Aristophanes, 210n10
Aristotle, 195
Arnold, Matthew: "The Scholar-Gypsy," 177

Baker, Carlos, 1, 25, 43, 79, 131, 205nn1,3, 207nn13,20, 210n5, 211n16, 214nn14,20, 218n5, 221n15, 224n5
Barnard, Ellsworth, 100, 216n13
Bible: Ezekiel, 217n15; Genesis, 119; Psalms, 184; Revelation, 119
Blake, William, 64, 70, 83, 90, 200
Bloom, Harold, 117, 150, 160, 167, 192, 196, 207n16, 217nn8,10,15, 219n16, 220n1, 221nn5,9, 224nn16,19
Boinville, Cornelia, 170
Boltzmann, Ludwig, 215n9
Bostetter, Edward E., 110, 216n1
Botticelli, Sandro, 191, 215n5
Brisman, Leslie, 191, 224n13
Brooks, Cleanth, 216n19
Brown, Nathaniel, 152, 211n18, 213n42, 220n20, 222n19
Browning, Robert, "Caliban upon Setebos," 14
Burke, Edmund, 67
Bush, Douglas, 113, 210n10, 217n5
Butter, Peter, 208n26

Byron, George Gordon, Lord, 5, 128, 146, 166–167, 219n6; *Childe Harold*, 145, 197, 225n21; *Don Juan*, 117, 145; *Manfred*, 33, 100; "Prometheus," 72, 75

Cameron, Kenneth Neill, 23, 57, 69, 103, 118, 119, 123, 172–174, 205n2, 206nn12,16,8, 212n31, 213n5, 215n5, 216nn17,18, 217nn12,13, 220n1, 222nn19,21,22,24, 223n32
Carlyle, Thomas, 78
Carothers, Yvonne M., 207nn19,20
Carpenter, Edward, and Barnefield, George, 212n26
Catherine of Russia, 195
Cenci, Beatrice, 5, 56, 127, 128
Chayes, Irene H., 216n20
Christ. *See* Jesus
Clairmont, Clara Mary Jane (Claire), 57, 59, 62, 143, 158, 170, 175–176, 183
Coleridge, John Taylor, 47
Coleridge, Samuel Taylor, 43, 106, 196; Ancient Mariner, 33, 52–54, 77; *Biographia Literaria*, 216n23; *Christabel*, 96
Colwell, Frederic S., 215n5
Cooper, Bryan, 208n23
Covent Garden theater, 127
Cronin, Richard, 147, 151, 218n1, 219nnll,17, 224n4
Crook, Nora, and Guiton, Derek, 222nn19,20
Curran, Stuart, 95, 96, 131, 215n4, 218nn7,13,15
Cuvier, Georges, 123

Dante Alighieri, 70, 167, 192; *Divina Commedia*, 117, 217n15; *Vita Nuova*, 181